AS SEEN ON TV

D.C. DENISON

PHOTOGRAPHS BY FLINT BORN

A FIRESIDE BOOK
PUBLISHED BY SIMON & SCHUSTER
New York London Toronto Sydney Tokyo Singapore

FIRESIDE
Simon & Schuster Building
Rockefeller Center
1230 Avenue of the Americas
New York, New York, 10020

Copyright © 1992 by David Denison

Designed by Quinn Hall
Manufactured in the United States of America

10   9   8   7   6   5   4   3   2   1

Library of Congress Cataloging in Publication Data

Denison, D. C. (David C.)
     As seen on TV / D. C. Denison ; photographs by Flint Born.
         p.   cm.
     "A Fireside book."
     Includes index.
         1. Television—Production and direction.   2. Television
broadcasting—United States.   I. Title.   II. Title: As seen on TV.
PN1992.75.D45   1992
791.45′0232′0973—dc20   92-15342
                                                        CIP

ISBN: 0-671-72619-6

To my wife. She knows who she is.

ACKNOWLEDGMENTS

Thanks: to Patricia Van der Leun, for her literary agentry; and to Kara Leverte, editor, for her many improvements.

CONTENTS

PREFACE

First, a warning: you are entering a celebrity-free zone. This is a book about television makers, not television performers.

"TV is a producer's medium," is a phrase one hears over and over in the television industry, to which I would add, "and a photographer's medium, and an audio engineer's medium, and a computer graphic artist's medium, and a lighting designer's medium . . ."

It's difficult to know when to end the list, because at this point the television industry is so sprawlingly diverse that any attempt to be definitive or comprehensive is doomed from the start.

There's a standard journalistic approach to sorting out this kind of mess: follow the money. Unfortunately, in the television industry that trail leads only to a succession of B-school grads and over-leveraged '80s-era takeover artists.

After a few dull trips down that road, I adopted a new scheme: follow the television signal—the pictures and the audio—back to the professionals at the producing end of the medium. That's where I found the people in this book, at work on productions in very different wings of the television complex.

For organizational purposes, I've divided the book into two large sections: TV/FACT and TV/FICTION. TV/FACT includes television productions that are news- or reality-based; TV/FICTION deals with television that's made up: stories, music videos, ads, etc. In both sections the approach is the same: Who's making these shows? How are they doing it? And what kind of equipment are they using?

Universal answers to these questions are annoyingly rare. But I have gathered lots of specifics. If these details do not exactly define the art of contemporary television, I hope, at least, that they serve as an interim report from TV's front lines.

TV
FACT

*John Baynard framing a
street-level shot of an
oncoming parade.*

1. ON ASSIGNMENT WITH JOHN BAYNARD

John Baynard is kneeling on the median stripe in the middle of Route 16 in downtown North Conway, New Hampshire. His camera is off his shoulder and on the pavement. He's getting a very low angle on the annual World Mud Bowl Championship parade, which is breaking around him like a blue and gold river of percussion and brass.

"It's a good, steady platform," Baynard explains later, speaking of the road, or maybe of the earth in general. "If I'm not using a tripod, I'm always looking for a large rock, or a car or a bench. Especially if I want to get a long shot, where you really notice any unsteadiness."

Baynard, who looks like the actor William Hurt, except more alert, is in North Conway shooting a ten-minute feature for "Our Times," a TV magazine-style show produced by WHDH-TV, Channel 7, the Boston CBS affiliate. The subject is North Conway's mud football championship, which takes place every year on a football field that's been watered and churned until it's covered by a thick chocolatey layer of mud.

Two weeks earlier Baynard had read a small item about the championship in a local newspaper, phoned up the organizers for some information, and made an easy ten-word pitch to the senior producer of "Our Times."

"I just said, 'There's a mud football championship every July in

North Conway,' Baynard recalls with a shrug. "It wasn't a difficult story to sell."

The story, as Baynard conceived it, would focus on one team, the Mass Muddahs. He planned to head up to New Hampshire the Friday afternoon before the championship weekend, attend a team meeting that night, and then shoot all day Saturday and Sunday.

On the Friday morning before the Mud Bowl weekend, Baynard drove into Boston to pick up his equipment from Channel 7: a Sony Betacam SP camcorder, five or six batteries, a battery charger, two dozen twenty-minute tapes, and two radio microphones. Later, when he got home, he added a few pieces of his own equipment: a tripod, a roll of duct tape, a light reflector, and two Lowel lights: one 1000 watts, one 600 watts. Baynard does not generally use a Sun Gun, the small battery-powered light that you often see perched on top of ENG cameras. "You don't get any depth with that kind of light," he says.

Most of this equipment was designed for ENG (electronic news gathering)—television at its most basic. Most of the time, the ENG product is thirty- and fifty-second segments that can be shot at 3:10 in the afternoon, hastily edited by 5:30, and thrown up on the screen at 6:14. ENG is angry-looking people in front of City Hall; ENG is blank faces atop bland suits saying, "We're talking about seventy-five million dollars in revenue"; ENG is women with stiff-looking frosted hair "coming to us from the scene of a Saturday night shooting that left one teenager dead." Two expressions appear to hold the whole news pastiche together: "back to you" and "still ahead."

For a photographer, ENG as it's practiced on the evening news is extremely formulaic: a medium shot of the smashed car; a close-up of the yellow barricade tape, with the smashed car in the background; a long shot from across the street showing a police car, lights flashing, next to the smashed car; and a close-up of a police lieutenant saying, "It appears the vehicle was traveling . . ."

ENG photographers also shoot a lot of fires for the late-night news. There are two reasons for this: (1) a fire gives the television audience the idea that something significant has happened since the six o'clock news; and (2) leaping flames, smoke, and flashing police lights look great against the black evening sky.

A veteran ENG photographer once told me his fire formula: "My major rule is always get the wide shot first," he said. "Because if you don't, by the time you go to do it, the fire may be out. So when you first get the camera out of the car, shoot an establishing shot: all the fire trucks, the flames shooting out of the building, and so on. After that go in and shoot a few tight shots of the flames. Then, start to look for burn-outs."

Hardware: The Sony Betacam SP Video Camera

When he shoots stories for Channel 7, Baynard uses one of their Sony Betacam SP cameras. If television cameras were cars, a Betacam SP camera would be a Mercedes convertible with MD license plates.

The Betacam format emerged as the prestige news-gathering format in the mid- to late 1980s. At the time it offered a number of improvements over the standard ¾-inch Umatic format. One major improvement was the Betacam tape decks were small enough to dock to the back of the camera. This reduced the manpower requirements by half: a news crew with a Umatic setup needed a cameraman, and another guy to carry the deck. Betacams made one-man bands like Baynard possible. A Betacam is a heavy package, about twenty-eight pounds with a battery pack attached, but the convenience of having everything in one tidy bundle more than compensates for the heft.

Betacams also engineer the television signal differently, sorting out the chrominance (color) and the luminance (whites and blacks) in a way that makes the image sharper and crisper than in the previous format. When Sony further refined the Betacam's engineering a few years after its introduction, an "SP" was added to the improved format's name.

The consumer videotape format, VHS, came along around the same time as Betacam, but it didn't make much of an impact on the broadcast market. Compared to Betacam, VHS images look dark and muddy.

Baynard has used consumer camcorders, but only in special situations. "I used one for a story on a bicycle messenger," he recalls. "I followed her on a bicycle, through traffic, using a consumer camcorder. It came out pretty well. I couldn't have done that with a broadcast camera. It's too heavy. The camcorder weighed only four pounds, I think.

"I also used one on a rafting story," he continues. "I didn't want to worry about wrecking a forty-thousand-dollar camera. Camcorders can also be useful for investigative stories. They're small enough and they're sensitive enough in low light so that you can get a picture even if you have the camcorder hidden in a gym bag. I worked on a story about teenage runaways, and we did some surveillance-type shooting with a broadcast camera in Times Square. So I spent a lot of time hanging around Forty-second street in New York carrying this huge, heavy bag with a hole cut in it. A camcorder would have been better."

Around 1990, two consumer formats emerged that began to approach the Betacam SP systems image quality: S-VHS and Hi-8. When Chuck Kraemer, a reporter for the Boston ABC affiliate, WCVB, bought a Hi-8 camera and began using it on stories he covered, it was difficult to detect any loss of image quality. Around the same time a television reporter in San Francisco bought a Hi-8 camcorder over the counter at an electronics store shortly before boarding a flight for Russia. When he returned, he edited his footage into a half-hour documentary that aired on the local PBS affiliate. Members of the local television union started to rumble about loss of jobs.

Then the Persian Gulf started simmering in late 1990; and when networks of various sizes started to send crews to cover the conflict, the Hi-8 format started to gain respectability, fast. Insurance doesn't cover losses in a war zone, it turns out. So suddenly the perceived difference in image quality between a $40,000 Betacam SP system and a $2000 Hi-8 camcorder began to shrink rapidly. A Scud attack looked about the same in both formats.

After the conflict, Hi-8 and S-VHS made more gains, particularly in the smaller television markets, but so far the high-end users are sticking with the Betacam format: for the image quality, which is still slightly superior, for the professional extras and options that are available only in Betacam, for the compatibility with the Betacam editing equipment back at the station, and for the rugged, work-a-day design of the camcorders. All of which means that camcorders like the Sony BVW-300, above, which sell in the range of $40,000, will probably remain news-gathering workhorses for a few years to come.

Burn-outs?

"Yeah. The people who've gotten burned out of their homes."

Baynard began shooting ENG stories in the late '70s, when he started working at WBTV in Charlotte, North Carolina. At the time he was a student at the University of North Carolina, and mostly interested in still photography, but he soon realized that a television station was a pretty good place to make pictures. "They kind of rely on visuals," he says dryly.

There are skills that cross over from still photography to video, according to Baynard, but not many. "You're painting with light in both mediums, but that's sort of where it stops," he says. "It's really two different languages.

"There's more to think about when you're shooting for television," he continues. "You're dealing with sound, for example, and how that relates to the picture, and how that relates to the story. Even if you're working with a sound technician, you have to think about what the person on one side of you is saying, and what the person on the other side is saying, and whether you should pan over to catch this or that. Or you might want to move in on something that's pertinent to what someone is saying. So even if you're not doing the sound, you have to shoot for sound."

After four years in North Carolina, Baynard moved to Boston, where he began shooting and editing news and documentaries for WBZ-TV and other outlets. When a popular local "Evening Magazine" host, Robin Young, was given a large contract at the local CBS affiliate, she hired Baynard as the principal photographer for her magazine show. Young and Baynard were given a lot of creative freedom; many of the show's segments were produced in the style of CBS' "Sunday Morning": meditative, with lots of natural sound. Although Baynard collected a local Emmy for his work on the show, the ratings never added up. After a few years, the show was canceled. The station bought out Robin Young's contract, and she went to California, where she later turned up as a host of "USA Today: The Television Show," a truly terrible project.

Meanwhile Baynard continued free-lancing, shooting segments for various local magazine shows, chasing down the Central American drug trade for the PBS series "Frontline," and riding with an emergency response team for "48 hours" on CBS ("It's like the Marines," he says. "You land, you do what you can, and you have to get out of there in forty-eight hours with your story.") Along the way his work was regularly recognized as being a cut above the local

TV camera product; Baynard was named New England Television News Cameraman of the Year three years running by the Boston Press Photographers Association, in 1986, 1987, and 1988. The following year, 1989, he began to contribute segments to "Our Times," a new weekly magazine show on Channel 7, the CBS affiliate.

One of the attractions of shooting for "Our Times," for Baynard, is that they give him the stylistic flexibility to shoot and edit natural sound (known as nat. sound) stories—tightly edited collages that attempt to tell a story using only the images, voices, and sounds that he can capture with his camera and microphones. Nat. sound stories, in other words, don't have a clean-cut reporter standing around looking concerned and nodding his head in one reaction shot after another.

Nat. sound is leaner, purer reporting: it allows the subjects to tell the story with relatively little interference from television reporters. Yet it is not a popular format. Many television producers believe that some of their viewers may need to see an on-the-scene reporter in order to relate to the story. They want to see the story through the reporter's eyes.

"Sixty Minutes" segments, for example, are generally put together by staff producers; yet the show always flies one of the hosts to the story's location. The host asks the questions the producer has prepared, and stands and sits and walks in front of the camera and pretends that he has been working on the story all along. That's why some "Sixty Minutes" hosts seem to be trying so hard to squinch their faces into the most interested, involved looks they can muster.

Fortunately for Baynard, "Our Times" adheres to the kind of high-toned style that station managers order up when they want to express their station's "commitment to local programming." So nat. sound stories are okay. Unfortunately, "commitment to local programming" usually means a hopeless time slot. The week before the Mud Bowl, "Our Times" was broadcast at 7:00 P.M. on Saturday night, one of television's undisputed dead zones.

A brief survey of "Our Times" competition turned up a weekend edition of "A Current Affair," an episode of the new syndicated "Star Trek," "Wheel of Fortune," some men arguing on CNN, wrestling, a PBS special on Nat King Cole, an episode of the new "Rin Tin Tin," and a repeat of "Star Search" with Ed McMahon.

But with so little at stake in terms of ratings, Baynard is able to corner a great deal of creative control for his "Our Times" segments. So driving up to North Conway, he knew what he needed to produce the piece he had in mind: enough good video and audio to edit into a self-contained, ten-minute montage of pictures and sound. If the story needed a little more exposition, one of the show's hosts would do a voice-over. Otherwise, a few Saturdays hence, they would just simply introduce the segment and roll tape.

Early Saturday morning, in North Conway, I track Baynard down to a Mud Bowl parade staging area, an open field a few blocks from the town's main street. He's on the edge of the field, behind an old bus, in the middle of three mud football players who are having a loose, warm-up catch. Baynard is wearing black jeans, a simple cotton shirt, and running shoes. A television camera is on his shoulder, and he's wearing a small backpack.

The first thing I write down in my notebook is, "He's right in their ears!" Because as the players warm up, Baynard is aggressively putting himself in the line of fire, walking up to the players with this bazooka-sized, bazooka-*shaped* instrument on his shoulder and aiming it at them at very close range—sometimes three or four inches away from their heads. He seems to be trying to fill the frame with big pictures, close-ups.

Once he's in the middle of things, Baynard carves the scene into medium and tight shots: a young woman pinning a pennant on a parade float; a mud football player going out for a pass, from behind the guy throwing it; two players in very silly looking costumes conferring very seriously about strategy. Baynard's approach appears to be very similar to that of newspaper and magazine photographers: try for a variety of different angles, don't worry about wasting film.

Except that occasionally Baynard makes these very deliberate movements, something you never see a still photographer do. At one point, for example, Baynard follows the parade marshal as he makes his way through the field shouting instructions into a bullhorn. When he follows someone with the camera on his shoulder, Baynard walks very deliberately, heel-toe, heel-toe, the way people walk when they're carrying a bowl of soup across an expensive new carpet.

Or Baynard plants his feet and slowly moves the camera in a small arc, panning by a cheerleader and a parade float to a quarterback who is moving in a wide circle, pumping the ball, then throwing. When the camera swings by, the lens looks like a dull, purpley mirror.

Often Baynard makes the same motion, with a few small variations, a number of times, as if he's thinking out loud or practicing or putting together a perfect seven-second sequence. Unlike still photographers, who think in lengths of a thirtieth or sixtieth of a second,

Baynard seems to be dividing the parade staging area into five- and ten-second chunks.

Baynard also gambles a lot. Just as the parade is about to begin, a player jumps into a parade trunk and guns the engine. Baynard hops on back and starts composing a shot from what will soon be a well-situated moving platform. Then the player, apparently having forgotten something, hops out and walks over to a teammate and they talk for a while. Baynard climbs down, looking like a hitchhiker whose ride just fell through. Or later, as the parade starts marching and playing, Baynard stations himself in front of a trombone player who is busily playing his part. Baynard hangs the camera down around his ankles, pointing at the trombone player's feet. Then very slowly and deliberately he raises it to the trombonist's face. Unfortunately, when he gets to the mouth, the trombonist's part is over. After that long climb, Baynard finds himself facing a grinning teenager holding his trombone at his chest. Another gamble that didn't pay off.

"Sometimes you set up for a shot that you think will happen, and you wait for a long time and nothing happens," Baynard tells me later. "You're not directing these people, after all."

Baynard's approach, the way he segments the wildly various pre-parade scene into discretely framed shots, reminds me of a conversation I once had with Dick Dunham, a Boston television photographer. As we sat in a television station cafeteria, he described how he approaches a new location when he's working.

"It's just like a person walking into a room" he said. "The first thing you see when you walk into this cafeteria is all the tables and everybody sitting around. That's your wide shot, and the first thing you shoot. Then, when you get inside, your vision usually narrows, so you go to a medium shot: the checkout area and the cash register, for example, or the coffee machine. Finally, you get the extreme close-ups: your hand on a cup, the pouring of the coffee, the cardboard box of plastic spoons, the money being passed from your hand to the cashier's hand, a reaction shot of the face of the woman at the cash register. You're drawing people in, and you're doing it in a way that's similar to the way people actually look at things."

I was surprised that none of Baynard's subjects appeared to regard his close-range reconnaissance as an intrusion. One explanation was that Baynard had effectively diffused objections the evening before—at the team meeting—when he explained what he wanted to do and received a carte blanche. Also, access—on these kinds of stories—is rarely denied. A television camera, today, is hardly an imposition; it's more like a validation, a conspicuous indication that what you're doing is noteworthy. Dealing with a television camera

John Baynard, left, shoots a member of the Mud Bowl parade from the ground up. The corresponding stills from his camera appear at right.

five inches from your face is merely the price you pay for significance. And resisting the urge to mug or ham it up in front of a television camera is a sign of media-age sophistication.

Still, capturing an event with a television camera without turning it into a television event is not an easy trick. "The hardest part of the job is getting people to accept you, to have people feel relaxed with you, so you can get the shots that tell the story," Baynard told me earlier. "The hardest shots are not a matter of having to climb a tree or go into a ditch, they involve making people feel comfortable enough with you so that they let you into their lives. Sometimes if the people are really aware of you being there, you have to stand back at first and use the zoom. You might even shoot from another room. Then as they get used to you, you can gradually work your way in. Even then, you're always telling people, 'Don't pay any attention to the camera,' or 'Act like I'm not even here.' But it's hard when you have two or three strange people in your house with cameras and microphones."

A few loud guys with whistles eventually wrangle the parade participants into some sort of rough formation. Baynard wades into the center of a drum and bugle corps toward the rear, places his camera on the ground, points it straight up through a snare drum, and waits for the drummer to start playing. After a few seconds of drumming, Baynard runs down the street, stations himself in the middle of the road, and allows the parade to wash over him. When a large white convertible lumbers by carrying a smiling "Miss Carabasett Valley Rat," Baynard swings the camera low to catch the sign on the side of the car, and then slowly straightens up to a shot of the waving beauty.

All along the route, spectators standing on the sidewalk are pointing their camcorders at the parade, presumably getting broad eye-level shots of the action. They look like fishermen, patiently waiting

A new angle on a parade drummer.

for good images to bite their cameras. Baynard, standing in the center of the street, dodging floats and ducking large wind instruments, looks like a skin diver, swimming against a strong current of pageantry.

At one point, Baynard slips a thin lens out of a small case and screws it onto the front of his lens.

"That was a wide-angle lens adapter," he tells me later. "Many photographers are reluctant to use an add-on lens. It's another piece of glass, so it could cut down the quality of the image. I thought that might be the case myself, but when I tried one, I noticed only a slight difference. Now I always bring one with me."

Later, when I saw the sequences Baynard shot using the wide-angle lens adapter, they appeared to have a little more breadth, slightly more peripheral vision.

When the parade dead-ends at the town common, the players spill off their floats onto the field and start running through plays, touch-football style. At one end of the field, I see a mud football team kneeling in a tight huddle, going over a playbook. Baynard is behind the team captain, shooting over his shoulder into the huddle. Then he shoots the captain's profile, close up, and pans the camera down so that it's pointing to the playbook as the captain turns the pages. A minute later, Baynard is kneeling down looking up into the huddle past the open playbook, framing close-ups against the blue sky.

Still later, he's standing where an opposing linebacker would line

The large attachment on the end of Baynard's lens is a wide-angle lens. He carries the lens with him in a stiff leather case; when he wants a shot with a little more breadth, he screws it on.

up. The players are running pass patterns around him as if he's an immovable object. On one play, a defensive player intercepts a pass and runs in a wide circle. Baynard follows him all the way around.

Occasionally Baynard asks a Muddah a question. Not major, "Meet the Press" questions, but simple questions that are meant to nudge the man into talking, like, "What does this game mean to you?" And then when the player turns to answer, beginning, "It means everything to me . . ." he's facing Baynard and the camera on Baynard's shoulder.

One of the players, a bald man with hair very short on the sides and a neatly trimmed mustache, has a profile that looks cut from granite; he looks like a nineteenth-century cricket player. He sets up at the end of the offensive line; Baynard walks up from behind him and moves his camera so that it looks across at the man in profile. Then the ball is snapped, and the player runs out of the frame.

A whistle summons the players from the practice area to the mud-covered field that is temporarily renamed the "Hog Coliseum." When Baynard sees a mud football player carrying a football on his hip, he runs over, holds his camera about waist high (about six inches from the ball and the player's hip), and walks backwards next to the player for about ten seconds. A minute later, he sees another player walking towards the playing field. Baynard asks him if he's feeling nervous. As the player responds, still walking, Baynard makes a wide circle around him, taking in the field, and the other players, and the mountains in the distance, and a lot of sky. As he circles the player, I notice that the front of the lens stays about the same distance from the man's face. Like a good hockey player, Baynard appears to be able to move smoothly in all directions.

As the players make their way to the field, the public address system is blaring the music to Bruce Springsteen's "Born in the USA," re-dubbed with new lyrics and a new chorus: "Born in the M.U.D." Baynard walks under the Hog Coliseum sign and down to the far sideline, where he gets down on one knee and points his camera at two players as they gingerly step into the mud and move their legs around. The players are both wearing thoughtful expressions, as if they are mentally gauging the mud's consistency.

Some of the things I see Baynard do once the game begins:

Hold his camera about a foot from a player's muddy hand, as he flicks mud off his fingertips. Baynard is so close that some of the mud splatters on the front of the lens. He slowly pans up to the player's face and holds the camera there awhile, as the player absentmindedly chews his mouthguard. Then Baynard wipes the mud off.

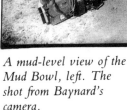

Set up a shot along the length of the sideline. In the foreground a man is squinting. He's wearing a plain red rubber bathing cap. Behind him you can see others on the sideline, lined up like a perspective exercise in a photography manual.

Shoot a few close-ups of the cheerleaders' pom-poms, which on a bright afternoon reflect a garish, electronic-looking light.

Frame a shot of two young male spectators, shirtless and tattooed, leaning back on their elbows on the hillside. When one of them yells "C'mon!" he comes off his elbows and his abdominal muscles ripple.

Use his camera to peer over the shoulder of two players on the sideline, who are scratching a play in the mud and talking vigorously about "taking out this guy" and "blocking that guy."

During the second quarter, Baynard takes a Vega wireless microphone unit out of his knapsack. The body-pack transmitter, about the size of a pack of cigarettes, looks like the one you see David Letterman wearing in the small of his back when the camera catches him from an odd angle. Baynard lifts up the captain's shirt and uses a long elastic bandage to strap the transmitter to the player's waist. He plugs a lavalier microphone into the unit, snakes the microphone inside the shirt, and clips it to the shirt collar.

The receiver, which looks like a thin portable radio, is inside his backpack. Baynard turns it on, uses his headphones to adjust the volume, and stuffs it back in his pack. When the captain rejoins the huddle, Baynard stations himself a few feet away, in one end zone. He's now shooting the outside of the huddle and listening to what's being said inside.

Later I asked him if the transmitter and microphone (list price: $1690) could stand up to the mud and the tackling on the field. "Oh sure," he said casually. "Those things are rugged."

After the last play of the first half, as the players climb out of the mud field and head for the bench, Baynard sort of falls into step with

them, pointing the camera just above the shoulder of the player in front of him. From his vantage, the team looks like weary mud-warriors slogging off a battlefield.

During the halftime, Baynard and I buy plastic-wrapped sandwiches from young volunteers under a large tent; then we sit down under a tree. I ask him a few questions.

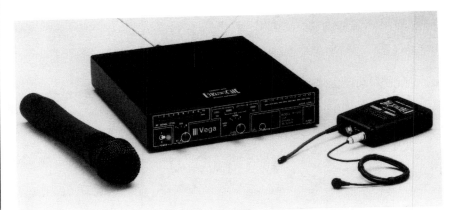

Hardware *A Vega Wireless Microphone System.*

"The use of wireless mics conveys a highly desirable image of professionalism and enhances the visual appeal of presentations and performances." That's according to Vega, the company that makes the wireless microphone that Baynard uses.

Actually Baynard likes wireless mikes for an entirely different reason: they follow people around and can send back high quality audio from as far away as two hundred yards: that's a baseball coach who's sitting on the bench on the other side of the field; or ballet director, on opening night, who's roaming the entire backstage area like a cat, talking constantly. Ideally, the person wearing the mike forgets about it, allowing Baynard to record his unguarded comments very clearly, even though Baynard is a hundred yards away shooting a close-up of someone putting on his cleats or ballet slippers. And if he decides to zoom in on the subject for a close-up, the audio matches. It sounds close-up.

Vega systems, including microphone, bodypack transmitter, and receiver, start at around $1500.

Q. Do you think in certain time units when you're shooting?

A. I usually figure around thirty seconds for a shot. I probably won't use all of that, but it gives me some room to work with in the editing room.

Q. How about continuity? What's going to hold all this together?

A. Well, I'm always looking for a scene that can lead somewhere. You know that scene in *2001,* when the bone gets tossed up in the air, and it comes down a few million years later as a satellite? That's the kind of thing I'm looking for.

Q. Do you usually work with a few microphones at a time?

A. Usually. I use a shotgun mike on top of the camera, and sometimes one or two wireless microphones, which I can monitor using meters in my viewfinder. It can be very difficult, like trying to shoot and play a video game at the same time. Sometimes you're shooting and you don't get the sound, and sometimes you shoot just for the sound.

Q. Do you worry about keeping your images steady?
A. I like to use a tripod as much as possible. But then again, with news and documentaries, you're often in settings where the best shot is off your shoulder—because you're moving with the people, or you're in a tight corner, or you want to go as unnoticed and unencumbered as possible.

As he's saying this, the PA system suddenly comes to life with "Born in the M.U.D." to kick off the second half. I follow Baynard to the open-air broadcast booth, which is built into the side of a hill overlooking the field. Baynard produces a battered-looking tripod from under a bench where he stashed it earlier. He mounts the camera on it; and after the kickoff, he shoots an establishing shot of the field from the booth. From the booth, it's difficult to tell who's really who, but you do get the big picture—players, mud, fans, some trees and sky. Afterwards, Baynard goes down to the field—with the tripod still attached to the camera—and takes more establishing shots: first from under one goalpost, then down the sideline from the end zone, then from under the opposite goalpost, and then down the opposite sideline. From where I'm standing, up in the broadcast booth, it looks as though he's framing a picture.

Frequently during the Mud Bowl I saw Baynard eject a videocassette from the back of his camera, quickly label it with a felt-tip pen, and stash it in his backpack. By Sunday night, he had filled twenty-one of these cassettes. At twenty minutes a cassette, that's seven hours of material. "I overshoot everything that I can," he told me a few days later.

When Baynard started working in television, in the late '70s, many news stories were still photographed in 16mm film. Because film is expensive and time-consuming to process, television photographers shot very conservatively. The advent of videotape—cheap, reusable, and easy to edit—allowed photographers like Baynard to be widely profligate. On most stories, he shoots at least twenty minutes of tape for every minute he uses. The shooting ratio on the Mud Bowl piece was much higher: he had more than forty minutes of tape for every minute of airtime.

Which meant that for a week or so following the Mud Bowl, Baynard spent large chunks of time at home in front of a television monitor, writing down on a clipboard the time-code location of promising pictures, quotations, and natural sounds.

After these good-looking and good-sounding sections are down on paper—next to their time-code locations—Baynard cuts them

Framing an establishment shot.

Baynard in his hotel room, after a shower, with his on-location equipment. Four canvas bags can hold it all: the radio microphones, the duct tape, the video-tapes, the cables, the batteries, the wide-angle lens, the hand-held microphone, and his Sony Betacam SP.

into strips and starts moving the thin pieces of paper around, playing with a variety of visual and audio chronologies and sequences. "It works a little like a poor man's word processor," Baynard says of his system.

The first elements that Baynard considers, generally, are the quotations. "Some quotations naturally take command, because you need them to tell the story," he says. "So you fit everything else around them. Other quotes can kind of float around. You can use them anywhere in the piece. There are also times during the editing of a piece when a certain visual, or a natural sound, is the most important element. So you're always moving things around as you go."

When the sequence of paper strips starts to look like a ten-minute television story, Baynard calls Channel 7 and reserves a few days in one of their editing rooms.

In the editing suite. The numbers along the bottom of the monitors are SMPTE time code, an electronic way of identifying each frame of videotape. At thirty frames per second, a half hour of video has 54,000 frames. SMPTE (for Society of Motion Picture and Television Engineers, the industry group that formulated it) time-code sort of lines the frames up and shuffles them into some kind of order, which is why it's come to be the dominant organizational tool among editors, special effects people, graphic artists, and musicians who work for television. Baynard's camera automatically records SMPTE time-code numbers on everything he shoots. Although most editing machines will display the time-code numbers, they aren't visible on the video image. Except if you want them to be, during the rough editing phase, in which case you can burn them in electronically. Time code is always displayed as eight digits, representing Hours:Minutes:Seconds:Frames.

A few panels are missing from the lowered ceiling in Edit Room B, a dark, shabby edit suite at Channel 7 where Baynard has settled in for the first of three day-long editing sessions. A cheap desk light, its neck twisted into an unnatural-looking position, splays a little illumination across a bare wall. Small groups of abandoned-looking videocassettes are gathered in the corners.

The editing system, which looks as if it's been hastily arranged on a few sturdy tables, comprises three Betacam videotape decks, a small audio mixing board, a large color television monitor, two small black-and-white monitors, a video switcher, a single speaker, and a computer display striped with three columns of time-code numbers.

A sheet of "Special Effects Patterns" is taped to a shelf above one of the monitors. There are twenty-three of these patterns, each a very specific way of bringing a new image over an old one. They look like nautical flags, with broad diagonal stripes and blocky geometric shapes.

I ask Baynard if he has a favorite special-effect pattern. He looks at them for a few seconds. "None of them," he says finally.

To Baynard, special-effect patterns are garish, tacky—the stuff of low-rent televised sports events and TV ads for car dealers. A special-effect pattern calls attention to the edit: "Look! A new image! And it's sliding down from the upper right-hand corner!"

Baynard is generally trying to achieve the opposite effect: he wants the transitions to be seamless, to look as if they're woven together. Most of the time, when he edits two segments together, he uses a dissolve. If he's looking for a more percussive effect, he uses a cut.

When he edits, Baynard often leads with the audio. This is called an "L cut" or a "split edit." For example: you see a shot of a player going out for a pass, and you're hearing the kinds of sounds that go with that picture: footsteps on the grass, grunting players, etc. But then after the player catches it and you're still watching him carry the ball back to the line of scrimmage, Baynard starts to bring up the audio track from the next segment, in this case the voice of a bandleader from the parade site, shouting: "one! two! three! four!" Then the picture changes to the parade. The two-second audio lead was the transition.

Or, at the end of the parade sequence, Baynard will use a split edit to make the transition to the next segment. When he gets to his last parade image—a police car with lights flashing, bringing up the rear of the parade—he starts to lower the parade audio and to bring up an entirely new audio track, with a man's voice yelling, "Hey Andy! Hey Andy Mello!" A second later we see a new visual: the mud

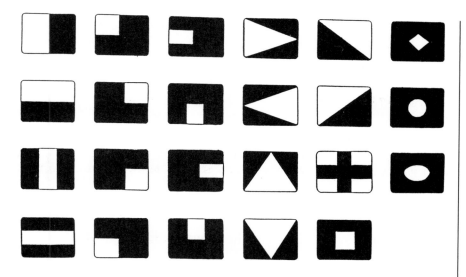

football quarterback, wearing a small microphone on his shirt, shouting at one of his players, a guy named Andy Mello. Now we're on an open field, watching a mud football team warm up. The captain is saying, "Andy Mello, you're playing center."

So Baynard gives you the new audio before he gives you the new picture, which accomplishes two of his editing objectives: he very subtly leads you along, by teasing you with the audio before showing you the picture, and he breaks up the choppiness that would result if the audio and video always changed at the same instant. "You want things to be smooth, to flow," he explains. "You don't want the audio changing with the video all the time."

Baynard has other ways of finessing the essential cut-and-paste nature of editing. One of them is the voice-over, where he uses an audio segment from one tape—usually a twenty- or thirty-second quotation from one of the players—over a series of visual images. If the quotation is coherent and understandable, the images can be nonsequential, almost unrelated.

In between edits, Baynard shuttles the tapes around, drums his fingers, and consults strips of paper that are loosely taped to a larger sheet. The strips of paper have quotations written on them, or descriptions of visual sequences, with time-code numbers to identify beginnings and ends. Occasionally Baynard reaches up and adjusts the contrast on a monitor.

The final piece inches forward as Baynard layers and overlaps the audio and video to cover his tracks, making things flow. Midway through his first afternoon, he's two minutes into the piece; according to the display on his monitor, he's made 109 edits.

Overall, the process does not seem linear—pasting segments together—so much as three-dimensional, an exercise in weaving together video and audio into unpredictable sequences and combinations. "I'm always trying to think of different ways to put it all together," he says. "You try to take a lot of different roads. You don't want to be stuck on just one road."

Three days later, Baynard turned in a copy of his segment to the "Our Times" producer. The length was just over ten minutes. He also wrote a short introductory paragraph for one of the cohosts to read; it explained how the mud football championship started, how it's become an annual event, and so on.

On the following Saturday night, at 7:00 P.M., I turned on the television just in time to hear the female cohost introducing Baynard's Mud Bowl story. She ended with, "Recently, photojournalist John Baynard followed the Mass Muddahs to the Mud Bowl finals as they battled their arch rivals, the Mount Washington Valley Hogs."

With that, the first image of the piece sort of unrolled onto the screen: a large shirtless player striking a Hulk Hogan pose in the pre-parade area. A two-word title, "Mud Bowl," scrolled across the player's chest in a plain typeface and disappeared.

Then the images and the audio segments started tumbling over one another. Even after watching Baynard in the field and in the editing room, I was surprised by the sheer quantity of images; and by the speed with which they were thrown up on the screen and then replaced. When I started counting out loud, I discovered that the average image was shown for about 2½ seconds. It was impossible to concentrate on a single image before another one tumbled over it. Sometimes it went too fast. Towards the end of the piece, I wasn't able to tell which team was winning and which was losing; it didn't help that the players and their uniforms were entirely covered with mud.

But the pace continued unabated, right through the piece, to the last series of images, which featured members of the winning team jubilantly frolicking in the mud, intercut with somber close-ups of the losers, the Mass Muddahs. "Born in the M.U.D." was blasting on the PA system. Then the co-hosts came back on; one of them made a weak pun about being a stick in the mud; and they previewed the next segment, about solid waste.

I once asked Baynard if it bothered him to see his carefully composed images flying by so rapidly. "That's what I miss about still photography," he said. "In television you have an image, but it's fleeting. With still photography when you see an image that makes you feel something, you can print it and put it on a wall or on a desk. With television, it's gone."

2. NEWSFEED, WASHINGTON, D.C.

8:15 A.M.

Twin fax machines are pumping out press releases as Steve Phillips, Newsfeed's assignment editor, looks through the latest update to the Associated Press Daybook.

"Colin Powell, the Chairman of the Joint Chiefs of Staff, will be speaking at a refugee program at two P.M.," he says, thinking out loud. "Bernard King, Washington Bullets star, will be speaking on a Congressional resolution declaring today 'NBA Stay In School Awareness Day,' at ten-thirty this morning."

Phillips taps his pencil a few times on his desk.

"I think we're still going to go with the Secretary of Transportation's news conference," he says finally, grabbing a few faxed press releases on very official looking Congressional letterheads and sorting them into small piles.

Newsfeed, a Washington, D.C.–based news service owned by Group W, a Westinghouse Company, is an efficient, television-age information processing unit. Ninety-five hungry television stations around the country—all with evening news programs to fill—rely on Newsfeed to sort through national news and the Washington political circus and bounce an hour of raw news off the satellite Telstar 301 every day from 4:00 P.M. to 5:00 P.M.

And one of the stories on today's feed, apparently, will be this news conference by Secretary of Transportation Sam Skinner. He's called the conference to mark the midpoint in the administration's

Steve Phillips checking out the Associated Press Daybook.

campaign for seventy percent use of safety belts by the end of 1992. Participants will include a variety of senators, congressmen, governors, and mayors, along with police representatives from cities and states where seat-belt compliance is particularly high. In a blatant pitch for television coverage, the press conference will also include the buckling of a three-hundred-foot safety belt, with the help of two crash dummies.

"It's basically an administration dog-and-pony show," Phillips explains. "It's not going to be a place where news happens, but we've gotten some requests from stations around the country for it. Their congressman or mayor is going to be there, and they want us to bag him for a news bite. We can put it on the satellite this afternoon, and they can use it on their news tonight."

8:45 A.M.

Reporter Jaime McIntyre and producer Karen Hendren are assigned the seat-belt story.

McIntyre is a free-lance reporter. He works for CNN three days a week and fills in at Newsfeed when they're shorthanded. He's already on the phone.

"I'm trying to find the other side," he says. "Someone to give me another point of view, maybe a critical point of view. It's not going to be easy. Who's against seat belts? Last week a consumer group criticized the Transportation Department for dragging its feet on safety issues. I'm going to try them."

Karen Hendren, the producer, is reading the press release.

"We'll be putting together two packages," she says. "The first one will be v.o./s.o.t."

"Huh?"

"V.O., voice-over, is material that the anchorpeople can talk over," she explains. "It will be shots of the news conference with a little natural sound in the background. Pictures to run while the anchorperson says 'Today at a news conference in Washington, D.C., Secretary of Transportation Skinner announced . . .'

"S.O.T. is sound on tape, basically sound bites from the people at the conference," she continues. "Today it will be a quote or two from Skinner, plus sound bites from the various participants, particularly some of the local politicians that we've been asked to get by their hometown stations.

"When we get back from the news conference, I'll put those segments together into a two- or three-minute package, and the local stations can use whatever they want from it," Hendren continues. "Meanwhile, Jaime will be writing the script for a two-minute self-contained package. He'll do the voice-over and a stand-up, and they can just run it as is. So the stations will have a choice: they can edit little pieces of the story into their own newscast—a news roundup or whatever—or they can run our produced package."

10:15 A.M.

Rich Guastadisegni, cameraman, will shoot the seat-belt news con-

phillips   Wed Oct 30 09:44   page   2

Location: Embassy of Zambia, 2419 Massachusetts Ave. NW
Contact: Bruce Kozarsky, 202-223-8700
10:15 a.m. JACOBS-GARNISHMENT — Rep. Andy Jacobs, D-Ind., holds
news conference on his efforts to end the exemption of federal
officials from garnishment to pay their bills.
Location: H-137 Capitol
Contact: David Wildes, 202-225-4011
10:30 a.m. WESTERN WATER — Rep. Ron Packard, R-Calif., holds
news conference to introduce two water bills. One is a
comprehensive wastewater and groundwater reclamation bill. The
other deals with desalination technology. Rep. Frank Riggs,
R-Calif., also takes part in announcement of the first bill.
Location: H-227, U.S. Capitol
Contact: Carole Suarez, 202-225-3906
10:30 a.m. HOMELESS — Photo op with Commerce Secretary Robert
Mosbacher and Veronica Parks, executive director of Martha's Table.
Mosbacher will present Martha's Table a collection of donated
clothes from Commerce employees for the area's homeless and will
help load it onto a shelter truck.
Location: Department of Commerce, North Court Parking area, 15th
Street between Pennsylvania and Constitution Avenues NW
Contact: Malcolm Barr 202-377-3142.
10:30 a.m. NBA-SCHOOLS — Washington Bullets player Bernard King
and other NBA players to join Rep. Cliff Stearns, R-Fla., and Sen.
Dan Coats. R-Ind., to speak on Congressional Resolution declaring
Oct. 30 "NBA Stay In School Awareness Day."
Location: U.S. Capitol, "Grassy Triangle" near House Steps
Contact: Marlin Collingwood or Mary Ann Maryn, 212-489-6900
11 a.m. KEARNS — Deputy Secretary of Education David T. Kearns
speaks at the United States Coalition for Education for All
meeting.
Location: Radisson Plaza Hotel, Alexandria, Va.
Contact: Etta Fielek, 202-401-3020
11 a.m. FIRES — Officials from California and Spokane, Wash.,
participate in U.S. Fire Administration videoconference on
wildfires.
Location: Originates from campus of National Fire Academy,
Emmitsburg, Md., uses'C-Band, Westar 4 satellite, transponder 10,
audio 6.2/6.8 MHz, downlink frequency 3920 MHz, 99 degrees west
Contact: Marvin Davis, 202-646-4600
11 a.m. REPUBLICANS-TAXES — Leading Republicans of the Joint
Economic Committee — Sen. William V. Roth Jr. and Rep. Dick Armey —
release a study of the correlation between tax increases and
federal spending. Study, prepared by two scholars at Ohio
University and the JEC Republican staff, concludes that Congress
spends $1.59 for every dollar it receives in new taxes. EMBARGOED
copies available.
Location: 526 Dirksen Senate Building
Contact: Ed Gillespie, 202-224-0374
11:30 a.m. SKINNER-SAFETY BELTS — News conference with
Transportation Secretary Skinner to mark midpoint in administration
campaign for 70 percent use of safety belts by 1992. Release of
figures on state-by-state use of safety belts, comparing with
national average. Buckling of a 300-foot safety belt with help of
crash dummies. Participants: Gov. Jim Edgar of Illinois; Sens.
Hatfield and Symms; Reps. Hammerschmidt, Coughlin, and Cardin;

phillips   Wed Oct 30 09:44   page   3

mayors of Denver, Colo., Sandy, Utah, and Grand Forks, N.D.; and
Commissioner Glen Walp of the Pennsylvania State Police.
Location: Capitol Hill, Upper Senate Park, Delaware and C
Streets NE (Across Delaware from the Russell Senate Building)
Contact: Shawn Sandor, 202-366-5563
APTV-10-30-91 0835EST +

*10:15 A.M. to 11:30 A.M.
in Washington, D.C.,
according to the
Associated Press
Daybook.*

ference. He'll also be responsible for the audio and will edit the produced package with Jaime McIntyre.

But first, Steve Phillips asks Guastadisegni to swing by the Department of Commerce for a photo op with Commerce Secretary Robert Mosbacher. Martha's Table, a local soup kitchen, is kicking off a clothing donation drive, and Mosbacher will ceremonially help the shelter's director load a box of Commerce Department donations into the shelter's van.

Richard Guastadisegni's press passes for Congress, and below, the Pentagon.

I accompany Guastadisegni down to a basement parking garage where he loads a Sony Betacam camcorder into the back of a Blazer-type vehicle. As we wheel out of the garage, I ask him if, like Baynard, he prefers to use Betacam SP videotape, the top-of-the-line news-gathering format.

"I use just plain Betacam," he says. "The Betacam SP format does give you a slightly better picture, but the tape is just too expensive. Washington news cameramen shoot a lot of tape; you'll find that most of them just shoot Betacam."

I ask Guastadisegni how he got started as a cameraman.

"First I majored in telecommunications/journalism at Kutztown University of Pennsylvania," he replies. "After that, if you want to get into television news, you have to be willing to go somewhere, to get the experience. I started at a station in Scranton, Pennsylvania. Then I worked in the corporate television department at New Jersey Bell Telephone and at another television station in Youngstown, Ohio. I came to Washington four years ago to work with the Medill

News Service; I started free-lancing for Newsfeed late in '90; I've been full-time since February '91.''

Guastadisegni usually covers the House of Representatives, the Senate, and the Pentagon. Recently he's also been spending a lot of time at the White House.

"Last year I'd say I spent about a hundred days at the White House," he says. "Most of us hate the White House."

Why?

"Everything's prearranged, staged," he says. "It's been that way ever since Reagan. The background is very important and the White House staff really restrict your angles, so you have to include it. I shot Bush the other day at the White House, and he was surrounded by flags and balloons and Boy Scouts. It was kind of ridiculous, but everybody's doing it now. They know it worked for Reagan."

Guastadisegni pulls up in front of a large Gothic-looking structure, slings his camera strap over his shoulder, and heads into an interior courtyard/parking area. A young blond female aide, dressed for success, comes out to greet us.

"We've already done it, but we'll do it again for you," she says.

Mosbacher, trim and tailored, is smiling and shaking hands and patting people on the back. Around him a loose circle of observers, many of them in khaki, are standing around holding clipboards or cameras. Rich puts the camera on his shoulder, makes a few adjustments, and nods to the female aide. Mosbacher and the executive director of Martha's Table load a box into a van, smile, and shake hands.

"Okay. Thanks," Guastadisegni says as he takes the camera off his shoulder and heads back to the car. Mosbacher, still smiling, exits amidst a small gaggle of khaki aides. Total elapsed time: three minutes. I feel as if I've just witnessed the filming of a tiny movie scene, the kind that's shot out of sequence and doesn't make sense until you see it in context, edited into the larger picture. Except there is no bigger context in this case, or maybe there is: the ongoing Washington political tableau, edited for television and shown in nightly installments at six and eleven.

From here, it's over to Upper Senate Park, part of the Capitol Mall, for the seat-belt news conference. On the way, I notice scattered groups of small children standing along the side of Pennsylvania Avenue. They look as though they are waiting for buses; but there are too many of them, and they are loosely strung along a number of blocks. Most of the kids look distracted, fidgety, as though they've been there awhile. Then, suddenly, the number of children swells and there, shaking hands and smiling amidst them, is the Reverend Jesse Jackson.

Guastadisegni shooting a photo op with Robert Mosbacher.

"It's supposed to be some kind of symbolic stand against violence, I think," Guastadisegni says.

"It looks like he's attracted a few cameras," he adds, pointing to two cameramen shadowing Jackson.

Another out-of-sequence scene hoping to be inserted in tonight's news movie.

Later I ask Guastadisegni how much it costs a local television station to hire a Washington news service to cover a story.

"Newsfeed works a little differently from the other news services," he replies. "Stations subscribe to Newsfeed. But there are contract news services that you can hire by the job. If you wanted Potomac News Service to shoot a story, it would probably cost you around three hundred and fifty dollars for just pictures and sound bites. If you wanted a produced package with an onscreen reporter, it would probably cost you around four hundred. There is a bargain alternative, the Medill News Service. They use professional cameramen—I worked there once—but most of the staff members are students from the Medill School of Journalism at Northwestern."

What does it take to work as a cameraman in Washington, I ask Guastadisegni.

"You have to be aggressive," he says. "And you have to know the rules."

What kind of rules?

"Well, for example, you can't use a tripod on the South Lawn of the White House," he replies. "They're afraid that you could sneak in a rocket launcher disguised as a tripod. There are some other places around Washington where tripods are also forbidden. Or if

How Guastadisegni and his equipment get around Capitol Hill.

you want to shoot a hearing on Capitol Hill, you can do one of two things: you can either 'spray,' which means you come in and spend two minutes in the room panning and zooming from a single location, or you can take a spot at the beginning of the hearing and stay the entire length of the hearing. There are a lot of rules like that.''

11:28 A.M.

A few minutes before the start of the seat-belt news conference, Guastadisegni is pulling a small luggage cart towards the Capitol Building. On the cart there's a large canvas bag containing batteries, cables, microphones, videotapes, and other miscellaneous equipment; on top of the bag a heavyset tripod is strapped to the cart with Bungee cords. Guastadisegni's camera, attached to a shoulder strap, is slung over his shoulder.

A long wooden platform has been set up for the cameramen. All of them arrive pulling similar luggage carts. They look like an efficient way to get around.

One problem is apparent right away. The organizers want the Capitol Building to be in the background, behind the speakers. This means that the cameramen have to shoot into the sun, which will cause problems with shadows and glare. There's some grumbling about this on the photographers' platform, but it doesn't last long. There's no way the organizers are going to give up their Capitol background.

Guastadisegni runs a cable up to the podium and adds his microphone to the half dozen already in place.

The speaker's platform is large, to accommodate all the politicians who want to share the credit for the seat-belt campaign. In front of the platform, dozens of state troopers are standing behind the three-hundred-foot seat belt. Legislative aides are everywhere; some of them are hanging around the perimeter talking into mobile phones. Most of the men look like Michael Kinsley, with gaunt faces slightly pink, and gray flannel suits. They look as if they've been shaving twice a day for twenty years. Most of the women are wearing stiff professional outfits, the kind they can't wait to change out of at the end of the day.

The TV photographers, by contrast, are wearing leather jackets, cotton shirts, blue jeans and sneakers; some of them are wearing the kind of sneakers that just barely pass for shoes. Jumbled together on the photographers' platform, they look much more like colleagues than competitors. When Guastadisegni returns from the speaker's platform, for example, he casually takes a roll of gaffer's tape from underneath a neighboring tripod and tapes down his microphone cable. A minute later, a cameraman a few feet away looks through his viewfinder with an expression of mild disgust.

"Who's got lens paper?" he yells. "Lens paper!"

Yet, it's very clearly a tenuous peace among equals. Soon after the start of the news conference, a heavyset newspaper photographer with a bulky camera bag over his shoulder clumsily tries to squeeze onto the photographers' platform.

"Get out of here!" a cameraman tells him sharply.

The bulky newspaper photographer starts to move to another part of the platform.

Guastadisegni adding his mike to the podium.

Jaime McIntyre (in sunglasses) and Karen Hendren flanking Guastadisegni at the news conference.

"Quit moving!" another cameraman says. "You're shaking my shot."

The frustrated photographer, looking like a moose stuck in a garden shed, finally lurches off the front of the platform and tries to compose himself.

"Down in front!" a third cameraman yells.

For the next twenty minutes, one by one, everybody on the speaker's platform comes forward to the microphones and thanks everybody else.

Jaime McIntyre and Karen Hendren stand close to Guastadisegni, taking notes and frequently checking their watches.

"Rich sets the time code on his camera to the time of day," Hendren explains. "So if I hear something I want to use, I look at my watch. If it's 11:42 and twenty seconds, I know that I can find that section by fast-forwarding to 11:42:20:00 on the tape."

An aide from the Department of Transportation taps Hendren on the shoulder and tells her that a video news release will be out by this afternoon. It will have some B-roll stuff and some clips and some sound bites. It will be available via satellite at 2:30.

Video news releases have become increasingly popular in Washington. When an agency or an industry group has a news conference, they hire a news-style crew to shoot the conference, add the best B-roll footage they can find—and some sound bites from their people—and put it up on a satellite for anyone and everyone to use as they wish. (B-roll is archival or file footage, basically good pictures. The seat-belt video release B-roll contained shots of crash dummies smashing through windshields in tests, and police checking seat-belt compliance at a road block.)

A good video news release, particularly one with dramatic pictures, will influence what gets covered, because the stations need the visuals. Video news releases can also show up almost uncut when news organizations get lazy, desperate, or cheap.

"Video news releases are very big now," Jaime McIntyre says. "When *Time* magazine published the first installment of Oliver North's book, they distributed a video news release via satellite. The slant of the release was 'North Makes Big Allegations.' I was working at CNN that day; we got the release, then we read the book. We used some parts of their release. We had to use their shot of the *Time* cover because it wasn't on the newsstand yet; but once we read the book, we changed the angle to 'North Supplies Little New Evidence.' That night we were watching NBC News and we were shocked. NBC basically ran the whole video news release: graphics, quote, archival footage—they even used *Time*'s self-serving slant. The only difference was that one of their guys, Robert Hagar, did the voice-over."

A podium's eye view of the press corps.

Behind the scenes at the news conference.

Up on the podium, after everyone has been thoroughly and pro-fusely thanked and a mother with a small child has testified how seat belts saved their lives, two men in crash-dummy suits help the little girl buckle the three-hundred-foot seat belt. The coupling is not perfectly choreographed: when the seat belt is buckled, the Secretary of Transportation finds himself obscured behind the buckles. ("He should be in *front* of the buckles, not behind!" a female aide behind me steams.) And the young girl finds herself alone in front of a three-hundred-foot seat belt, facing fourteen television camera crews and a lot of aides. After a few awkward seconds, the Secretary of Transportation parts the buckles and scoots her inside.

Cameramen, hard-wired into their microphones.

Then someone up on the podium thanks everybody for the last time, and the feeding frenzy begins: the television photographers yank their cameras off their tripods, consult with their reporters and producers, and go off to bag some sound bites.

In quick succession, Guastadisegni, Hendren, and McIntyre very quickly conduct short interviews with three representatives, a governor, and the Secretary of Transportation himself.

In each case they turn the subject around so the sun falls squarely on his face, ask a few questions, and wait for the sound bites to tumble out.

1:30 P.M.

Karen Hendren is in the edit room, putting together the opening package. She starts with a ten-second wide shot of the speaker's stage, with Transportation Secretary Skinner behind the podium. She adjusts the audio level so that his voice is audible but not intelligible.

Next, Hendren adds a couple of three-second cutaway shots: one of the television cameras lined up, shooting the news conference; another of a reporter taking notes in a notebook. Again there's some low-volume sound in the background.

"These opening shots are v.o., voice-over shots," Hendren explains. "The anchorperson at the local station will be talking over them."

Why the low-level audio?

Karen Hendren and Guastadisegni bagging a sound bite from Rep. Benjamin Cardin, (D-Maryland).

File Video
Much of the footage that Newsfeed ships up to the satellite every afternoon is file video: it's World War II footage for a subscriber station that's doing a Pearl Harbor special; it's a file shot of Imelda Marcos on the eve of her return to the Philippines; it's a few seconds of former Supreme Court Justice Thurgood Marshall. Newsfeed's resources are deep in this department. They keep just about everything they shoot, and a lot of it turns out to be valuable later on. Just two weeks after Guastadisegni shot Transportation Secretary Samuel Skinner, for example, there was a shake-up at the White House and Skinner was named Chief of Staff. A tight shot of Skinner from the seat-belt conference went out to all the subscribers that afternoon. The major networks provide a similar file

"When you're watching television news, you're usually hearing the sound in the background, even if a reporter or an anchorperson is talking," Hendren says. "You might not be aware of it consciously, but if there was no sound, you'd notice it. The natural sound makes you feel like you're there. So you always want to have some audio in the background."

Now Hendren is fast-forwarding through the tape, checking her notes for time-code numbers.

"I'm looking for my sound-on-tape, my sound bite," she says.

She chooses a twenty-second segment, a tight shot of Sam Skinner at the podium that begins with his saying, "I'm delighted to announce today that we've reached a milestone in seat-belt usage . . ."

After the Skinner segment, Hendren assembles a series of thirty-second sound bites from the local politicians in attendance. She begins each bite with a shot of herself, from behind, reaching a hand-held microphone up to the politician's face as he says something inaudible; then she quickly cuts to a head shot of the politician delivering his thirty-second sound bite.

I ask why she includes a shot of herself from behind in each section.

"You need that two shot to lay into the bite," she says.

After the fourth sound bite, Hendren glances at her notes.

"That's everybody," she says as she hits the Eject button on one of the video decks. "The length is 2:32, and it's ready to use."

2 P.M.

Rich Guastadisegni has just gotten back from lunch. Now he's waiting for Jaime McIntyre to finish writing the script, so they can do the stand-up for the seat-belt story.

"We'll probably do it out front, with the Capitol in the background," he says.

I ask Guastadisegni about popular "locator shots": shots that proclaim "I'm in Washington, D.C." loud and clear.

"Follow me," Guastadisegni says as he walks to the far end of the office where a few very large windows offer an unrestricted view of the Capitol Building. Two small television studios, carpeted and muffled with dark acoustical foam, have been set up to shoot studio-style interviews with a Capitol background.

"This is a good shot if you want to say Washington, or Congress," Guastadisegni offers as we walk into one of the studios.

"TV 3 in Spain anchors their Washington report from here," Guastadisegni says.

A dapper man in a European-style suit, TV 3's Washington correspondent, enters holding a script; we move into the studio next door. It's empty and very quiet; a chair and a lavalier microphone are waiting for the next "coming-to-you-from-Washington-D.C." interview.

"During the Clarence Thomas hearings, there was a line outside these studios," Guastadisegni says. "We had so many senators and media people coming through, we had to shoot some interviews up on the roof, to keep up with the demand."

Guastadisegni walks over to the window.

"On the other side of the Capitol Building, there are two very popular stand-up areas. If you're doing a story about the Senate, you generally do your stand-up on the swamp site, with the Senate chambers behind you."

"If you're doing a House of Representatives story," Guastadisegni continues," you want to be on the other side of the Capitol, under the elm tree. Go up to either site and you'll see a row of small metal boxes against the wall. They call those 'coffins.' They belong to the networks and the news services. You plug your camera and

video service for their affiliates.

When independent producers need file video, they usually work through an archival footage house like Sherman Grinberg in Manhattan. Bargain hunters start with a visit to the National Archives (Audiovisual Division) at the Library of Congress, which has motion pictures on over a hundred thousand subjects, most of them from old newsreels, government films, and educational films. The best part about the collection is that the majority of it is the property of the U.S. Government, and free. The only charge is for duplication. The shot of Elvis and Priscilla, above, is one gem found in The National Archives collection. It's one of thousands of such stories included in a Universal Newsreel series donated to the U.S. Government.

For an interview with a view: one of Newsfeed's studios between senators.

microphone into one of those boxes, and the signals go directly to your broadcast center. That way you can do a stand-up live, from in front of the Capitol or the House of Representatives."

How about White House shots?

"Most White House correspondents use the South Lawn for stand-ups," Guastadisegni replies. "But if you're in a hurry or you don't have a pass, you can shoot either from the Ellipse, in front of the White House, or from Lafayette Park across the street."

2:10 P.M.

Jaime McIntyre walks over holding a script.

"Let's do my stand-up in a car, with me clicking on a seat belt," he says.

Guastadisegni picks up his camera.

"Let's use my car," he says.

"After about your tenth stand-up in front of the Capitol, you get pretty sick of it," McIntyre says on the way to the elevator.

Guastadisegni drives to a nearby parking lot, opens the passenger door, and sets up his camera on a tripod, pointing in. After checking the viewfinder, he pulls a light out of the trunk and starts setting that up.

Meanwhile, Jaime McIntyre is sitting in the driver's seat, looking in the rear-vision mirror, putting on makeup.

"First I put some theatrical makeup under my eyes, to make me look like I've gotten more sleep than I have," McIntyre says. "Of

Some coffins under the elm, Capitol Hill.

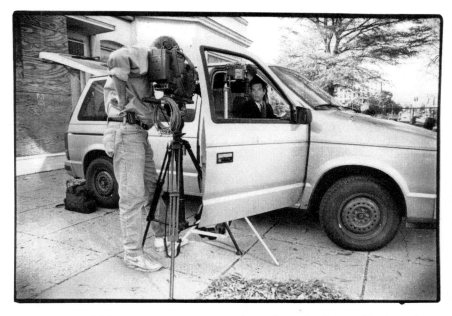

Jaime McIntyre's sit-down stand-up.

course, I could just try to get more sleep, but that's not likely. I have two very young children. After that, if I haven't had time to shave, I put on 'beard cover.' Then something to give me a darker complexion. And finally, powder, so my face doesn't look shiny."

McIntyre finishes applying his makeup; his face now looks as if he's just come back from a restful week in the Bahamas. Now he starts reciting his stand-up section for the camera, suddenly lowering his voice about an octave and adding the kind of emphatic inflection that actors use when they are playing TV news anchors.

After a few takes, Guastadisegni changes the camera angle slightly and McIntyre does a tease.

"The government says that more people are buckling up and living to tell about it," he says in his low, news-reporter voice. "In Washington, I'm Jaime McIntyre and I'll have the story."

On the way back to the office, I ask McIntyre how he writes the script. I had noticed that he didn't work in an editing room.

"I use a tape recorder to make an audio copy of the sound bites," he explains. "And then I listen to the tape on a Walkman, and I write my piece around the bites. When I'm happy with the script, I go into a booth and record my voice-over; I'm going to do that as soon as we get back. That way, when I come into the edit room, I've got my voice-over, I've got my stand-up, and I'm ready to edit."

3 P.M.

With the stand-up and voice-over done, McIntyre and Guastadisegni trundle their tapes and notes and press releases into a small edit room. They have exactly one hour to crank out a 2½-minute package for the 4:00 P.M. satellite feed.

Guastadisegni sits at the controls: shrinking news budgets have turned many cameramen into cameramen/editors.

The video news release has arrived by this point. Guastadisegni puts it into one of the decks. The opening shot is very wide, with the Capitol very prominent.

"That's wider than my shot," Guastadisegni says. "Let's use theirs."

The rest of the release looks like a typical television news story, right down to the conservatively dressed female reporter. The B-roll footage features many shots of crash-test dummies smashing through windshields.

"I think that footage is overused," McIntyre says. "Let's skip it."

McIntyre's voice-over is already recorded. It begins, "The government says that the safety-belt message is clicking with Americans . . ."

McIntyre wrote the opening to accompany a shot in which the three-hundred-foot seat belt is ceremoniously buckled. Using the time-code numbers in his notes, he and Guastadisegni quickly find the segment and edit it in. After that, they start improvising—assembling a collage of establishing shots, close-ups, sound bites from middle-aged men, and file footage of auto accident scenes. Towards the end of the piece, McIntyre seeks out the segment from the news conference in which a mother, holding a young girl in her arms, gives a testimonial about how seat belts saved their lives.

"I'm setting up the McIntyre moment," he says half facetiously as Guastadisegni edits the sequence into the piece.

Putting the package together: Gustadisegni (left) and McIntyre.

The McIntyre moment?

"That's what one of the producers at CNN calls it," McIntyre says. "I like to end a piece with a little bit of a kicker, sort of a signature-type thing. So now, when I turn in a piece, this producer often asks, 'Does it have a McIntyre moment?' "

McIntyre then reads some time-code numbers to Guastadisegni, who fast-forwards to the part of the news conference in which the three-hundred-foot seat belt is buckled. Once again we see the little girl temporarily trapped outside the seat belt until Sam Skinner parts the buckles and brings her inside.

Guastadisegni inserts the footage under McIntyre's closing words.

"And at today's news conference a bit of unintended symbolism as young Emily Main once again sought safety behind a seat belt. This is Jaime McIntyre in Washington."

"A classic McIntyre moment," McIntyre says, leaning back in his chair.

4 P.M.

The Newsfeed uplink starts at exactly 4:00 P.M. Newsfeed has an hour of satellite time to move its daily blast of raw news fodder. Managing editor Dave Foreman and feed producer Kia Johnson are sitting on the edges of their seats in a high-tech control room, sending the news up to the satellite. Today's transmission includes two seat-belt stories: Karen Hendren's raw v.o./s.o.t. piece, and Jaime McIntyre's more polished package. Also in today's feed: forty-five seconds of auto factory footage to accompany the news that Chrysler has reported big losses in the third quarter; forty seconds of Imelda Marcos returning to the Philippines; two minutes on a gubernatorial debate in Louisiana; 1:10 on jury selection for the William Kennedy Smith trial; two minutes of weather footage of a severe storm that has hit the Massachusetts coast.

As the uplink continues—with sports highlights from last night's action—staff reporter Andy Field walks over to the doorway and watches a few segments on their way up and out to the ninety-five news programs that Newsfeed supplies.

"There are a lot of hungry monsters out there to feed," he says.

4:55 P.M.

A lush glade, verdant and placid looking, is displayed on a monitor in a control room on the other side of the office.

"That's the South Lawn of the White House," Steve Phillips

explains, looking up from a computer printout. "Bush's helicopter is due to land in a few minutes. That's the pool feed."

On another monitor, there's a wide shot of the Senate floor.

"More pool coverage," Phillips says. "I've been taping the Senate all day just in case fireworks erupt. If something dramatic happens, I've got it and I'll look like a genius."

Phillips goes back to reading his computer printout, scanning tomorrow's Associated Press Daybook for newsworthy events.

```
    denison              Tue Nov  5 15:32  page   1

SLUG                      FROM     MOVED              STATUS TIME  NUMBER
AX-NF-DAYLIST-FINAL       MLvwnewsvr Wed Oct 30 17:27  WIRE   3:02 2592
=================================================================================
bc-NF-DAYLIST-FINAL
-------------------------------------------------------------------------------
---------             GROUP W DAYFEED FINAL LIST                    ---------
---------         Copyright 1991 Group W Television, Inc.           ---------
---------                                                           ---------
-------------------------------------------------------------------------------
ATTENTION STATIONS:  This is a list of slugs, formats, timecodes and run times
                     for our most recent DAYFEED satellite transmission


-------------------------------------------------------------------------------
SLUG: SECRETARY SKINNER MARKS SEATBELT CAMPAIGN MID-POINT
FORMAT: VO/SOT                         TIME CODE:  02:55      RUNS:  02:30

SLUG: CHRYSLER REPORTS BIG LOSSES IN THIRD QUARTER
FORMAT: VO                             TIME CODE:  05:3?      RUNS:  00:45

SLUG: C.P.S.C. HALLOWEEN RECALL: PUMPKIN OIL LAMP, AND HALLOWEEN TRUMPET TOYS
FORMAT: VO                             TIME CODE:  06:47      RUNS:  01:00

SLUG: CONSUMER: AIR BAGS ARE PROVEN TO BE SAFE WHEN USED WITH SEAT BELTS
FORMAT: PKG-HERB WEISBAUM              TIME CODE:  08:00      RUNS:  02:09

SLUG: HTS REQUEST: NHL: ISLANDERS CAGE SHARKS 8-4
FORMAT: VO                             TIME CODE:  10:46      RUNS:  00:50

SLUG: HALLOWEEN: SCARY MOVIES ARE EVERYWHERE THIS TIME OF YEAR
FORMAT: MOVIE CLIPS                    TIME CODE:  12:05      RUNS:  01:59

SLUG: FILE: WORLD WAR I, WORLD WAR II, KOREAN WAR AND VIETNAM WAR
FORMAT: FILE VIDEO                     TIME CODE:  14:15      RUNS:  01:44

SLUG: FILE:  DEVIL'S NIGHT 1990 IN DETROIT
FORMAT: FILE VIDEO                     TIME CODE:  16:08      RUNS:  00:40

SLUG: FILE:  GORILLA TIMMY/ANIMAL RIGHTS GROUPS WANT HIM TO STAY IN CLEVELAND
FORMAT: FILE VIDEO                     TIME CODE:  17:00      RUNS:  00:35

SLUG: FILE: IMELDA MARCOS/LEAVES FOR PHILIPPINES THURSDAY
FORMAT: FILE VO                        TIME CODE:  17:47      RUNS:  00:40

SLUG: WJBK REQUEST: REFEED: PAT LAFONTAINE GOAL ON SUNDAY NIGHT FOR SABRES
FORMAT: VO-REFEED                      TIME CODE:  18:32      RUNS:  00:40

SLUG: KENS FILE REQUEST: FORMER U.S. SUPREME COURT JUSTICE THURGOOD MARSHALL
FORMAT: VO/FILE                        TIME CODE:  18:35      RUNS:  00:50

SLUG: DAVID DUKE AND EDWIN EDWARDS HOLD A FORUM IN BATON ROUGE
FORMAT: VO/SOT                         TIME CODE:  22:26      RUNS:  02:04

SLUG: SNOW IN WICHITA TODAY
FORMAT: VO                             TIME CODE:  25:00      RUNS:  02:00

SLUG: JAMIE MCINTYRE PACKAGE- GOVT SAYS SAFETY BELT USAGE UP
FORMAT: PACKAGE- MCINTYRE             TIME CODE:  27:22      RUNS:  01:42
```

```
denison              Tue Nov  5  15:32  page   2

  SLUG: JURY SELECTION BEGINS TOMORROW FOR WILLIAM KENNEDY SMITH RAPE TRIAL
  FORMAT: VO/SOT                  TIME CODE:  29:35      RUNS:  01:10

  SLUG: FILE: POTTS TOWN, PENNSYLVANIA
  FORMAT: FILE VIDEO              TIME CODE:  31:48      RUNS:  01:25

  SLUG: WEATHER VIDE:  SEVERE STORM STRIKES MASSACHUSETTS COASTLINE
  FORMAT: VO/NAT-SND              TIME CODE:  34:05      RUNS:  02:00

  SLUG: MASSACHUSETTS CHURCH TIES IN ABORTION ISSUE WITH HALLOWEEN
  FORMAT: PKG/TED WAYMAN          TIME CODE:  36:31      RUNS:  01:50

  SLUG: PLAY OF THE DAY: WE WENT TO A BOXING MATCH AND A HOCKEY GAME BROKE OUT
  FORMAT: VO                      TIME CODE:  38:48      RUNS:  00:47

  SLUG: BOXING: RIDDICK BOWE WINS DISQUALIFICATION AFTER BRAWL
  FORMAT: VO/SOT                  TIME CODE:  41:30      RUNS:  01:18

  SLUG: NBA NEWS: TODAY IS NBA "STAY IN SCHOOL" AWARENESS DAY
  FORMAT: VO/NAT-SND              TIME CODE:  43:11      RUNS:  01:11

  SLUG: NFL NEWS: LIONS ACQUIRE D.J. DOZIER AFTER BEING RELEASED BY VIKINGS
  FORMAT: FILE VIDEO              TIME CODE:  45:30      RUNS:  00:18

  SLUG: BREEDERS CUP: POST DRAW HELD TODAY/IN EXCESS WILL ONLY ENTER ONE RACE
  FORMAT: VO/NAT-SND              TIME CODE:  46:04      RUNS:  01:30

  SLUG: ANDY FIELD PACKAGE-  FOOD STAMPS
  FORMAT: PACKAGE- FIELD          TIME CODE:  50:30      RUNS:  01:54

  SLUG: WDTV REQUEST: WEST VIRGINIA ADVERTISMENT FOR UNWANTED ANIMALS
  FORMAT: VO/SOT                  TIME CODE:  53:36      RUNS:  00:30

  SLUG: NBA NEWS: BARKLEY CALLS PHILADELPHIA A "RACIST" CITY/ENCITES FANS WRATH
  FORMAT: SOT                     TIME CODE:  55:28      RUNS:  01:20

   APEX-10-30-91 1725EST
```

"The Minnesota Twins will be at the White House. Our stations in Minnesota will want that," he says aloud. "After that, there's an EPA news conference on pesticides, a forum with Oliver North, a news conference on the Exxon *Valdez* settlements . . ."

Phillips doesn't look particularly impressed by any of his options.

"I'll look this over again on the train home," he says, standing up and folding the long printout into a neat pile.

"And you never know, something might happen overnight," he adds almost hopefully.

The Newsfeed rundown of the stories they transmitted to their subscribers during their 4:00 P.M. uplink.

3. HOW-TO TV: "THIS OLD HOUSE"

Nonfiction television is choppy by nature. Reality won't stand still long enough for leisurely, artfully composed visual ruminations. So nonfiction television generally takes its cue from the news, cobbling together short shots into choppy, quick-cut segments.

"This Old House," the home improvement show on PBS, takes the opposite approach. "This Old House" is about as fluid as non-fiction television gets. When Norm Abram (one of the hosts) is standing on top of a steep gable talking to a roofer about asphalt shingles, and he says, "Let's go look at the chimney flashing," cameraman Dick Holden is likely to follow, camera running, as the host and roofer climb down from the gable, walk across the roof, and climb another peak to the chimney—where they'll talk for a few more minutes.

Every year since 1979, "This Old House" has taken on a challenging piece of domestic architecture: a crumbling old Victorian house, a condominium that needs renovations, a historic mansion that's fallen on hard times. Then, over the course of roughly twenty half-hour episodes, we watch as the project proceeds, sometimes lurches, towards completion. The style of the show is straightforward and unpretentious, almost improvisational. The people on camera don't look like they're reading cue cards, or mouthing scripted stuff they've memorized. "This Old House" is actually more "real" than most reality-based programs. Dealing with a $5000 estimate to repair a worn-out furnace is arguably more real to most people than the two-bit drug dealers and prostitutes they bust every week on "Cops." Yet at the same time, the show really *flows*: from room to room, down to the basement, around to the backyard, and in the back door to the kitchen.

Which is why, while host Steve Thomas is talking to a visiting plumber about heating systems, I usually find myself wondering how they managed to get from the kitchen to the living room so smoothly. Another thing I find myself doing: keeping track of the length of the individual shots. When Steve walks from the living room through the dining room and into the front hall while he's talking to a wallpaper guy about period patterns—and the sequence has been going on for over two minutes without an edit—I completely lose track of what they're talking about.

So when I heard that "This Old House" was taking on an aging triple-decker in Boston's Jamaica Plain neighborhood for its twelfth season, I drove out to the site—not to find out how the restoration was going, but how producer/director Russell Morash, cameraman Dick Holden, and the rest of the crew makes "This Old House."

"I believe that the television camera should behave as the human eye does," Morash tells me right off, as he stands next to a white picket fence in front of this season's star, a drab triple-decker in transition. "The eye doesn't cut: it pans, it tilts, it zooms, but it never cuts. That's something that's imposed on us by modern-day movies. But I feel that often it's very disorienting to cut, so that if I can attach

Dick Holden looking for a good vantage point.

scene to scene to scene, image to image to image, then I'm able to convey an orientation that's not possible with the cutting technique. I think television direction should be like a good haircut: you should never be aware of it. If it draws attention to itself, then there's something wrong."

How do you attach image to image to image?

"You have to be able to direct the scene so that things are connected. You can't say, 'I want to shoot that bed, and talk about it for fourteen seconds, and then we'll talk about that light up there.' You need to think about the transition. You'll see a lot of that transitional stuff on this show. So there's sort of a choreography that you learn how to do. Yesterday we did a great piece where Steve comes through the door of a mansion; we walk through a living room, with many different zooms and pans and tilts; and then we move into a dining room, into a hallway, and into a kitchen—and it goes on for six or seven minutes. As long as the content is there, I think that's a more acceptable way to go than the cut, cut, cut approach. Of course, to pull it off you also have to be blessed with a great cameraman."

Right now, Dick Holden, the cameraman Morash has been blessed with, is about twenty feet above us on a granite promontory. Holden is trying to get a dramatic angle for the opening of Show #1014, in which host Steve Thomas drives up to the house in his pickup truck.

Russ Morash is down at sea level, watching the signal from Holden's camera on the small portable television he's holding in his left hand. A half dozen crew members are bustling about; every one of them is wearing some combination of corduroy, denim, and all-cotton flannel. Morash, who likes to direct from the middle of the fray, uses a walkie-talkie to communicate with Holden and distant crew members.

"When you drive up, Steve," Morash is saying to host Thomas, "I want you to talk your way up to the house from the truck. Say something like, 'Look what Norm's up to.'"

"I'll need a little noise from you, Norm," Morash says to Norm Abram, the show's carpenter, who's kneeling on the porch next to the front doorway.

On "Action," Abram starts hitting the porch with his hammer. He sounds convincingly busy. Steve Thomas drives up in the pickup and talks his way up to the house. He looks loose and natural, as though he were just back from the hardware store.

Now Morash wants Thomas to do it again, "bigger and to the camera up on the cliff." Then again: "This time, Norm, stop hammering when Steve starts talking." And again: "Don't throw it so

Holden (left) and cable puller Derek Diggins follow the door into this season's "This Old House." Producer/director Russell Morash watches the signal from Holden's camera on his hand-held television. He's listening to the audio on his headphones.

much to Norm. Throw your voice up here, to the camera." And again: "Perfect."

After Thomas has talked his way up to the house for the fifth time, Morash and Holden choreograph a series of overlapping shots that move the show's two hosts out to the truck to get a new door and then back to the doorway to start the installation. The pace is deliberate and strictly sequential. Morash first makes sure he's happy with the move from point A to point B; then he starts planning the move from B to C. Scene by scene, "This Old House" is laid out visually like a straightaway of interlocking train tracks: a tight fit, end to end. Which gives Dick Holden a little creative slack. In fact, Holden's loose camera work plays well against Morash's straight-ahead style; it keeps the show from turning into a blocky, Lego-like structure.

An example: when Norm and Steve walk from the house to the pickup truck to get the new door, Holden walks backward in front of them until they get to the truck, then he veers off and takes the long way around the front bumper to the other side of the truck, taking in a lot of shiny red sheet metal as he moves along the outside of the cab and truck bed until the camera meets up with Norm and Steve at the back of the truck. Then, when they lift the door and start to head back to the house, Holden again takes the scenic sheet-metal route around the outside of the truck and catches up with them as they carry the door up the pathway to the house. Although Holden is shooting a show that preaches efficiency and economy, he rarely travels the most direct route between two points.

Dick Holden. Like John Baynard, Holden uses a Betacam SP camera. He wears a headset to communicate with director Russell Morash.

When he's holding a camera, Holden's bearing is somehow taut and relaxed at the same time, like that of a confident defensive cornerback. The camera he uses, an Ikegami 79E, weighs twenty-two pounds. They make lighter ones now, but Holden likes the weight.

"A heavier camera is easier to keep steady," he says. "The weight cuts down on the shakiness when I'm moving."

And when Holden moves, he likes to stay close to the action.

"I like to stay close, rather than zoom in from a distance," he says. "If you're close you can move better, you can move laterally. If you're zoomed in on a tight shot, you're trapped: if the person moves, or if something moves in the foreground, you have to zoom out, move, then zoom back in. All that zooming can give the viewer vertigo. If you're close, you can move with the action much better."

Holden began his career as a studio cameraman, at the Hartford, Connecticut, public broadcasting station. He arrived at WGBH just as Russell Morash was launching "The Victory Garden" in a garden he planted in the WGBH parking lot.

"I was a junior man, a very junior man," Holden recalls. "During the first year of 'The Victory Garden,' I would appear from time to time as a cable puller, stage manager, grip. Then one of the show's two cameramen went off on paternity leave and I took his spot. I've been with Russell ever since, working on 'The Victory Garden,' 'This Old House,' and various Julia Child programs."

Along the way, Holden's fluent approach carved out a distinctive

THIS OLD HOUSE
PRODUCTION SCHEDULE
Wednesday, November 28, 1990

==

7:00	Station call; travel to Jamaica Plain

==

7:30-8:00	Set-up kit

==

8:00-9:00	Open for Show #1014; front door installation, intro to Workshop drop-in, intro to Bill Richardson

==

9:00-10:00	Shoot scene with Bill Richardson of Sentry Protective Systems

==

10:00-12:00	Shoot installation of de-leaded doors; intro to PFD drop-in and Close for Show #1014

==

12:00-1:00	Lunch

==

1:00-2:00	Shoot open for Show #1015, Abel installs vinyl flooring

==

2:00-4:30	Shoot floor sanding scene; intro to Salem drop-in and Close for Show #1015

==

4:30-5:00	Travel back to WGBH

==

THIS OLD HOUSE #1014 PROGRAM RUNDOWN

==

LENGTH ALLOWED	ACTUAL TIME	SCENE DESCRIPTION	REMAINING TIME
	:35	WGBH Logo, Uwr. Credits	
	:30	Tease (post-build)	
2:00		Sc. 1: Open; Steve meets Norm installing the front door.	
:30		Intro. Workshop Flashback	
5:00		Sc. 2: FLASHBACK: At Workshop Norm installs the front door's electric buzzer/lock.	
2:00		Sc. 3: Back at the house, Norm completes front door installation.	
:30		Intro. to Bill Richardson of Sentry Protective Systems	
5:00		Sc. 4: Bill Richardson of Sentry Protective Systems discusses security measures for the house.	
2:00		Sc. 5: Norm and Abel install de-leaded doors	
:30		Intro to Public Facilities Dept. Tour	
8:00		Sc. 6: Steve meets Amy Wrigley for a tour of three PFD properties on the market.	
1:00		Sc. 7: Close. Next week: Floor sanding, installation of vinyl flooring, and a visit to the Essex Institute in Salem (floor cloths).	
	1:10	End Credits	

A "This Old House" production schedule and program rundown.

(as of 11/21/90)

style for the Morash programs. It's significant that the very first Emmy nomination for "The Victory Garden" was for outstanding achievement in technical direction/electronic camera/video control. Holden has since won two national Emmy Awards for his work on "This Old House."

Although he now works almost exclusively with ENG-style equipment, Holden's shooting style is heavily influenced by his studio experience.

"I'm a fugitive from ENG," he says. "As far as the style goes, I was a studio cameraman for many years, and happily so. I used to love to dolly the camera. I was proud to be a member of the million-mile club. I love a shot with movement in it. And out here, that style is still the Platonic ideal: a moving camera that looks the way a studio dolly shot would look. Smooth, like the feeling you get with those wonderful rolling Vinten pedestals you use in the studio. That's something I keep in the back of my mind, something I aim for."

Inside the house, plaster dust is everywhere; the floor is littered with plywood scraps and nails; and it is dark, compared to the bright day outside. Before Norm and Steve start working on the door, Holden sets up a tall light stand and aims a 200-watt HMI light at the scene. To soften the glare, he covers the light with a single layer of fiberglass fabric called "spun." When he turns it on, the hallway looks much brighter, but in a muffled kind of way.

Holden shooting Norm Abram and Steve Thomas talking doors. The light in the upper right hand corner is an HMI light, very powerful and very expensive. A single 200-watt HMI bulb throws off more light than two similar traditional quartz bulbs; it also costs $250. Holden thinks the HMI lights are worth the money. Frequently, on location he has to work with household current. An HMI light gives him the most light for the least power consumption.

"I'm always trying to create that perfect cloudy day," Holden says.

When Norm and Steve start discussing the door's installation and Holden frames a steady wide shot, I trace his camera cable up the stairs and into a small makeshift control room. Here I find Bill Fairweather and Francis X. Coakley monitoring the production amidst scattered, well-beaten equipment cases. Coakley, the show's audio technician, is sitting in front of a portable Betacam SP deck, watching the audio meters very carefully. Four antennas are pointing straight up from behind the deck.

"Two of the antennas are getting signals from the radio mikes on Norm Abram and Steve Thomas," Coakley explains. "We're also sending out audio and video signals to Russ. He can hear the audio on his headphones; he can watch the video on his Watchman."

Bill Fairweather is sitting to Coakley's right. On the credits, Fairweather's job is listed as simply "video/videotape." He's watching the picture from Holden's camera on a small television monitor; he's also watching a waveform monitor, an oscilloscope that measures and displays various properties of the television signal. When Holden moves his camera towards the open front door, Fairweather turns down the camera's iris; if he didn't, the bright daylight would blast the image.

"Normally a cameraman would do this himself," Fairweather says, "but Dick's got enough to think about already. And if I continually adjust the iris, he can walk from a dark hallway into a bright

Bill Fairweather (left) and Francis Coakley in their ad hoc control room.

room—or pan across an open window—without worrying about screwing up the signal. I keep it pretty even.

"It's really a terrible day today, from our point of view," Fairweather continues, pointing out the window at the bright, cloudless blue sky. "Ideally, we like some clouds to soften the light and give us some fill. I have to be very careful to turn down the iris every time Dick shoots near a door or window. Otherwise, the image would fluctuate wildly."

If you have a good television monitor, I ask Fairweather, why do you need a waveform monitor?

"Because you need a waveform to set up your television monitor, so you know it's good," he says. "It's like flying an airplane. You don't just watch your altitude or your rate of climb, or your turn and bank. You correlate all these things. That's also how you make the proper television exposure: you correlate the information you get from the waveform monitor with the picture you see on the television monitor."

Downstairs, Norm Abram and Steve Thomas are installing the door, talking and hammering. I ask Frank Coakley how he's mikeing the scene.

"Everything you're hearing is coming over the radio mikes on Norm and Steve," he says. "That's usually enough. Every once in a while I'll use a shotgun microphone; I used one when Steve drove up in the car, to get the humming engine and the truck door's closing. I wanted you to really feel like the truck was coming into the frame."

The radio mikes that Coakley uses are Vegas, the same brand that John Baynard uses for his ENG work. I mention to Coakley that the Vega manual says that sometimes "tempers flare" in the field when different television crews discover that they are using the same RF frequency.

"Sure. Happens all the time," Coakley says, "and who's right?"

How do you handle it?

"I just find the guy, slap him around, and tell him to get off my frequency," Coakley says deadpan.

"Seriously, most of us are pretty cooperative," he adds. "We're all in the same business. Say I'm on 184.5, you're on 185.4. We're too close. So I'll say, 'Can you move to another frequency? Or else I'll move.' We do that kind of thing all the time, because chances are that if I'm hearing him, he's hearing me. Fortunately, this system can operate on eight different frequencies, so you have some room to move."

What's the range of a radio microphone?

"Very limited," Coakley says. "Maybe a couple of hundred yards."

"So you can also just move one block down, and the problem is solved," Fairweather adds. "The real problem comes when you're in an urban area, a high RF environment."

What does he hear, police radios?

"It's hard to identify," Fairweather says, "because you don't hear the modulated signal."

"You hear chucch, chucch," Coakley says.

"You hear the splatter," Fairweather says.

"I hear taxicabs occasionally," Coakley says.

Midway through the conversation it occurs to me that Fairweather and Coakley have spent so many hours together, monitoring and adjusting video and audio signals, that it's possible to get two very informed views with one question. A rare two-for-one journalistic bargain.

What kind of sound quality are you looking for, I ask Fairweather and Coakley.

"I just want it to sound natural," Fairweather says.

"What I try to do when I'm miking somebody is get a mix of what's happening in the room," Coakley says. "But mainly the voices. On this show Russ wants to hear every line, every word. He wants everything to be perfectly clear. He wants the viewers to understand what's going on. And that can be a problem if you've got power tools going."

"It's also a problem if you're standing outside and the wind is blowing at thirty-five knots," Fairweather adds. "Then you've got to bury the mike in the person's clothing. And the more you bury it, the more you lose the sibilance, the high end. It gets muddier and muddier."

"It's a compromise," Coakley says.

"Then there's clothing rustle, and silk ties," Fairweather adds.

"There's a whole science to miking people with radio mikes," Coakley says. "You have to use all sorts of little tricks to deal with different kinds of clothing."

"Like turtlenecks," Fairweather says.

How *do* you deal with turtlenecks? I ask.

"You come up behind them, generally," Coakley says.

"You also have to be kind of a diplomat," Fairweather says. "Like if you have to hide a microphone in a woman's leotard."

"And actually, the best place to put a mike, in that case, is right between a woman's breasts," Coakley says. "There's a little space there, and there's no clothing rub. You do have to be pretty diplomatic about it. For professional actresses it's no problem. They just drop their clothes and say 'Where do you want to put it?' But if you have some woman who's just visiting the show one day and she's a homeowner, it's a different story.''

How long have radio mikes been part of the production scene?

"They've been a reliable tool since the mid eighties," Coakley says. "Before that they had radio microphones that worked, but they were so big and so clunky that you couldn't hide them on anybody. When they got them down to small body packs, they took off.''

Do you think they've influenced the way television is made?

"Definitely," Coakley says. "Look at 'Sixty Minutes.' " (Coakley often works for "60 Minutes" on a freelance basis.) "Or 'Evening Magazine.' Radio mikes allow the camera to move around quite a bit more. They give people the freedom to go where the action is.''

"We couldn't do this show without radio mikes," Fairweather adds. "That's one of the strengths of this show: it breaks down the studio door and goes places you don't expect television to go. We couldn't do that without radio mikes. I mean, the idea of trying to use a boom mike on this show, forget it. You could never get the mike where it needs to be so you can hear them. The radio mike is really the only way to go.''

I mention to Coakley that I've recently seen positive articles on low-priced radio microphones in the television-production trade magazines. Some of the radio microphones sell for as little as $200. Is a $2000 Vega really that much better?

"I've listened to them, and I'm unimpressed," Coakley says. "They don't have the fidelity that I want, but what I really worry about is the reliability. You want a solidly built product that will perform well day in and day out. The difference between a $150 radio mike and a $2000 radio mike is dependability.''

A production assistant arrives with word that the burglar-alarm guy is in the kitchen, ready to discuss electronic security with Steve Thomas. Frank goes downstairs to wire him with a radio microphone. I follow him down to the kitchen, where I find Holden bouncing a light off the ceiling.

"A lot of people bounce lights off umbrellas or something," he says, "but I bounce it off the ceiling. I want there to be shadows, if possible, under the chin. I think that helps with the definition.''

Holden is aiming the light so that everybody's shadow falls on the floor, not on the walls where they might get in the picture.

"Shadows are my enemy," he says. "Once again, I'm basically

Dick Holden, cable puller Derek Diggins, director Russell Morash, and host Steve Thomas rehearsing with home security consultant Bill Richardson. Note the HMI light behind Holden, bouncing light off the ceiling. Another attempt by Holden to create a "perfect cloudy day."

trying to create that perfect cloudy day. Then, if circumstances permit, I'll throw in a kicker, a small light to bring out the eyes. But that's extra credit."

Russell Morash, Steve Thomas, and the alarm guy are standing around the kitchen counter, improvising Steve's opening lines.

Morash says, "How about an opening line like, 'It's a sad but true fact of modern life that a burglar alarm is not a luxury, it's a necessity.' "

Holden is conferring with Derek Diggins, his cable puller. They are trying to plot a camera move that will allow Holden to shoot continuously without getting any camera cables in the frame.

"Cables are another enemy," Holden says. "I have an enemies list, but they're all inanimate."

After some paranoia-inducing tips from the alarm guy ("now, if someone smashes the first-floor window . . ."), the production breaks for an alfresco catered lunch. Holden and I grab crusty overstuffed sandwiches, some bottled water, and drag a pair of canvas chairs to a large overturned box.

I ask him if he feels free to improvise when he's shooting "This Old House?"

"I try to mimic the human eye," he says. "That's what's behind the whole concept. We try to show things the way you would see them if you happened to walk into a room. On 'The Victory Garden,' when we're on a garden tour we try to approach the garden the way people do when they walk into a backyard garden. If the layout permits it and the light permits it, that's the ideal way. But it involves a big investment up front. For instance, the cable. You can't just lay it out and have it follow you. It has to be laid out ahead of time. It's really kind of a teleological approach: where the end dictates everything that comes before. It's like we're being rewound into the spool.

"And if everything comes together—the conditions and the planning—you can end up with some pretty long shots that really work," Holden continues. "In the early days of 'The Victory Garden,' we did a shot that lasted fifteen to eighteen minutes, probably a personal record. We've also done a 'This Old House' show that had just five shots in it: one nine minutes long, one ten, and three short shots. We didn't plan it that way, it just happened. That was really the epitome of our style."

Russell Morash walks by, stops, and sits down for a minute.

"If you're collecting camera moves, there's a great one in the Scorsese movie *GoodFellas*," he says. "It's a single camera move that he uses coming into the Copacabana, following the people in. It's the same kind of stuff that Dick does, except Scorsese was probably working with a Steadicam or tracks."

I ask Holden if he's ever thought about using a Steadicam, the stabilization system that smooths hand-held camera shots into dolly-like fluidity.

"Not really," he replies. "The Steadicam hardware is pretty cumbersome. It's a moose to get on and off. And I just couldn't do it, the way we shoot here. It's just too tight, plus it takes up so much room. If I were wearing all that Steadicam gear, I couldn't get nearly as wide a shot."

A linoleum installer arrives, ten minutes early for the first after-lunch segment. Morash gets up, greets him, and heads inside to the kitchen. As Holden starts packing up his lunch, I ask him if he is frequently hired free-lance to shoot fledgling how-to television shows and perhaps add a little PBS luster to the project.

"I've been hired to do the 'This Old House' look," he says. "But when I get there, the director often loses his nerve. He'll start saying stuff like, 'Maybe we should try a tripod on this shot.' I've discovered that most of these shows are jerky, badly planned, and badly lit, with a lot of fussy little shots. I don't do them anymore.

"Everybody seems to love this style," he says finally. "But nobody else seems to have the guts to do it."

4. FOURTEEN WINNING TIPS FOR BETTER TALK-SHOW SEGMENTS

1. Know who's plugging what.

Joanne Tardieu booked William Devane for today's "Live with Regis & Kathie Lee" about a week ago, after she got a call from a publicist she knows at CBS. Devane, who has played the relentlessly rich and powerful Gregory Sumner on "Knots Landing" since 1983, was planning to be in New York to do some publicity for an upcoming appearance in the made-for-TV movie *Nightmare in Columbia County*.

"I thought he'd be a good guest," Tardieu recalls. "The viewers all know him from 'Knots.' "

Tardieu is one of six segment producers who work on "Live with Regis & Kathie Lee." She's been with the show since 1988, just before it went from being a hot local program to a nationally syndicated success. Before that she was a segment producer for "Good Day," a similar show in Boston. Recently, Tardieu's job has grown in importance. In a television industry that's currently talk-crazy, executives have come to realize that it's the segment producers like Tardieu who push the programming along; it's the segment producers who provide the hosts with something to talk *about*.

This morning, as Tardieu produces the William Devane segment, I'm watching and taking notes, in an effort to see how a segment producer works. Already I've learned that it helps if you can break down a how-to segment into a number of discrete tips: earlier in the week, for example, a segment with Richard Simmons featured "Five

Tips for Keeping Weight Off During the Holidays." Maybe this approach has wider applications.

2. Pre-interview the guest.

The first thing Joanne Tardieu did after she booked William Devane on the show was schedule a pre-interview.

"Obviously he's here to plug the movie," she says, "but I wanted to get some personal stuff: family, hobbies, background, children. That's what works on the show."

Tardieu has no trouble steering a conversation into these areas. Within five minutes of our first meeting, she knew how many children I had, their ages, where I grew up; I knew that she had married very young, and that for four years she lived in Brookline, Massachusetts, which has an excellent school system. Her daughter, who's now in college, had a terrific four years at Brookline High School.

When Tardieu reached Devane at his New York hotel yesterday afternoon, she found him easy to talk to. They quickly dispensed with the made-for-TV movie he was supposed to be plugging and talked about his horses, his polo playing, and his family life. He's been married to his wife, Eugenie, for twenty-nine years; they met as students at the American Academy of Dramatic Arts. They have two sons in their twenties. The sons help run Devane's Italian restaurant. When Tardieu asked if the restaurant's cuisine was Northern or Southern Italian, Devane said, "New Jersey Italian."

When she asked about "Knots," casually, Devane mentioned that actually there had been some trouble with the writers; most of them had just been fired and the show was going on a short hiatus to regroup.

"Yesterday's New York *Post* had an item about it," Devane said.

After the interview, Tardieu sought out yesterday's *Post*, clipped the article, and added it to her manila folder marked "Devane."

"That's a great bit of newsy information," she says. "It's something Regis can ask him about."

3. Get a "hot" clip.

Tardieu already had a cassette from CBS with three short scenes from the made-for-TV movie. It came with the press kit.

"They were fine," she says of the clips. "I looked at them upstairs, and chose a suspenseful scene. But I also wanted a 'Knots Landing' clip, so I called CBS and asked them to send me some 'hot' clips, like bedroom scenes."

When the tape arrived via courier, Tardieu quickly screened it and chose a scene with William Devane and a young blonde lying in bed, scheming.

4. Send some information home with the hosts.

Late yesterday afternoon, Tardieu had typed out two cards to include in the daily package that's sent home with Regis and Kathie Lee.

First she wrote an introduction for Regis that played off the hot clip from "Knots," briefly mentioning Devane's polo playing.

She also sketched out three questions having to do with turmoil on the set of "Knots Landing," Devane's polo ranch, and his polo injuries.

Then she wrote a short introduction to the clip from the made-for-TV movie, described what's in the clip, and finished with the plug: one sentence, underlined.

"That's the way we always structure the segments," she says. "First personal stuff, then the plug."

The second card contained background material: Devane's marriage (*29 YEARS*), his sons, the restaurant, including the "New Jersey Italian" joke, and a sentence about how he started out onstage in New York, working for Joseph Papp.

All the information is typed in capital letters, with lots of white space and underlining. Kathie Lee Gifford will be able to read it easily during the limousine ride back to her house in Connecticut; Regis will be able to quickly scan it during the commercial break before Devane's appearance.

SEG. 2   WILLIAM DEVANE   REGIS & KATHIE LEE   12/10/91 Joanne
(BUMPER CLIP IN FROM "KNOT'S LANDING" - WILLIAM DEVANE IN BED WITH A BLOND)

THAT WAS VETERAN ACTOR, WILLIAM DEVANE IN A COZY SCENE FROM "KNOT'S LANDING"
HE'S PLAYED THE RICH AND POWERFUL GREGORY SUMNER ON THAT SHOW SINCE 1983,
AND ALSO FINDS TIME TO RAISE HORSES FOR POLO AND PLAY THAT GAME AS WELL!

-WHAT'S BEEN HAPPENING ON "KNOT'S LANDING" - (PROBLEMS, THE WRITERS WERE
    FIRED, ETC. SEE ARTICLE FROM YESTERDAY'S NEW YORK POST)

-WILLIAM LIVES IN THE DESERT AREA NEAR PALM SPRINGS, ON A LARGE RANCH
    THAT IS PART OF A GROUP OF RANCHES FOR PEOPLE WHO RAISE POLO HORSES,
    AND PLAY THE GAME AS WELL..ASK HIM HOW IT GOT STARTED?

-HAS HE HAD ANY POLO INJURIES? (YES, BROKEN SOME PARTS, BUT STILL PLAYS,
    JUST NOT AS ROUGHLY..HIS WIFE TRIED IT ONCE, GOT HURT, STOPPED)

-TONIGHT ON CBS, WILLIAM STARS IN "NIGHTMARE IN COLUMBIA COUNTY" - BASED ON
    A TRUE STORY, HE PLAYS A SHERIFF TRYING TO SOLVE A KIDNAPPING...

-***CLIP** WILLIAM WITH THE KIDNAPPED GIRL'S OLDER SISTER, DAWN.
            WILLIAM WANTS DAWN TO TALK TO THE KIDNAPPER IF HE CALLS AGAIN.

PLUG "NIGHTMARE IN COLUMBIA COUNTY" AIRS TONIGHT AT 9 ON CBS

SEG. 2 WILLIAM DEVANE   REGIS & KATHIE LEE   12/10/91 Joanne

   BACKGROUND MATERIAL

  -WILLIAM STARTED PLAYING POLO APPROX 6 YEARS AGO, ACTUALLY PUT THIS
      RANCH PROPERTY TOGETHER - IT'S LIKE A POLO COMMUNITY.

  -HE AND WIFE, EUGENIE, HAVE BEEN MARRIED 29 YEARS..THEY MET AS STUDENTS
      AT THE AMERICAN ACADEMY OF DRAMATIC ARTS.

  -THEY HAVE TWO SONS, JOSH AND JAKE IN THEIR 20'S

  -THE SONS AND WILLIAM'S BROTHER RUN HIS RESTAURANT, "FABS" IN INDIO..
      GREAT ITALIAN FOOD, LIKE "FABS" IN LOS ANGELES" ..WILLIAM IS IN ON
   IT WITH AN ITALIAN FAMILY FROM NEW JERSEY! (THEY HAD THE RESTAURANT IN
      LOS ANGELES, WHICH WILLIAM DOESN'T HAVE A SHARE IN)

  -ASK HIM IF THE RESTAURANT SERVES NORTHERN OR SOUTHERN ITALIAN?
      (HE'LL PROBABLY SAY, "NEW JERSEY")

  -HIS YOUNGER SON, JAKE IS LEARNING TO COOK, WORKS IN THE KITCHEN OF
      THE RESTAURANT..OLDER SON AND HIS GIRLFRIEND RUN THE PLACE, IT'S
      A REAL FAMILY AFFAIR..

  -WILLIAM SAYS ORIGINALLY HE CAME TO NEW YORK, STUDIED ACTING AND
      WO
      RKED WITH JOSEPH PAPP. BOTH ACTING, DRIVING A TRUCK WHATEVER PAPP NE__

5. Get some photos.

A head shot of William Devane came with the press kit. Tardieu threw it out.

"Head shots don't elicit conversation," she says.

What Tardieu really likes is personal photos; she almost always asks a guest to bring them. Many guests are happy to comply. Earlier in the week, Debby Boone arrived for her segment with a thick pile of photos; William Shatner brought nearly an entire photo album. Lucie Arnaz showed home videos during her segment.

During the pre-interview, Tardieu asked Devane if he had any personal photos: of the ranch, his family, his horses. He didn't.

"He told me he's not a picture-taker," she says with a shrug.

So a few days ago, Tardieu put in a call to Jerry Ohlinger (she calls him Jerry O), who has a show-business photo archive in Manhattan. She asked for "anything Devane." Also, because Devane got his big break playing John F. Kennedy and looks quite a bit like him, she asked Jerry O to send her two roughly comparable shots of Devane and Kennedy.

The package arrived yesterday afternoon, but now, standing in the hallway about an hour before show time, Tardieu is taking her first close look at the file, trying to choose a few for the segment. There's Devane as Kennedy in *The Missiles of October*; Devane embracing Natalie Wood in a still from the television version of *From Here to Eternity*; an odd, unlabeled photo of a young Devane sporting a shaggy beard; some "Knots Landing" stills; Devane embracing a partially clothed Vanessa Redgrave in *Yanks*; Devane with Dustin Hoffman in *Marathon Man*. There's also a head shot of John F. Kennedy and a head shot of a younger Devane; they look like brothers.

Tardieu sets five or six photos aside.

"I'll get these mounted and labeled and show them to Reege," she says.

Couldn't you just bring them into the control room and display them on the television monitor?

"We could do that, but it's not as folksy. It's much better if Regis is holding them."

6. Make some cue cards.

Tardieu began the morning at 7:00 A.M., carrying her Devane folder. The manila folder contained a few script notes and two press releases. An hour ago, she added the unwieldy package of photos. Now at 8:30 A.M., she's also carrying around a half dozen large white cardboard cards and a black marker, looking for a space to write

OPPOSITE
The two cards that went home with Regis and Kathie Lee.

some cue cards. First she stakes out a small, wobbly table outside the green room. There's already a small Christmas tree and a few notebooks on the table, but there's just enough room to sort of lean the cards on the table, as she writes, WHAT'S GOING ON AT "KNOTS LANDING"? (SOME STAFF HAVE *BEEN FIRED*) and WHEN NOT WORKING, WILLIAM LIKES TO BE ON HIS *RANCH,* FOR *POLO.*

Tardieu has a desk upstairs, but almost all of the show's pre-broadcast business is conducted on the fly, in the corridors and on the edges of the stage. As technicians and assistant directors and prop people whisk by, the segment producers flag them for favors, questions, and updates. When Bob Nimmo, the show's prop master, goes by, Tardieu quickly bundles up her folder, her photos, and her cue cards and follows him into the studio.

"Bob, Bob, can you mount these pictures for me?" she asks. "Devane is segment two today."

Nimmo takes the photos. Tardieu turns to head back to the corridor, but her place on the rickety table is gone. Another segment producer is using it to write her cue cards. Tardieu finds a space in an empty aisle in the audience section, and starts to write the plug.

"I always put the plug on a clean card," she says as she writes *PLUG:* "NIGHTMARE IN COLUMBIA COUNTY" ON CBS. *TONIGHT AT 9 PM.*

"And I always keep one blank, just in case I have to write something at the last second."

Writing cue cards.

7. Try to get one last-minute session with the host.

At 8:50, ten minutes until airtime, Joanne Tardieu is stationed just outside the studio's main makeup room. Another segment producer is standing next to her.

"Regis will be arriving any second," she says. "This is the last chance you have to catch him and get a minute or two of his time before the show. Sometimes there's a line of segment producers waiting outside the makeup room, waiting for their two-minute shot with Regis. I'm here because I want to run some of the Devane pictures by him. I also just found out that the blonde who's in bed with Devane in the 'Knots' clip is now off the show. I want Regis to know that going in."

Does he always come down at exactly the same time?

"Exactly, like three, two, one," she says, counting down, looking at a hallway clock. "Gee, he's a little late."

Just then Regis, under a full head of steam, swoops around the corner and turns into the makeup room. Tardieu falls in behind him. As soon as he sits down and the makeup artist starts powdering and smoothing, Tardieu quickly starts showing him photos.

Yes, he likes the shot with Vanessa Redgrave; yes on the shot with Natalie Wood. No, he doesn't like the Kennedy comparison. That's out.

Joanne tells him that the blonde in the opening clip is no longer on the show. She's out.

Running some pictures by Reege.

Today's short rundown.
Opposite, a more
detailed script. Note
Tardieu's initials on both
sheets; all questions
about the segment are
referred to her. Note also
the staging (downstage
stools), the two clips,
and the promo for one of
tomorrow's guests (Ed
Marinaro).

By now the stage manager, Julian Abio, has moved in. He's massaging Regis's shoulders.

Tardieu shows Regis one last photo, the unlabeled picture of the young, bearded Devane.

"Don't show this to Devane beforehand," Regis says. "Let me show it to him."

8. Use the element of surprise.

"Did you catch that?" Tardieu asks as we leave the makeup room.

LIVE Regis & Kathie Lee   **SHORT RUNDOWN**

DATE: TUESDAY, DECEMBER 10, 1991

SEG. #1	HOST CHAT
SEG. #2	WILLIAM DEVANE - JT
SEG. #3	KARYN WHITE - VL
SEG. #4	CLAUDIA COHEN - SH
SEG. #5	JOEL RAPP - RK
SEG. #6	JOEL RAPP - RK
SEG. #7	CLOSE
PROMOS:	ON CAMERA CHRISTMAS PROMOS (5) - KGS
POST TAPE:	KIMBERLY WILLIAMS - BF

SEG 2(R&KL) (JT)	C:12				UL
9:17:20 BUMPER IN	SOT:21	CLIP			
WILLIAM DEVANE/WALK-ON/DOWNSTAGE STOOLS	3RF				6:00
CLIP	SOT:1:04 CLIP				
9:22:20 (B.O.) TOMORROW: ED MARINARO	C:11			01:33:45	X

CX 2 - 1 min. barter spot +(1:02 black)					

SEG 3(R&KL) (VL)	C:11				UL
9:25:22 BUMPER IN	SOT:15	CLIP			
KARYN WHITE/WALK-ON/DOWNSTAGE STOOLS	3RF				6:00
PERFORM TO TRACK/3 MIC STANDS/HANDHELD CD	SOT:2:00 MUSIC				
	2 HAND MICS				
	1 HAND HELD RF				
9:31:22 (B.O.) TOMORROW: BILLY FALCON	SOT:15	CLIP		01:33:45	
CX 3 - (2:02 Black)					

SEG 4(R&KL) (SH)	C:12			01:29:05	LL
9:33:24					
CLAUDIA COHEN/PRE-SET/HOMEBASE/MONITOR UP	3RF				6:00
SS TBA					
	C:11				
9:39:24 (B.O.) THURSDAY: CLINT HOLMES	SIL:20	CLIP		01:32:35	
CX 5 - (2:02 black) SUSAN DEY				01:32:35	X

SEG 5(R&KL) (RK)	C:12				LL
9:41:26					
JOEL RAPP/PRE-SET/DOWNSTAGE DEMO TABLE	3RF				6:00
9:47:26 (B.O.) NEWSLETTER #97	C:12			01: :	
CX 6 - (2:02) 9:55:10 at the latest					

SEG 6(R&KL) (RK)	C:11				LL
9:49:28					
JOEL RAPP/CONTD.	3RF				5:00
	C:12				
9:54:28 (B.O.) FRIDAY: DUSTIN HOFFMAN	SIL:20	CLIP		01:33:10	
CX 4 - (2:02 black)					

SEG. 7 (DEAD ROLL AUDIO CART AT 56:18)	C:12				UL
9:56:30 R & KL PRE-SET/HOMEBASE/CLOSE	2RF				1:00
9:57:30 ROLL FEE SPOTS/AUDIO PRECEDES					
9:57:35 FEE SPOT AUDIO					
9:58:05 CHYRON/STUDIO SHOT - CLOTHING					
9:58:20 BUENA VISTA ANIMATION					
9:58:26 BLACK					

"Regis wants to surprise Devane with that last photo. He thinks he can do something with that."

Across the hall, Kathie Lee is sitting in her makeup chair. Her hair is in rollers.

Is she going to show the photos to Kathie Lee? I ask.

"No, Kathie Lee doesn't like to see photos ahead of time," Tardieu replies. "She likes to be surprised on the air. Sometimes we'll also hold things back on Regis, to encourage that element of surprise."

For example?

"A few days ago, Julia Sweeney, a cast member on 'Saturday Night Live,' was on the show. She told me during the pre-interview that her mother was a huge fan of Regis. She said her mother likes him because he's a Catholic, and because he's 'funny but not irreverent.' I told her it would be cute if she mentioned that on the air, if it came up naturally. But I didn't tell Regis. And she did mention it, and it kind of caught Regis by surprise and was a nice moment."

9. Make the guest comfortable, then turn him over to an intern.

William Devane is scheduled to appear in the first segment after host chat, at 9:17. His limousine pulls up to the studio at 9:07. Tardieu escorts Devane, his wife, and a few publicists into the green room. Regis and Kathie Lee are already halfway through their opening host-chat segment. Regis is complaining about how much a Christmas tree costs in New York City ($75). As soon as Devane has a cup of coffee, Tardieu turns him over to an intern.

"I've got to be on the floor," Tardieu says. She's now wearing an intercom system so that she can communicate with the control room. She has also drafted another segment producer, Tisi Aylward, to help her choreograph the cue cards.

As the host-chat segment draws to a close, Tardieu is standing just offstage sorting through her cue cards. A few seconds later—when the first commercial break arrives—Tardieu walks up to the table next to Regis and checks to see that the photos are there.

"I can't touch them," she says, "Union regulations. But I can make sure the prop people put them out."

Then she positions herself right next to the camera; Tisi stands directly behind her. Regis has Tardieu's background cards in his lap.

The "Knots Landing" clip rolls, the one that features Devane in bed with a blonde.

When Devane walks on, Regis is reacting to the clip.

Joanne Tardieu and William Devane in the green room.

"How come I don't have a job like that!" he's yelling. "Laying around with starlets all day. What do I get? I get Kathie Lee!"

Everybody's smiling. Tardieu is holding her first cue card. It reads: WHAT'S GOING ON AT "KNOTS LANDING"? (SOME STAFF HAVE *BEEN FIRED*) and WHEN NOT WORKING, WILLIAM LIKES TO BE ON HIS *RANCH,* FOR *POLO.*

Regis starts by asking Devane about his early acting career in New York, and why he moved to Los Angeles. They talk about this for a few minutes. Then Regis looks at Tardieu.

"So, William, what's going on at 'Knots Landing?' We've been reading about staff changes, turmoil . . . "

By the time Devane responds to the question, it's time for the clip. Tardieu is holding up her "clip" cue card with all the information that Regis needs to set it up. Regis reads it verbatim.

The clip lasts about a minute. While it's running I'm surprised to see that both Regis and Kathie Lee are watching it intently. When it ends, Regis and Kathie Lee compliment Devane on his performance. Tardieu is holding up her "plug" cue card.

"All right, William," Regis says, looking directly at Tardieu's cue card. "That's *Nightmare in Columbia County,* on CBS, tonight at nine. We'll be back with singer Karyn White, after this. . . . "

Tardieu escorts Devane offstage to the green room—where Devane's wife and publicists are waiting—and then out to the limousine. The limousine's engine is still running; it's 9:25 when Devane and party climb in; they were in the building less than twenty minutes.

*Joanne Tardieu during
her segment.*

"I think it went pretty well," Tardieu says as she walks back to the studio.

I mention that Regis didn't use any pictures.

"That's all right; he was rolling," she replies. "The pictures are kind of a fallback. He didn't need them. If Regis and Kathie Lee get off to a good start, they can take it from there, because they actually listen to what the guest is saying, and they respond to it. A lot of times the people doing interviews are so uptight, thinking about the next question or where they want the interview to go, that they don't really listen to the answer. They're just anticipating asking the next question. Our hosts really visit. Once they get on a topic, the segment can really go in any direction, because they're listening."

Now we're just about to enter the studio; the red "On Air" light is bright red. Tardieu pauses at the door.

"Did you notice how Regis responded to the clip of Devane in bed with that blonde?" she asks. "The schtick about 'How come I don't have a job like that?' I didn't say anything to him beforehand, but I had a feeling that might get him going."

10. Try to attend to the right detail at the right moment.

Inside the studio, the show's resident gossip columnist, Claudia Cohen, is talking about Warren and Cher as if she had dinner with them last night. Cohen has just come back from a pair of West Coast press junkets, for the movies *Hook* and *Bugsy*. She and Tardieu have to edit her interview with Dustin Hoffman into a six-minute segment for an upcoming show; Tardieu has reserved an editor and an editing room so she and Cohen can work on it after her segment. Then Tardieu has to do a phone pre-interview with Clint Holmes for a segment she's producing in two days; she also has to make arrangements for a very big two-part, on-location segment next week in which Barbara Bush will give Regis and Kathie Lee a personal tour of the White House.

"It's a constant juggling act, attending to the right detail at the right moment," Tardieu says. "The priorities change moment to moment. That's kind of the key to this job."

At this moment, the right detail is exactly where the *Hook* film clip should go in Claudia Cohen's Dustin Hoffman interview.

"You know where Dustin starts talking about how he modeled some of Hook's mannerisms on William F. Buckley?" Tardieu is saying to Cohen as they head upstairs to an editing room. "I think that's the place."

In the edit room, I ask Cohen how the junkets are run.

"Very efficiently," she says. "You get six minutes with someone like Dustin. You walk into the room and they have two cameras running: one on you, one on the star. They record the whole thing, and then as you leave they give you the two tapes. You bring them home and edit them together. It's pretty frantic. They really hustle you in and out. I was supposed to get eight minutes with Annette Bening for *Bugsy,* and then suddenly they made an announcement: 'All interviews with Annette Bening have been reduced to five minutes. Everybody will get just five minutes with Annette Bening.'"

Tardieu and Cohen and a staff editor start fast-forwarding and rewinding the interview. Hoffman looks professional and courteous; Cohen looks very happy to be in the same room with Hoffman. Eventually, Tardieu and Cohen find the perfect place to insert the film clip. Tardieu says she'll check on the segment a little later.

That done, the next most important detail concerns next week's visit to the White House. Tardieu, still carrying manila folders, walks down the hall to the segment producers' office, a large, long room jammed with desks and wallpapered with multicolored Post-its. Each Post-it, depending on the color, represents a possible segment, a confirmed segment, or an idea for a segment. Future shows are tentatively lined up in vertical stacks of Post-its, each one labeled with the initials of the responsible segment producer. It looks like an extremely fluid setup.

Tardieu's desk is covered with press kits, videotapes, and glossy photographs. Virtually every horizontal surface in the office—chairs, file cabinet tops, shelves—is stacked with teetering piles of glossy, brightly colored publicity materials.

A fresh copy of today's *Celebrity Bulletin,* just off the fax machine, has been placed on top of the stuff that's piled on top of Tardieu's desk.

The front page lists the latest on upcoming celebrity arrivals in New York; the reason for each celebrity arrival; and the names and phone numbers of the celebrity's agent and publicist.

NEW YORK ARRIVALS   **TUESDAY DECEMBER 10, 1991**

OLIVER STONE
arrives from the West Coast for the December 18 invitational screening of his new Warner Bros. film "JFK" with KEVIN COSTNER, SISSY SPACEK, GARY OLDMAN at the Museum of Modern Art.

WILLIAM DEVANE
has arrived from the West Coast on hiatus from his CBS-TV series "Knots Landing" for interviews and tv appearances(incl. "Live with Regis & Kathie Lee") to promote his new movie-of-the-week.

WARREN BEATTY
BARRY LEVINSON
BEN KINGSLEY
JOE MANTEGNA
MARK JOHNSON
have arrived for the Tuesday, December 10 invitational screening of their new Tri-Star feature "Bugsy" at the Museum of Modern Art.

MARTIN SHORT
who stars as the 'official wedding coordinator' in Touchstone's "Father of the Bride" arrives from Toronto for a December 18 appearance on "Late Night with David Letterman."

BRENDA FRICKER
Academy Award winner for "My Left Foot," has arrived from Ireland to film her role in the 20th Century Fox feature "Home Alone 2 - Lost in New York."

KIMBERLY WILLIAMS
who plays STEVE MARTIN's daughter in "Father of the Bride," has arrived from the West Coast for interviews and tv appearances to promote the Touchstone Pictures feature; here thru December 11.

ERIC BURDON
formerly of the '60s British rock group THE ANIMALS, will be in town this month for interviews in connection with the release of his new home video by A*Vision "Finally...Eric Burdon & The Animals" & his local concert dates including Wetlands from December 27 to 31.

JOHNNY MANDEL
has arrived from L.A. to co-porduce the new SHIRLEY HORN album for Polygram as well as the score for the film version of "Glengarry Glen Ross."

Today's Celebrity Bulletin.

"This is something we all use," Tardieu says as she picks the *Bulletin* up and glances at the front page. "It's part of a service. If you're a subscriber, you can also call them up and get information on how to contact any celebrity in the United States—who the agent is, and so on. It's not cheap, though. I think it's around fifteen hundred dollars a year."

So if you want to reach Arnold Schwarzenegger's management, you can just call them up?

"I already know how to contact Arnold Schwarzenegger's management," Tardieu replies. "But if it were someone I didn't know, yes, I could call them."

The person at the White House whom Tardieu wants to reach is in a meeting. I ask her how the segment business has changed since she got into it in the mid eighties.

"The biggest change is the onslaught of the tabloid stuff," Tardieu replies. "Your standard talk-show fare used to be much more polite and schmoozy and classy and fun. And I happen to still prefer that, tastewise, which is one reason why I prefer doing our show.

"I would not want to work on a 'Sally,'" Tardieu continues, gesturing to a single television set in the middle of the office. The sound is off, but it is clearly Sally Jessy Raphael gesturing to a man and two women on a dais.

"I wouldn't want to book, and interview, and be responsible for those kinds of guests," Tardieu continues. "I would find it depressing and bizarre. It's like a *National Enquirer* on the air."

Tardieu dials another number. I watch Sally Jessy Raphael. Today's topic is "Gay Men Who Have Fathered Babies for Lesbian Couples."

11. Involve the hosts, if the hosts are Regis Philbin and Kathie Lee Gifford.

"The segments that work the best on 'Regis & Kathie Lee' are the ones that truly involve the hosts," Joanne Tardieu says a few minutes later as she sits at her desk, on hold. "Some shows are content driven or guest driven. People tune in for the topic or the celebrity. 'Good Day,' the show I worked on in Boston, was that way. But this show is host driven, meaning that our viewers tune in first and foremost to see what Regis and Kathie Lee are up to, and whom they're up to it with. We get name celebrities, and the ratings show that people tune in for that; but even when we don't have the best bookings, our ratings are pretty steady. So if Regis and Kathie Lee are involved, the viewers are involved. Even if it's just a guest they're really interested in talking to. Like when Kathy Bates had that sudden success in

Misery, the audience picked up on how Regis and Kathie Lee were excited to talk to her about it. Or it can be Kathie Lee singing with Clint Holmes, or Regis doing schtick with a cook. Recently we had on that artist who does that painting show on PBS, and Regis and Kathie Lee both made a painting. Those are the things that work the best for us."

12. Brainstorm.

Every day after the show, the segment producers meet with executive producer Michael Gelman. Today's meeting is a little late, because Gelman has been in the studio taping promos with Regis and Kathie Lee. But as it gets towards 11:00 A.M., the seven segment producers—all women, and all holding manila folders full of notes—are loosely gathered at one end of the office. Most of them are sipping coffee from paper cups. The talk is wide-ranging and gossipy, like a ladies' lunch that's gone slightly out of control. Listening to the segment producers, it's clear that although Michael Gelman is

A segment producers' meeting.

ostensibly in charge, "Live with Regis & Kathie Lee" is a matriarchy. The personality of the show comes directly from the values and interests of the women in this room.

"This meeting usually ends up being a brainstorming session," Tardieu says. "Everybody talks about their segments, whom they're trying to book, who's been pitched to them, and everybody feels free to jump in and add their own suggestions and ideas. And usually the segments get better. We do this every day; we also work in the same room. Now it's almost like we're one brain. I'm only going to be able to stay for about half the meeting today; I have to get back to the Dustin Hoffman segment."

Gelman walks in and sits down at one end of the room.

"Let's meet, guys," he says as he unfolds a long computer print-out. "First, yesterday's ratings. They were good. Donahue's doing nothing against us; Chuck Woolery, nothing. We were consistent throughout the show: once we had 'em, we had 'em."

"Today's show . . ." he continues. "Devane was good, chatty. Maybe a little low key, but good. Mr. Mother Earth on flowering plants—good. The singer was very good, strong."

Gelman is moving right along.

"Tomorrow's show?"

"Ed Marinaro is the first segment," a producer says.

"Plugging what?" Gelman asks.

" 'Sisters,' on NBC," she says. "He's also being inducted into the College Football Hall of Fame."

For the next five minutes, the segment producers conduct an open forum on Ed Marinaro's career, his best roles, his sex appeal, his reputation in college ("he went out with all the best-looking girls"), and his current status: 41 and not married. This last fact draws a surprised chorus of ahhhh's.

Next?

"Billy Falcon, who'll be singing," a producer reports. "His story is heartbreaking but inspirational. Last year his wife died of breast cancer (sympathetic ohhh's from the segment producers), but now he's coming back from that. . . ."

From here the meeting segues from how Billy Falcon hooked up with Jon Bon Jovi (he knew Bon Jovi's gardener), to a segment on "TV Guided" fashions. ("We're going to have five models dressed in the styles of five popular shows," the producer reports.) Then a description of a segment on *People* magazine celebrity photographer Harry Benson, and the problems one producer is having getting "L.A. Law" clips for an upcoming segment with the actress Susan Dey. The group is still discussing "L.A. Law" and Dey (Gelman to segment producer: "Can you find out if she's chatty?") when Regis

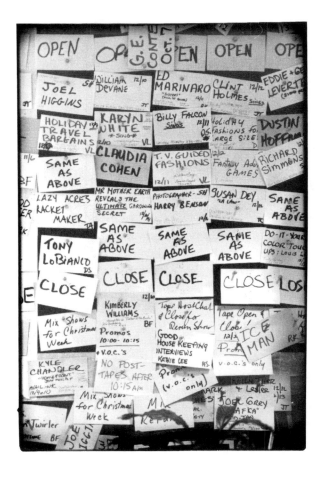

A week's worth of shows lined up vertically on the segment producers' office wall.

Philbin steps into the office and scrutinizes tomorrow's show, a vertical stripe of Post-its on the wall.

"Same old show," he says glumly. "I'll tell you what, let's shake it up. Let's start with the photographer from *People*. Do something different. Shake things up. We always start with the celebrity; let's surprise people."

Regis leaves; Gelman adjusts the Post-its; and he moves on to the rest of the week.

"John Denver. What's he selling?" he asks.

"A Christmas television special," somebody says.

By now Tardieu is edging towards the door, heading back to the edit suite. I follow her out. As we head out the door, Gelman is looking over today's *Celebrity Bulletin*.

"Bonnie Raitt's in town," he says.

"I talked to her people," a producer says. "She doesn't really have anything to push."

How about Christian Slater?

"He turned us down a million times during *Robin Hood*," someone reports.

Gelman still looks interested.

"Let's try him one more time," Gelman says.

13. Be on the lookout for real people stories.

After some more work, the Dustin Hoffman interview is down to a neat six-minute segment and Tardieu is back at her desk. Most of the segment producers are still in the office, talking on the phone. I ask Tardieu if she specializes in any particular kind of segment.

"The only segments I won't do are cooking segments," she says. "I just don't feel like I'm good at them. But I'll do everything else: I do a lot of celebrities; I also do a lot of real people segments. Real people segments are a challenge. They're the hardest segments to really get to work on the air."

What's an example of a real people segment?

"I'll give you an example of a real people segment that didn't work as well as I hoped," Tardieu replies. "I was reading the New York *Post* a few years ago, and there was a picture of a woman in Brooklyn who was finally going to meet the pen pal she had been corresponding with for the last forty years. They had started writing to each other during World War II. So I read this and I said to myself, 'I've got to book this so that they meet for the first time on our set, live.' So it was really exciting. We flew the woman in; sequestered her in a hotel. And we got photos of both of them from the forties, when they first started writing to each other. And we really hyped: today they'll meet for the first time. . . .

"So when the morning arrived, we brought one of the women on first, and chatted with her a little bit, and then we brought the other one out. And it was a little weird. It wasn't like a big hugging reunion, because they had never seen each other. It was like, 'God, maybe it was better when they just wrote to each other.' The actual moment was kind of a letdown. The hype was great. I know we had people tuning in because the story was so sweet. But when they actually met, they were sort of stunned. They didn't have much to say to each other; there wasn't a whole lot of emotion, as you would expect from two people who were reuniting. Because they weren't reuniting. They were being introduced for the very first time. Those things happen."

14. Don't be a nervous wreck.

Tardieu takes a call from someone at a Washington, D.C. limo company; he needs some very specific instructions for the day of the White House tour. Tardieu talks to him for a few minutes, detailing pickup times and locations, White House drop-off logistics, and estimated waiting times. When she hangs up, I ask her what she's still worried about, in regard to the White House tour.

"The biggest challenge will be to do this tour in twenty to thirty minutes, which is all that we've been given," she says. "The next biggest challenge will be editing it for air. We'll probably show it in two days, in two six-minute segments. If we end up shooting way more than we can use, it's going to be a bear to edit. I recently worked on a Bette Midler interview that Claudia did. It ran forty-five minutes, almost all of Midler nonstop talking. It was great, but to eke eight good minutes out of that, with continuity, so that it sounded like one question after another—that was a challenge. And that will be the challenge if we end up shooting a ton of stuff at the White House."

I ask her if she's nervous.

"I'm not nervous. It's going to be fine," she replies. "I've been through enough situations to know that there will always be problems, but they can always be solved without my turning into a nervous wreck. Besides, nervous-wreck producers cannot do live television. Because the hosts pick it up. And that knocks them off base—to have a bunch of nervous, hysterical people around them. So I'll be at my best if I'm calm and I can just be there. I'm not really planning on having any major terror conniptions."

TV

FICTION

**LEMON SKY PRODUCTIONS WILL BE FILMING
PART OF A SERIES
FOR FOX TELEVISION**

**ON: <u>FRIDAY DECEMBER 14, 1990,</u>
FROM: <u>7:00AM</u> TO:<u>11:00PM</u>**

**WE HAVE PERMITS FROM THE CITY OF BOSTON DEPARTMENTS
OF TRANSPORTATION AND PUBLIC WORKS TO OCCUPY
PARKING SPACES IN THIS AREA.**

**WE WOULD APPRECIATE YOUR COOPERATION
BY NOT PARKING IN THE DESIGNATED AREAS
AT THE ABOVE-MENTIONED TIMES
(PLEASE TAKE NOTE OF SIGNS POSTED)**

**WE ARE CONCERNED ABOUT YOUR QUALITY OF LIFE
IN THE CITY OF BOSTON AND ASSURE YOU
THAT THERE WILL BE PERSONNEL AVAILABLE ON OUR SET
AT ALL TIMES TO ANSWER ANY QUESTIONS
OR DEAL WITH ANY INCONVENIENCES THAT MAY ARISE.**

**SGT. J. MICHAEL CROSSEN IS OUR CITY OF BOSTON POLICE
LIAISON WITH THE DEPARTMENT OF TRAFFIC AND PARKING.**

**HE CAN BE REACHED MONDAY THROUGH FRIDAY
FROM 6AM TO 7PM AT 725-3441.**

THANK YOU FOR YOUR COOPERATION.

SARABANDE PRODUCTIONS 10,000 W. Washington Blvd. Suite 3012 Los Angeles, CA 90232   213 280-6462, FAX: 213 836-1680

LEMON SKY PRODUCTIONS   32 Cobble Hill Road   Somerville, MA 02143   617 776-4500, FAX: 617 625-1029

A Sarabande Production in association with Lemon Sky Productions.

*An "Against the Law"
flyer.*

5. "AGAINST THE LAW": EPISODE 11, EAST COAST

Jan Egleson, who will be directing the eleventh episode of "Against the Law," a dramatic television series on the Fox network, is the first to arrive.

"I just saw Phil and Steve," he says. "I think they're looking for a place to park the van."

Standing just inside the doorway of Jacob Wirth's, a Spartan, old-world German restaurant/beer hall in a charmless section of downtown Boston, Egleson looks leonine. His beard and shaggy brown hair give him the appearance of a Shakespearean actor on the way to being eminent. (I learn later that in fact he started out as a Shakespearean actor. He trained at the Bristol Old Vic and the Yale School of Drama before joining the Theater Company of Boston, where he hyphenated himself into an actor-director.)

A few weeks ago, when I asked Egleson if I could follow the making of an episode of "Against the Law" from the time the script arrived until the broadcast date, he shrugged and said "Sure" in a way that indicated he wasn't quite certain why anyone would like to do such a thing. Then he told me that the script for Episode 11 was due in a few days, and he'd call me as soon as work on the show began.

"Against the Law" is an hour-long dramatic serial, a popular prime-time genre that includes shows like "thirtysomething," "L.A. Law," "Hill Street Blues," and "Twin Peaks." At the dramatic center of the show is maverick attorney Simon MacHeath (played by Michael O'Keefe), a "street-smart, unconventional Boston attorney," according to a Fox press release. The concept is not particularly original, particularly this television season, which has seen a glut of street-smart, unconventional attorneys. Still, there's plenty of room for stylish execution, and besides, producing a show like "Against the Law" is not about originality, anyway, at least according to Egleson.

"Shows like this are the American Noh drama," he tells me. "It's a very stylized form: the good guys and the bad guys are clearly identified; the action and dramatic development proceed in very traditional ways. That's what the audience wants, that's what they expect. You can stretch it a little—I think 'thirtysomething' has stretched the form—but only a little."

One of the conventions of the hour-long dramatic genre is a big-budget, film-style look. Unlike situation comedies, which are flatly lit and simply staged, hour-long dramatic shows must have what's referred to as "high production values": the lighting, the sets, the camerawork—all must approach feature film standards. And although "Against the Law"'s scripts have been wildly erratic (some of them, in fact, have been truly awful), the production values have been uniformly high.

I had imagined that work would start on Episode 11 with a formal production meeting around a large conference table. Photocopied scripts would sit at each place; there would be plenty of strong coffee and upscale pastries. As it turned out, the luxury of a production meeting evaporated when the filming of Episode 10 started running behind. The script for Episode 11 was also late; just a few days ago, Egleson had only a very general idea of the plot.

"A guy whom MacHeath put in jail years ago comes back and stalks him, looking for revenge," he told me. "Also, there's a B story about a kid with dyslexia whom Mac tries to help."

Then this morning Egleson called. The script was still running late; only two of the four acts had been completed; but since filming was scheduled to start in just four days, the preproduction process was going to start today. At 1:00 P.M. he was meeting the location manager, Philip Alvare, and the first assistant director, Steve Wertimer, at Jacob Wirth's to "put together some days."

When Steve Wertimer and Philip Alvare arrive and we all sit down at an old wooden table in the middle of the restaurant, I ask what it means to "put together some days."

Wertimer, who as first assistant director is responsible for the day-to-day planning of the episode, takes the question.

"You can't shoot a show in sequence, the way it appears in the script," he says. "It would be too expensive, and it would take too long. So you try to group all the like scenes together so you can shoot them most efficiently. That's what we'll be doing today: seeing how many scenes we can organize into twelve-hour days, so we can spend the most time shooting and the least time in transit and in setting up."

"A television production is like a big, powerful, expensive train that's moving down the tracks," Wertimer continues. "The most important thing is to keep it moving, not to let it grind to a halt. That's the cardinal sin. There are about seventy people on this production, thousands of dollars an hour, and tight deadlines. You have to keep everybody working together, everything moving forward. And that can be difficult because everybody is totally obsessed with his or her particular job."

"I remember hearing a story about an executive producer who decided to visit the set of a film he was working on," Egleson adds. "He flies down from New York to Arizona where they are shooting, and he gets picked up at the airport by a production assistant.

" 'How's the production going?' he asks as they're driving to the set.

" 'Terrible, just terrible,' the production assistant says, shaking his head. 'The photocopy machine is broken.'

"To be honest," Egleson continues, "I don't think the director is that important on a television serial. The consistency of the show comes from the crew. They're like a machine that was set in motion at the beginning of the show, and they work on it every day. The directors, on the other hand, change from show to show. Doing a show as a director is like coming into a new high school senior year. The crew has been together for weeks, months, just about every day. Most of the time, the crew doesn't even know what episode they're shooting."

This afternoon, Wertimer, Egleson, and Alvare will be scouting four locations for Episode 11: an artist's loft, a working-class bar, a hospital, and a waterfront seafood restaurant. They'll be looking for locations that will look good on camera, that can accommodate a large television crew, and that don't involve too much traveling.

•　•　•

Philip Alvare shooting a location. Note point-and-shoot camera, and the compass around his neck.

"Normally people will take as long as they possibly can to scout locations," Philip Alvare says. "It's a way of diffusing neurosis. In their defense, before you can create, you want to have all the elements in front of you. And locations are some of the first elements that you have to deal with. It's your stage.

"On this show, we're always on the fly. We have two, maybe three days to scout locations. But on a feature film, they'll spend months scouting locations. I heard that Paul Mazursky spent a year scouting locations for one of his films.

"Scouting for advertisements can also go on forever," Alvare continues. "The worst is when they want this one place, with the bannister on the left, not the right, and the Victorian wallpaper, and the duck on the newel post. And then you watch the ad, months later, and you can't see any of those details. You can hardly see the locations. It's tight shots all the way through."

A Philip Alvare montage of a possible Chelsea location for "Against the Law." Note the compass reading (S.E. 140) and the time of the photos (2:45)

After lunch we all climb into Alvare's van and drive down to the industrial waterfront in South Boston, to an old four-story building that stretches about three city blocks. It looks like a skyscraper that someone knocked over. It was a marine terminal; now most of it is a design center. A large chunk on the top floor belongs to a fashion photographer who has decorated it in SoHo-inspired industrial style.

"We're thinking of shooting the opening scenes of the show here," Egleson says as he walks into the loft, looking all around in a kind of distracted, dreamy way. "In the opening scene of the show, MacHeath is supposed to be in a loft in lower Manhattan, with a woman he's romantically involved with. And the man who's stalking him is watching them from the next building."

Suzanne Cavedon, the production designer, arrives. She and Egleson consult briefly with Alvare; the loft is fine. Approved.

"I think this is the right combination of raw and finished," Cavedon says. "A lot of lofts are too finished."

Downstairs, Alvare introduces everybody to the building superintendent, who escorts us into a large, brightly lit, windowless hallway in the basement.

"I was thinking that this hallway could be the hospital," Alvare says.

In the middle of Episode 11, apparently, MacHeath gets stabbed by a poison dart and ends up in the hospital.

"I think it could work," Cavedon says. "If we put some tape on the floor, and bring in some hospital props—those rolling beds, IV bags, that kind of thing."

"This could be good," Wertimer says. "Shoot those scenes upstairs in the morning, then move down here in the afternoon."

After checking out the building's security guard office—to see if it could be made to pass for a hospital room (it could)—we bundle into the van for the trip to the other side of Boston Harbor, to the Chelsea Yacht Club, which Philip Alvare thinks will work as a blue-collar waterfront restaurant.

Is it really worth all the trouble to shoot on location instead of in the studio? I ask.

"Yes," Egleson replies. "Because of the variety, and the texture."

"And the funkiness," Alvare adds. "You can't get that in a studio."

At the Chelsea Yacht Club, Alvare negotiates with the manager while Egleson and Wertimer look around. Then, later, driving through Chelsea, Egleson spots a neighborhood tavern that might work for a scene in which MacHeath gets stabbed in the leg with a poisoned dart. Again, Alvare negotiates with the bartender while Egleson and Wertimer discuss possible camera setups. Back in the van, I ask Alvare how he approaches the job of negotiating for locations.

"There are so many things to take into consideration," he says. "The area, what the market is, how savvy people are."

I had heard that the going rate was $1000 a day for an interior location, at least in New England.

"That's probably too general," Alvare says, "simply because there are so many variables. Like the impact of the production. If you're going to be shutting down a top restaurant that makes ten thousand dollars a day, you better believe they want to be compensated. On the other hand, a lot of places like the publicity and the excitement. So you really have to feel it out.

"I usually start by asking, 'What do you think a fair price would be?' " Alvare continues.

Are the responses all over the map? I ask.

Alvare rolls his eyes.

"I've had people say, 'A price? You mean I have to pay you?' At that point I try to be fair. There's really no point in trying to get a place for nothing. On the other hand, you don't want to get involved with people who will try to inflate things: 'You're not going to shoot here for less than five thousand dollars.' That just brings up the price for everything. Those negotiations can be tough. You often run into that kind of thing when you deal with lawyers. Because this is a law show and we're frequently looking for law offices as locations, I talk to lawyers a lot. Dealing with law firms is the worst.

"And then sometimes we have to paint a location, which can make negotiations more difficult. For example, we don't want white walls, white doesn't read well. Also, the show has it's own palette, so we'll come in and paint the walls a kind of ochre/yellow. I tell people it's 'period' color. But if you asked me which period, I'd have to say 'late Halloween.' "

Now we're driving through industrial East Boston, past huge oil storage tanks and electrical power stations, on our way back to the "Against the Law" production office. Steve Wertimer is in the backseat, studying his notes; Jan Egleson is staring distractedly out the window; Alvare is telling a story about a location manager and a director who were scouting locations in Boston's North End. "They went scouting for a period streetscape, from the early 1900s, with no success," he says. "And then, finally, they found a location that's perfect, except for one thing: a single air conditioner, very visible, sticking out of the front window of one of the houses. The director says, 'Lose the air conditioner.' So the location manager finds the man who lives in the house and gives him a hundred dollars to take the air conditioner out. Fine. No problem. Then they come back two days later for the shot, and there are about a dozen air conditioners sticking out of windows everywhere."

The "Against the Law" production office is located across the street from an auto tow lot with a snarling cur on a chain and a trailer with a large sign taped to the front door: ATTENTION: IT'S NOT THE DISPATCHER'S FAULT THAT YOUR CAR WAS TOWED. The building that houses the office and studio is a solid, unimaginative mass of brick and concrete. The neighborhood, in outlying Somerville, looks as if it's trying to make a modest leap from freight yard to light manufacturing. As we pull into the parking lot, I ask Jan Egleson how, and why, they chose this location.

"It was cheap," he says. "There was really only one studio in Boston, the place where they made 'Spenser for Hire.' But it wasn't big enough for us. So we decided to build our own set: this place had a lot of empty warehouse space, plus some offices. It also turns out to be near a lot of highways, so it's good for the trucks."

Inside, the production office looks like a business crash pad: a boiler-room operation where the wall-to-wall carpeting is cheap, all the furniture is rented, and the phone lines are barely concealed under long strips of gray duct tape. On the bulletin board, there are flyers from pizza places that deliver, an ad for a local masseuse, and a photocopied review of the "Against the Law" pilot from *People.* At one point in the review, which is generally positive, the critic praises "O'Keefe's jacked-to-the-eyeballs performance"—an accurate description of his energetic approach to the role of MacHeath. Next to it, there's another review, from *Variety,* praising the "engaging new Fox Broadcasting skein."

Twenty or thirty people are scattered about, separated by room dividers and temporary walls. Most of them are on the phone. Their conversations bounce among four different episodes: Episode 8 is on television tonight, at 9:00 P.M.; Episode 9 is in postproduction on the West Coast; the crew is out shooting Episode 10 now; Episode 11 is just gearing up.

Steve Wertimer grabs his phone messages and spreads his notes on a large table next to a room divider. "They told us this morning that there was going to be a car chase in the show," he says. "I'm hoping they'll cut it out. Nobody likes car scenes. Very difficult to do well. Very intensive to shoot."

A few minutes later, I find Philip Alvare in a barren-looking office, sorting out folders, each marked with a location: "East Bos-

A few questions for director Jan Egleson the next morning, while he's waiting for Yale Udoff, the script-writer, to finish the third and fourth acts of Episode 11:

Q. You've directed feature films and television shows. What's the difference?

A. Two things, and I guess they're related. First, the size of shots. Television is physically smaller, so you want to be close to things on television. You tend to see less of the landscape in which people are moving, which I don't like. I think that's a real loss. The second thing is that because television is a fairly brief medium—an hour show is only forty-four minutes—you really have to make your points and make them clearly. So you're always watching to make sure that things are clear. People are engaged in a different way, and listening in a different way, when they're watching television. So you really have to show people the face, get right close to it, and be clear about how the story is progressing.

The other thing that's interesting is that people are impatient with television when people aren't talking, unless there's a car crash. I've noticed that at the editing stage, the stuff that gets cut out is the stuff where people aren't talking. I think that's a shame. I think it has something to do with the fact that when you go to a movie theater, you're there, you're committed, and it's a more over-whelming visual experience. And you like those moments between people where there are no words. That's something that film does very well. In television you tend to lose those moments. Also, there's the pressure to get the shows out, and everybody is working fast, flying along. So in the cutting, the stuff that goes first is the stuff that doesn't seem immediately necessary. It just gets thrown out right away. To get that back in is a very time-consuming process. Usually you don't have the time.

Q. So you're looking to drive the plot, all the time?

A. That's right. You're always looking for that energy.

Q. Doesn't the shape of the television screen differ from the shape of a movie screen?

A. The standard-aspect ratio of a television screen is 1 to 1:33, which is a slightly elongated square. A movie screen is 1 to 1.85, which is wider and which I think just feels better. It fits your eye better, it frames things better. You also cut less, because you can include more in the frame. But what happens if you're shooting in 35mm for television is that when you look through the camera, you'll see a smaller, circum-scribed box that indicates TV-safe. That's what they guarantee that the worst-adjusted set in America will actually show. So you try to stay within TV-safe.

ton High," "Summer House, Topsfield," etc. Each folder contains a series of snapshots, roughly arranged to provide interior and exterior panoramic views.

I mention that they look like David Hockney photo collages from the early eighties.

"I heard that Hockney actually got the idea for his collages from a location director he knows," Alvare says.

Alvare stacks the folders in an upright stand marked "Episode 11"; then he turns his attention to a large weekly grid on the wall. Two or three days are either blank or have question marks on them.

"We'll know a lot more when the script is finished," he says.
The notice on the bulletin board says,

"COLLINGE/PICKMAN IS SEEKING
FOUR JAPANESE MALES FOR
PRINT WORK IN A BROCHURE
TO BE DISTRIBUTED IN JAPAN."

Collinge/Pickman is a casting agency located just outside Harvard
Square, in Cambridge. The waiting room is exactly the kind that
actors universally bemoan: drably decorated (with movie posters,
mostly), with uncomfortable plastic seats lining the walls. The bulletin board is tacked with flyers for dinner theaters, improvisational
groups, and community theaters. Eight-by-ten glossies of actors al-
ternate with advertisements for head-shot photographers.

This morning, two actors—a middle-aged man and an older
woman—are sitting in the waiting room, leafing through scripts,
early for their appointments to audition for a few small parts in
Episode 11.

On the other side of a large blond door, in a long, narrow room
also drably decorated, Jan Egleson is sitting with Patty Collinge, a

Jan Egleson directing Michael O'Keefe in an episode of "Against the Law."

principal in the casting firm; she also happens to be his wife. On the other side of the room, an industrial video camera is sitting on a tripod pointing nowhere. A few videotape decks, one ¾ inch, the other VHS, are stacked on a console. The time is blinking on the VHS deck. Carolyn Pickman, the firm's cofounder, drops in occasionally, but she's very busy on another account: by the end of the day she has to find a young African-American boy, preferably a drummer, for a Burger King advertisement.

Tomorrow Jan Egleson will take the shuttle to New York, to cast the major roles: a love interest for MacHeath, a black teenage boy, and a Mac-stalking ex-con. Today, Egleson and Collinge will be trying to populate the rest of episode 11; they're looking for a high school teacher, a principal, a bartender, a mother of an adolescent black boy, and a detective. The actors they select will get $441 a day. In forty minutes they audition five actors:

Some of the actors they see:

A middle-aged actress from Providence, a member of the Trinity Square Repertory company. She could be the teacher or the principal. She has an Irish accent.

Patty Collinge stands up. "I'll be everybody else."

They do a scene where Collinge plays a young black adolescent and the actress plays the teacher. Then they do another scene where Collinge plays the parts of MacHeath and the child's mother and the actress plays the principal. Egleson watches the scenes, doodling absentmindedly between takes.

"Great, great," he says when she's finished.

Patty Collinge being "everybody else" at a casting session; Jan Egleson and Carolyn Pickman look on.

The next audition is a patrician-looking man with a remarkable resemblance to George Bush. His readings of the principal and teacher parts are convincing, although both characters sound as though they belong in a prep school, not in an inner-city public school.

"He was good," Egleson says afterwards, "but you know, both the teacher and the principal are disciplining Cleon, the young black kid; and I don't think we want a white, Waspy guy beating up on a black kid. That's not the message I'm trying to get across. This story isn't about racism."

Egleson jots a few notes on a casting log, then looks up.

"Episodic television is really a blunt instrument, isn't it?" he says. "You can only say one thing at a time."

A light-skinned black man is next. Collinge asks him to read a scene in which the teacher, out for a jog, accidentally meets up with MacHeath and they discuss young Cleon's future. The actor takes the script, walks to the other side of the room and starts running in place; then he runs over to Collinge and does the scene convincingly out of breath.

A heavy white man is next. He is asked to read the part of the detective in a scene that begins with the detective dusting for prints. He drops down on one knee and starts making dusting movements on a chair leg, then he rises, holding the script, and begins reading.

During a short break, I ask Collinge how she decides whom to invite to an audition.

"I want somebody who's done a few things, who's consistent," she says. "You don't really get to rehearse on this kind of show, so you have to be ready to give a good performance on short notice."

Does her husband have certain preferences when it comes to actors?

"He likes to use people who kind of play against the script," she says. "If it's a sentimental scene, he wants actors who aren't bang-on sentimental. He wants slightly quirkier choices."

J. W. Winston, a young casting assistant, arrives with a copy of the current version of the script. He's about to do an extras breakdown. I follow him into a small office he shares with two other casting assistants.

"The first thing I look for is court scenes," he says as he flips through the script. "That can mean an extra three hundred extras right there. I don't see any here. Here's a classroom scene: that will mean probably twenty or thirty kids. A barroom scene will mean another fifty adults. A seafood restaurant—that's another dozen. We're probably talking a hundred and fifty extras overall for the episode."

Where does he find these people?

"You can't just call your friends," he says. "A friend will work one fourteen-hour day and never talk to you again. The way we did it is, we had a big open casting call in July. We took a few ads out in the local papers, and just invited anybody who wanted to come in. It was a zoo, but we wound up with a lot of names, and a lot of people whom we've used on different episodes. We also keep up relationships with various organizations, like local churches, who help us out. There's a minister in Roxbury whom we call whenever we need black kids. We have to keep working at it, though: we don't want the same faces turning up all the time."

According to an agreement with the actors union, J. W. is required to hire at least 35% of his extras from the union; the rest can be non-union. A union extra earns $91 a day; a non-union extra gets $50.

"The union extras are usually out-of-work actors," he says. "They can use the money, and it helps them with their pension plans. Most of the non-union extras are in it because it's fun, and different. It's funny: if a non-union extra is in a scene that's cut, he's disappointed. He wants to see himself on television. If a union extra's scene is cut, he's happy. He knows we can use him again sooner, maybe in a bigger role."

The "Against the Law" set, which consists of Simon MacHeath's office and living area, is a tightly constructed bandbox in the middle of a large, cement-floored warehouse. It opens up in a few unexpected places—like the top—but most of it is tightly enclosed by layers of interlocking stud walls, false doors, and faux windows.

Inside, it all makes sense, right down to the law journals on the coffee table. Outside, you see the propped-up, unfinished backs of everything, the large lights that peer over the top of the set, the thick cables snaking off to some remote power supply, the scattered canvas chairs, and cast-off props from the previous show. The light, which is pretty low to begin with, gets dimmer and dimmer the further you get from the set, until it trails off into a kind of warehouse murk towards the outer edges of the building.

Today, "shoot day 1 of 8" on Episode 11, begins with a lot of banging at one end of the set. A bright splash of light is focused on an outside corner where carpenters are hammering fake brick facade and copper flashing around the exterior of a few windows.

A few days ago, Egleson and producer Marcus Viscidi reevaluated the opening of the show; they elected not to use the photographer's studio they had scouted. Instead, the stalker would spy on MacHeath and his girlfriend while they were in MacHeath's apartment, on the set. But Egleson still wants to shoot from outside the apartment; this means that some of the set's windows, which have always been shot from the inside, now have to look good from the outside as well. So the show's carpenters were summoned at 8:00 A.M. today to put up the brick and granite facade around the windows. They are still hammering away at 10:00 A.M. as the film crew starts to gather for shooting the first scene of the day. A young man

Director of Photography Tom Priestly (left) checks out a scene through a window. First assistant director Steve Wertimer is looking over his shoulder. Jonathan Burkhart, the first assistant camera operator (rear, standing next to the dolly), will be responsible for adjusting the camera's focus; dolly grip Tony Campenni (right) will push the dolly.

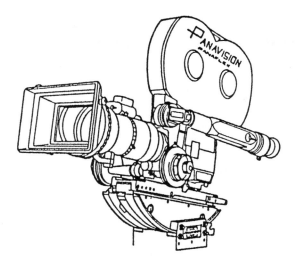

A Panavision Panaflex Gold 2 camera. Although there are few concrete differences between Panavision and its closest competitor, Arriflex, camera preferences die hard, and Panavision is the sentimental favorite of a majority of American directors of photography. You can't buy a Panavision camera even if you want to; you have to rent it from an authorized dealer for somewhere between $6000 and $10,000 a week, depending on the model and the extras. You can buy an Arriflex, but few DP's choose to do so. The maintenance costs are too high; and if a camera breaks down in the middle of a tight shooting schedule, you want a replacement fast. Renting from a large camera company gives you that protection.

holding a boom microphone is already sitting on top of one of the walls, waiting for rehearsals to begin.

A few feet away, Marcus Viscidi is nervously surveying the construction.

"I'm trying to keep the construction crew ahead of the film crew," he says. "Right now they're about five minutes ahead. And since we brought them in at eight A.M., we're already into heavy overtime."

Viscidi is also worried about finding a location for some upcoming school scenes. "On another show we used a Catholic boys' high school downtown," he says. "But we wanted something grittier for this show. So we looked at a school in Roxbury. But the police just told us that there's a gang in that area. If we shoot there, they want us to hire thirteen policemen with bulletproof vests. I don't think we want to get that gritty."

A photograph of the Boston skyline, about the size of a football field, hangs on one side of the set, just outside the windows. Six very large, very bright lights, on stands held down by sandbags, shine through it from behind, lighting it up like a giant slide. Suzanne Cavedon shot the photograph of the skyline with a 4″ x 5″ camera; a Los Angeles–based company, Pacific Studios, blew it up to almost life size. From inside the set, the effect is surprisingly realistic.

The day-sized chunk of work that Steve Wertimer has put together is neatly detailed in a pair of call sheets, which serve as the production company's morning paper. After shooting ten episodes in succession, the cast and crew now live like a traveling circus, isolated from the rest of the world by their long hours and skewed circadian rhythms. The daily call sheets, which usually come out late the previous night, convey the kind of essential information this

The Boston Skyline by Pacific Studios, outside the set's windows.

small community needs to keep functioning. Among the information: sunrise and sunset times, scenes to be filmed, pickup time for the cast members, reporting time for the various departments, when breakfast and lunch will be ready, the props required for today's scenes, and the tentative schedule for the next two days.

Attached to the call sheets are the script pages for the scenes scheduled to be shot today. In the first scene, which takes place in MacHeath's kitchen, MacHeath confers with a police detective about the man who is stalking him.

Jan Egleson, who arrived a few minutes ago, is talking with Tom Priestly, the director of photography. They are standing behind a large camera mounted on a dolly. The camera is a Panaflex Panavision 35mm film camera; the dolly is a Chapman PeeWee.

Although the scene takes place in MacHeath's kitchen, Egleson wants to shoot it from outside the newly renovated wall and windows.

"I want to shoot a lot from the outside looking in," he says to Priestly. "You should never be sure whether you're seeing things from the perspective of the guy who's stalking MacHeath."

Now Egleson and Priestly start to block out the shot: the camera, mounted on the dolly, will move along the outside wall of the set and then shoot the scene through one of the windows.

Nearby, dolly grip Tony Campenni and first assistant cameraman Jonathan Burkhart are watching and listening. Campenni will push the dolly; Burkhart will adjust the focus.

Everybody runs through the scene a few times. As Campenni

WEATHER: SUNRISE: am SUNSET: pm

CALL SHEET
AGAINST THE LAW

DIRECTOR: Jan Egleson   Production office:
PRODUCER: Marcus Viscidi   (617) 776-4500
FIRST A.D.: Steve Wertimer
SECOND A.D.: Alan Breton   "PAST PRESENT"
PRODUCTION MANAGER: Daniel Lupi
DATE: **TUES. DEC. 11, 1990**   CREW CALL: 11:00A
SHOOT DAY: 5 OF 8

SCENE	SET	CAST	DAY	PAGES	D/N	LOC.
9	INT Mac's apartment reception area	3,9	2	5/8	N	Studio
	Elizabeth gets a strange visitor					
49	INT Mac's apartment reception area	1,5,6	6	1 0/8	N	
	Cleon arrives for the weekend					
51	INT Mac's kitchen	1,5	6	6/8	N	
	They prepare dinner, Vanessa goes to Cleon					
53	INT Mac's kitchen	1,5	6	1 0/8	N	
	Mac drops veggies, he's tense					
61	INT Mac's kitchen	1	6	2/8	N	
	Mac talks to Meigs on a stake out					
58	INT Various rooms	1,5,6	6	1 2/8	N	
	Vanessa and Cleon scare Mac					
65	INT Mac's bedroom	1,5	6	1 2/8	N	
	Vanessa tells Mac she is going to teach					
68	INT Mac's bedroom	1,5	6	2/8	N	
	Mac and Vanessa awakened by scream					
69	INT apartment reception area	1,5,6,9	6	3/8	N	
	Dartman is in the apartment					
55	INT Mac's apartment reception area	5,6	6	1/8	N	
	POV of apartment through skylights					
64	INT Mac's apartment reception area	6	6	1/8	N	
	Cleon is asleep					

TOTAL PAGES: 7 1/8

#	CAST		CHARACTER	W/MU/HR	ON SET	REMARKS
1.	Michael O'Keefe	(W)	MacHeath	12:00N	1:00P	PU @ DENTIST
2.	M.C. Gainey	(H)	Meigs	—	—	—
3.	Elizabeth Ruscio	(W)	Elizabeth	11:00A	12:00N	PU @ 10:45 @ Comm Ave
4.	Suzzanne Douglas	(H)	Yvette	—	—	—
5.	Christine Moore	(W)	Vanessa	11:30A	1:00P	PU @ 11:15A @ Sonesta
6.	Jason Boyd	(W)	Cleon	TA	TA + 15	PU @ TA @ 808 Memorial Drive B708
9.	Steven Keats	(W)	Dartman	11:00A	12:00N	PU @ 10:45A @ Sonesta
13.	John G. Phillips	(H)	Det. Shaner	—	—	—

EXTRAS
Mac/Dartman SI   RPT TO LOC @ 11:00A
Elizabeth/Vanessa SI RPT TO LOC @ 11:00A
Cleon SI   RPT TO LOC @ 12:00N

TUTOR REPORT TO LOC @ 12:00N

SPECIAL INSTRUCTIONS ON OTHER SIDE...   ALAN AT HOME: 242-5969

TUE DEC 11, 1990

CREW CALL 11:00A

DIRECTOR:	11:00A	SOUND:	11:00A	WARDROBE:	11:00A
ASST. DIR.:	PU 10:45A	GRIPS:	11:00A	MAKEUP:	11:00A
2ND A.D.:	11:00A	ELEC.:	11:00A	HAIR:	11:00A
2ND 2ND:	11:00A	PROPS:	11:00A		
PA'S:	10:30A	ART DEPT:	O/C	COFFEE/BKFAST:	Ready @ 10:45A
SCRIPT:	11:00A			LUNCH:	FOR: 80
DP/OP:	PU 10:45A				READY @ 4:30P
CAMERA:	11:00A				
UNIT:	PER COLLINS				

ADVANCED SCHEDULE   ADVANCE SCHEDULE

STUDIO   WED 12th | STUDIO   Thurs 13th
   + |
KILL SHANER |

TRANSPORTATION		PROPS	RAIN
HONEYWAGON AT LOCATION @	10:30A	manilla envelope	Hudson sprayer up to Sc65
ALL OTHER EQUIPMENT @ LOCATION @	10:30A	sign/tear sheet	
		pen	
BLUE VAN LVS Sonesta @	10:45A	wrapped package	**WARDROBE**
w/S. Wertimer, T. Priestley, D. Gillham, R. Reis,		w/tape cassette	body stockings
P. Cote, Paul K., A. Priestley, STEVEN KEATS		knapsack	
		dinner fixings (Sc51)	
BROWN VAN PU ELIZABETH RUSCIO @	10:45A	knife	
@ Comm Ave		glass of water	
		aspirin	
VAN PU CHRISTINE MOORE @	11:15A	bowl	
@ Sonesta		spilled vegetables	
		harmonica	
UNIT PU JASON BOYD @	TA	phone	
808 Memorial Drive B708 @		firewood	
		tray of ice	
VAN PU M. O'KEEFE @ Dentist @	TBA	soda, wine, scotch	
		shotgun	

Call sheets for Episode 11, Day 5.

Two of the five strong lights illuminating the Pacific Studios' skyline from behind. A grip (right) is making a minor adjustment.

pushes the dolly, Priestly turns a steering wheel on the side of the dolly, cranking the camera up very slightly, and very smoothly. The dolly moves as if it's finely geared and well greased. The shot sort of flows along the wall and up to the window.

Now they try the shot again, while Michael O'Keefe and the detective rehearse the scene. They then shoot it for real, twice.

When the scene is completed, O'Keefe, who's tall with long brown hair swept back, walks over to where I'm standing and sits down on a canvas chair.

I ask him how he approaches the first day of shooting a new episode.

"I like it," he says. "I like it when the actors who'll be working on the episode first arrive. It's like bringing fresh players into the game. It energizes everybody. That's one of the best parts of this job: working with the actors who come in for the different episodes."

Has he offered any script suggestions on this episode?

"Just a few," he says. "You know, I remember watching 'Combat' with my father when I was like twelve, and the hero would be hanging from a cliff, and I'd say to my father, 'He's not in any trouble. Because he's the star. They can't kill him. But those two other guys, the guest stars, they're going to die before the next commercial.' So I think that when you're working on a show like this, you have to try to work against that kind of predictability. That's what I try to do, anyway."

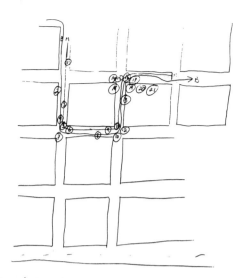

① Mac thinking - front mount - 1st unit

+ ② bad guys car squals out in pursuit (Mac passes, sedan squeals cy) - passby - 2nd unit

③ Mac checks rear view mirror - front mount - 1st unit

+ ④ sedan roars up blowing horn - cam on insert car - 2nd unit

+ ⑤ sedan in Mac's rear view mirror - cam inside corvette over Mac's dbl's shoulder to mirror
  to sedan, hand reaches up to mirror - 2nd unit (maybe 1st unit)

- ⑥ Mac makes left onto another street - front mount - 1st unit

- ⑦ 'Vette turns left, sedan follows - passby - 2nd unit

+ ⑧ sedan pulls even, veers very close to 'Vette - cam on insert car - 2nd unit
  starts to force it over

⑨ Mac screams at other car - cam in 'Vette back seat - 1st unit
  sees pedestrian

  pedestrian leaps out of the way of 2 speeding cars - passby w/stuntman - 2nd un

⑪ Mac, panicking, hangs left into alley - front mount - 1st unit

+ ⑫ Vette makes turn, sedan follows - passby - 2nd unit

+ ⑬ 2 cars race down alley - low angle passby or crane w/ 2 cars speeding underneath
  2nd unit

⑭ Mac looks up, sees red light, - front mount - 1st unit
  screams

+ ⑮ insert light turning red - 2nd unit

+ ⑯ insert Mac hitting brakes - 2nd unit

  insert Mac's tires squealing to a stop - 2nd unit

+ ⑱ sedan gaining on Vette, swerves past it at last moment - passby - 2nd un

+ ⑲ two cars squeal to a stop at intersection - passby - 2nd unit

⑳ shot past Mac to sedan pulling alongside, Mac screams as car pulls
  away, pan with it - passby - 1st unit

㉑ Mac reaction to pull up and peel away of sedan - cam inside 'Vette
  1st unit

21 shots - 13 2nd unit
        8 1st unit (5 are front mount reactions,
                    1 OTS, 1 inside 'Vette,
                    1 outside 'Vette)

A thirty-second car chase as diagrammed by first assistant director Steve Wertimer.

A few minutes later, as the grips and gaffers are moving equipment to the other side of the set where the next scene will be shot, I wander through a few thick doors and down a narrow corridor into the production office, where I find Jan Egleson on the phone trying to set up another casting session. Yesterday in New York, he was able to fill all the major roles except one: the part of Cleon, the dyslexic teenager whom MacHeath helps.

"The kids are too cute in New York, they're too sitcom-professional," he says when he gets off the phone. "Get them with a laugh track, great. But they won't work for this kind of story."

A few yards away, Steve Wertimer is leaning over his desk, plotting the proposed car chase. The diagram looks like a connect-the-dots puzzle, with twenty-one clearly labeled circles, each representing a camera position and a shot. Eight of the shots would be first unit—that is, with Michael O'Keefe in the picture; the remaining thirteen shots could be shot second unit, without O'Keefe or with a stand-in. According to Wertimer's calculations, the chase would take an entire morning, maybe a day, to pull off. Wertimer doesn't think it's worth it.

"A thirty-second chase will take twenty-one shots and a lot of set-up time," he says. "If you're going to do it right you've got to go back and forth, back and forth, bang, bang, bang (he's snapping his fingers now). Mac goes around a corner; the other guy goes around a corner; Mac hits a hydrant; the other guy goes through the water—it has to go like that, or it just won't look right."

Day two, and the production is already starting to run late. Last night the crew worked until midnight; today things got rolling around noon; lunch was at 6:00 P.M. Now, just back from lunch, the crew is setting up to film a short three-line, eight-word, almost inconsequential scene.

According to the script, MacHeath has just received another missive from the stalker. His secretary, Elizabeth, walks from the reception area into his office.

> ELIZABETH
> (concerned)
> Are you okay?
>
> MAC
> (looking worried)
> Fine. Are you okay?
>
> ELIZABETH
> (still looking concerned)
> Fine.

Two grips carry the Chapman dolly into the reception area outside MacHeath's office. Egleson stands next to it, then walks around. Above, grips and gaffers are bustling around in the rafters, adjusting lights.

"Can I get Elizabeth on the set?" Egleson says.

The request reverberates like an echo, from production assistant to production assistant: "Elizabeth on the set, Elizabeth on the set . . ."

When the actress arrives, looking kind of taut, Egleson starts describing the scene to Elizabeth and to Tom Priestly, the director of photography. As Egleson speaks, he holds his hands out as if he's framing a small television picture.

"I want you to walk slowly from the reception area to the doorway of MacHeath's office," he says to Elizabeth.

A Fisher Ten Dolly, which, along with a Chapman PeeWee, saw a lot of action on the "Against the Law" set. For roughly $160 a day, it will move the camera in any direction with super pneumatic smoothness.

J.L. Fisher Inc.

Model **TEN** CAMERA DOLLY

STANDARD EQUIPMENT

HIGH AND LOW SIDE BOARDS
INTERCHANGABLE FRONT BOARDS
ADJUSTABLE SEATS
PUSH POSTS
CARRY HANDLES
POWER CORD
BATTERY TRAY

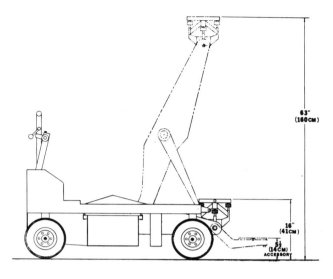

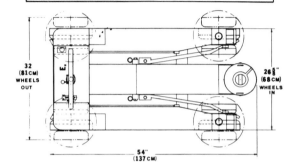

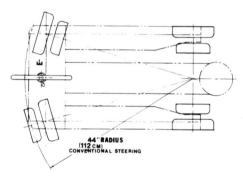

44" RADIUS
(112 CM)
CONVENTIONAL STEERING

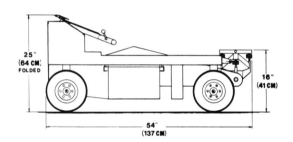

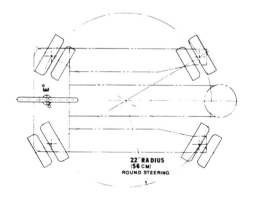

22" RADIUS
(56 CM)
ROUND STEERING

OPTIONAL ACCESSORIES

RISERS: 3", 6", & 12"
CAMERA OFFSETS: 10", 24" & ROTATING
90° ANGLE PLATES
PAN/TILT ADAPTERS
MONITOR RACK
LOW LEVEL HEAD
SEAT OFFSETS
SEAT RISERS
SEAT PLATFORM
EXTENDED HIGH SIDE BOARDS
SQUARE TRACK (STRAIGHT & CURVED)
TRACK RAMP
SHIPPING CASE

J. L. Fisher, Inc. • 10918 Burbank Boulevard, North Hollywood, California 91601 • (213) 877-9966

"Tom," he continues, "I want you to be right behind her on the dolly, following her, slowly moving the camera down, so that when she gets to the door, the camera is about waist high looking past her into MacHeath's office, at MacHeath sitting at his desk. I want a sense of menace, a sense of creeping around."

Elizabeth and the dolly crew try the move a few times. The dolly moves the camera very smoothly in two directions at the same time. As Campenni rolls it towards the office door, Priestly turns a steering wheel on the side, lowering it very slightly. The action is so fluent, so deliberate, it looks inevitable.

Satisfied with the shot, Egleson turns control over to Priestly, who begins to light the scene, directing the gaffers and grips to position and adjust lights, flags, peppers, foam-core sections, and silks. Priestly spends the next ten minutes carefully sculpting the light: highlighting a wall on one side of the office, training a small light to illuminate Elizabeth's face when she reaches the doorway, and bouncing light off a foam-core panel so that it catches Mac-Heath's face when he leans back in his chair.

When Priestly is satisfied, they call the actors back and film the scene twice, with Michael O'Keefe saying his line from behind the desk.

They then break down the scene and put the camera behind Mac's desk for a reverse angle looking out at Elizabeth standing at the door.

Priestly takes over again and relights everything.

"Coverage," Priestly says. "We want to give the editor a lot of angles to choose from."

Elizabeth stands in the doorway; she and MacHeath do the scene for the second time.

Then another camera move, and another lighting scheme, for a close-up of O'Keefe as he and Elizabeth do the scene for the third time.

Three angles for a three-line scene. I feel as though I'm in the middle of a cubist composition.

Finally when Egleson says "Cut" for the last time, the set quickly fills up with technicians, grips, and gaffers. The lights, so precisely placed, are now bouncing randomly off the tops of everybody's heads.

As the crew regroups for the next scene, I calculate a box score: eight words, three setups, one hour and forty-five minutes of elapsed time for eight seconds of screen time. The result, however, is a spacious, three-dimensional feeling. Maybe there's no other way to get it.

• • •

Paul Cote on the set, monitoring a scene. Note the television-style antenna for picking up radio microphones. The boom microphone is sheathed next to his left hand.

Paul Cote, the sound mixer, is sitting behind a sturdy cart loaded with electronic equipment, trimmed with coiled cables, and topped off by what looks like a fifties-era television antenna. Cote always speaks *sotto voce,* even between scenes when the first assistant director is yelling at the second assistant director about the prop that should have been on the set five minutes ago.

"It's for receiving the signals from the radio mikes, the lavaliers," Cote says quietly when I ask him about the antenna. "I usually wire up everybody who has a speaking part."

What about the guy who's sitting on top of one of the set's walls dangling a boom microphone over the actors?

"Basically, when I set up for a scene, I put the boom up and I hook up the lavalier mikes," he responds. "Then I compare them; I do an A/B reference. If you're within a controlled environment like this set, and the boom is in an acceptable range, then the boom is the way to go: you can get better sound. But in some cases, especially on location, the boom picks up more sound than you want to hear. Then you go to the radio lavalier microphones. And sometimes you can't use a boom because of the lights."

The lights?

"The boom man has to watch his shadow—you don't want to cast a shadow. So you're always trying to finesse around the lights. But on some scenes, you just can't use the boom at all. Then you go with the radio mikes."

Do the radio mikes give pretty good sound even in noisy environments?

"No, not always. Fortunately, you can always dub the dialogue in later, in postproduction. You can't dub the picture. So if you're in a place where the picture looks great but the sound is impossible, the picture takes precedence."

When Cote was in high school in Florida, he visited the set of a television commercial that was filming nearby. By the end of the afternoon, he had one strong impression: "This is what I want to do." He subsequently attended Florida State University as a communications major; when he was graduated in 1975, he moved to New York City and got a job with a small production company.

In 1979, Cote decided to go freelance as an audio man. His first challenge was getting work, and getting the equipment to do the work.

"The bigger the job, the more I would invest in my equipment," he recalls.

His first purchase was a Nagra tape recorder. The model he currently uses, the 4.2, sells for around $11,000.

"The Nagra is almost a given," he says. "One reason is that a movie camera runs at crystal speed, and the Nagra has an internal crystal that you can sync up with the film camera. You need that for lip synchronization. The other reason why the Nagra is a workhorse is that it was developed to really take a beating. On 'Against the Law' alone, we've worked outdoors in the middle of winter, at night, and in the sun, midday, when it's above ninety degrees and humid. So you need a machine that's built to take abuse."

Cote also bought a mixer and a variety of radio and boom-mounted microphones. The mixer he uses today costs $6500; the microphones range in price from $1200 to $3400. He estimates that the current value of his equipment hovers around $50,000.

Most of Cote's early work was on documentaries, but recently

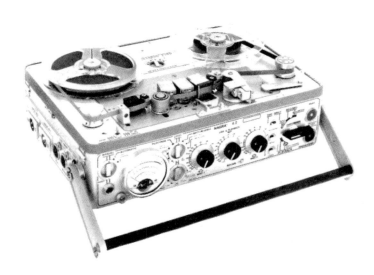

The Nagra 4.2. At the heart of Paul Cote's setup.

he's been working more on feature films and television shows where the money is a little better.

"Documentaries are great training," he says. "You're out there running and gunning, flying by the seat of your pants."

At the moment, the audio industry is abuzz over digital audio tape, DAT. Will Cote eventually have to trade up?

"Eventually," he says. "But right now it's just not cost-effective to spend twenty thousand dollars on a DAT deck. All this technology is great, but it could be going a little too fast, a little too . . . do you remember disco? This might be a poor analogy, but you know how slick that was, how glitzy? That's the way it can get with equipment. And sooner or later, people just want to get back to basics. So I don't think it makes sense to become obsessed with obsolescence: Is your equipment state of the art, and so on. Basically my equipment package is strong enough to do a feature film. And if I have to go beyond that on a given job, I rent."

On a cold, raw December morning, six large tractor-trailer trucks are lined up side by side in the parking lot of East Boston High School.

Today, a Saturday, the production crew will be shooting ten scenes at East Boston High, interiors and exteriors. Outside, Tom Priestly and Jan Egleson are planning a scene in which someone (the stalker presumably) tries to ram MacHeath's Corvette as he starts to pull out of the high school parking lot. Inside, production designer Suzanne Cavedon and a few members of the prop department are dressing a principal's office, a school cafeteria, a hallway, and a classroom. Walkie-talkies and intercoms are crackling with communiqués between the two groups.

Outside, in the school's parking lot, I ask Priestly how he's going to choreograph the near miss.

"We want it to be staccato, like commercial editing, to heighten the excitement," he says. "We want it to go boom, boom, boom."

As he says this and claps his heavy gloves together, his windbreaker makes a rustling nylon sound.

Brian Ricci, "Against the Law" 's stunt man and special effects coordinator, is driving the stalker's car, a beat-up Chrysler New Yorker.

Michael O'Keefe is behind the wheel of his character's sixties-era Corvette.

They rehearse the scene a few times. O'Keefe starts to pull out; Ricci zooms towards him; then as O'Keefe jams on the brakes, Ricci swerves by and speeds around the corner, tires squealing.

A rail shot assembled and executed.

When the sequence starts to look realistic, Priestly shoots the sequence three times: from the right of the Corvette, then from behind, then from the left.

"Now I want a shot from the stalker's point of view," he says as he stands behind the old Chrysler, looking at the Corvette.

"Let's do a track shot," he says finally.

Almost immediately, the words "track shot" start echoing, grip to grip, back to the unit truck. A few minutes later, a bunch of grips are kneeling down on the cement banging together sections of tubing. When they have a thirty-foot section together, they carefully move it into position, lower it into place, and level it off with wooden shims. The Chapman PeeWee dolly is bolted to a wooden dolly and loaded onto the tracks. They run the camera down the track a few times; the sequence looks like a very short roller-coaster ride that dead-ends at a Corvette.

Priestly describing his approach: "We'll put Michael in the Corvette and we'll zoom towards him. And as we're going down the track, I'll also be zooming the camera in, so you'll get this sort of vertigo effect. We'll also be running the camera a little slow, so at regular speed it will seem slightly faster."

After his last screeching drive around the corner, Brian Ricci returns and pours himself a cup of coffee.

In addition to stunts, Ricci also does special effects for the show.

"I did a nice explosion the other day. Did anybody mention it?" he asks.

I ask him what he'll be contributing to Episode 11.

"This, some rain later, and a shotgun hit—those are fun, and kind of gory," he says.

Jan Egleson walks over. "Brian, that shotgun hit, I want a real guy in the car, with a pump that will splash blood against the windshield when he gets hit. Can you do that?"

Tom Priestly supervising the lighting of Michael O'Keefe, who's in the car.

Michael O'Keefe as the shot appears in the show.

"You got it," Ricci says confidently.

The crew moves on to the next shot: a stunned reaction from MacHeath as the car disappears around the corner.

The camera and dolly are unloaded from the track and placed on the passenger side of the Corvette. A large light is moved into position in front of the Corvette and trained on O'Keefe sitting inside the car, giving his face a warm glow.

Is his face maybe too bright, compared to the generally drab surroundings?

"It is brighter," Priestly says. "But he's the star. We want to see his face."

Suzanne Cavedon supervising the transformation of a guidance counselor's office into a principal's office.

Inside the school, someone is sawing the legs off two chairs, then carefully gluing them back on.

"Cleon, the kid, is supposed to smash a chair against a wall," he explains. "We want the legs to break off easily."

Down the hall, Suzanne Cavedon is transforming a guidance counselor's office into a principal's office. She covers floral contact paper on a bookcase with wood grain paper; she moves out the plastic chair behind the desk and replaces it with a higher-backed, executive-looking chair; she puts up an American Presidents calendar and a picture of Albert Einstein; she moves in a beat-up leather couch and a small potted plant; she puts up a few diplomas. On the desk she places a small, severe-looking book, the official Boston Public Schools Code of Discipline.

In Scene 11, MacHeath gets out of his car outside the high school and walks inside. A few menacing-looking teenagers check out his Corvette, possibly with larcenous intentions, but then the stalker arrives. (MacHeath's stalker is never given a name in the script; most of the crew refers to him as "Dartman"—a reference to Scene 15, when he stabs MacHeath with a poison dart.) Dartman scares the teenagers off, jimmies the lock, and leaves an audiocassette on the seat.

The production has rented Tom Doran's crane for the scene. Doran, the key grip on "Against the Law," bought the crane from the Universal lot a few years ago and refurbished it. The crane is primitive by today's standards: Doran simply loads one side up with

Tom Doran's crane, in action, making the move from a high establishing shot to a street-level angle.

counterweights until he gets the balance he wants; then he controls it with a rope, pulling it down in one smooth, slow motion.

Egleson requested the crane because he wants to start out high, with an establishing shot of a busy urban schoolyard, and then slowly descend as first the teenagers, then the stalker, approach the Corvette. When the platform reaches the ground, Egleson wants the cameraman to step off the crane and move in on the stalker and the Corvette.

The cameraman, Richard Reis, wants to stop the shot when the platform hits the ground; he doesn't want to step off the platform with the camera running.

"He thinks it will look shaky," Egleson says. "I don't mind shaky, but that's a major point of pride to cameramen, smoothness."

Egleson calls over an extra, a black teenager.

"When the platform reaches the ground, I want you to walk in front of the camera, towards the Corvette," he says to the extra.

"Okay, the kid will walk ahead of you," he says to Reis. "Follow him with the camera, and it will distract from any shakiness. The kid will take the bumps off."

While the camera crew is fussing with the crane shot, Steve Wertimer is organizing the extras into three distinct clusters around the schoolyard; a production assistant with a walkie-talkie is stationed with each group. Then, just before each take, when Wertimer gives the signal via walkie-talkie, each cluster breaks up like a rack of billiard balls. By the time the camera starts rolling a few seconds later, their combined movements look like natural schoolyard activity.

Paul Cote is traveling light on this scene, carrying his Nagra in a shoulder bag, using a single boom microphone.

"I'm doing this documentary style," he says.

Standing next to the crane, Cote has been using the boom to keep the microphone as close to the camera as possible. As the camera descends, so does the microphone.

"I'm trying to get sound that matches the perspective of the camera," he says. "I try to match the point of view of the lens: If the shot is wide, you want a wide sound. If it's tight you want something tight. If the camera is tight on something, and I'm not, I'm in trouble. It's not so bad the other way around: If I've got tight sound, and the camera is wide, they can add air to it in the edit room."

I ask Cote if he tries to capture some of the audio ambiance of a location, along with the dialogue.

"No, not really," he says. "On location, you just want the clean-

Paul Cote, traveling light.

est, strongest dialogue tracks you can get. They can add all the ambiance they want in postproduction. I'll give you an example: We recently had a scene where a guy was talking through a megaphone. I decided to just record him talking, without the megaphone, and they muddied it up in postproduction to get that megaphone sound. That way if they wanted to use the voice without the megaphone for some reason, they could."

Although the boom that Cote is holding looks like a glorified broomstick, I take a wild guess that it is costlier than it appears.

"A good boom pole will cost you around six hundred dollars," Cote says. "And then you also need a shock mount to reduce the handling noise that the microphone will pick up."

At the end of the boom, the microphone looks like it's been covered with the pelt of a small furry animal.

"Dealing with wind is a gradual process," Cote says. "If you're outside and there's no wind, maybe you can get away with just a foam screen. But now the wind picks up, the foam can't tolerate the wind, and the microphone is starting to break up. So the next degree of wind protection is the zeppelin, which is a very thin housing. Then the wind picks up a little more. The next degree is a wind sock, which is like a very light sweatshirt material, and it goes over the zeppelin. Now if the wind picks up more, as it has today, then you take off the wind sock and put on the windjammer, which is made from synthetic fur.

"The theory behind the windjammer is actually kind of interesting. It's based on the idea that when wind hits an animal's fur, it rolls off the fur and kind of wraps around it. It's really amazing. I've used the windjammer in some really windy situations, and you just don't hear the wind."

Don't you want some wind noise, to convey a sense of the location?

"Sure," Cote replies. "But you want to hear the wind like shh-hhh, not like bughhhhhhh."

After the scene is over, I ask Doran about his crane.

"It's great for steps," he says. "You can stay with the person as he comes down some courthouse steps, for instance. It's also good for establishing shots of the Corvette. A Tulip or Piccolo crane will go as high as my crane, but they're designed for inside use, so it can get kind of scary up there when you're outside. This crane gives you a sturdier platform."

I ask Doran if he's had enough business to repay his investment in the crane.

"It goes out quite a bit," he says, "but it will probably take me three years to pay it off. Every producer is the same, 'Can you cut me a deal?' I'm always knocking my price down."

Back at the production office, Dan Blatt, the show's executive producer, has just arrived from Los Angeles on the red eye, the overnight flight; he's planning to put in some days on the set. All morning he's been popping in and out of his office. Sometimes he only opens the door about a foot and yells something to his intern/assistant, Deborah; sometimes he just sticks his arm out, holding something to be photocopied.

Blatt, who looks as if he's trying to shake off a persistent case of jet lag, was brought in as the show's executive producer after the show's sixth episode. Fox felt that the original producer, David Manson, was making MacHeath too quirky, too offbeat. An industry veteran, Blatt was asked to steer the show back towards the middle of the road.

When Blatt shoehorns me into his schedule later in the afternoon, I don't expect to get his undivided attention, and I don't.

"I started out as a lawyer in New York," he tells me, "and then I got involved with the civil rights movement. You know who I worked with? Gary Bellow, a professor at Harvard Law School. Now he's a consultant on this show—"

Blatt lunges at the door.

"Deborah? Deborah! Can you get Joan-Ellen Delaney in New York to fax up that bio on Gary Bellow? Thanks."

Blatt closes the door, then opens it again.

"And Deborah? Could you call the Harvard Square Army-Navy store and reserve that white coat with the hood. It was a hundred and nineteen dollars."

Now he's back inside. He flops into his chair.

"Anyway, a guy I grew up with in Brooklyn, Dan Curtis, asked me if I wanted to work in motion pictures. It sounded interesting, so I went out to the West Coast. I worked on films like *Sleuth, Heartbreak Kid, The Stepford Wives.* After that I began producing TV movies: *Raid on Entebbe, V, Common Ground*—"

Deborah opens the door and hands Blatt a four-page fax. It's a bio of Gary Bellow from the Fox publicity office. Blatt stands in the middle of the office and reads the entire four pages, aloud, at 78 RPM.

When he's finished, I ask him about the job of producing "Against the Law." What changes did he make?

"What I'm trying to do here is put a lot of production value up on the screen," he says. "I want it to look like real life."

Deborah buzzes. It's Marty on line two.

"Thanks," Blatt says. "And Deborah? Get me some cold medicine. Anything."

Now Blatt is speaking on the phone.

"Marty, did you see the clips I sent you? Either his price is going to go up after this picture or he's going to have no price. What's your feeling?"

Blatt conducts some business with Marty, hangs up, and looks at me as if I'd just arrived.

"Okay, where were we?"

The changes you made when you started producing "Against the Law."

"Oh yeah, I didn't know what MacHeath's MO was. We wanted the scripts to be cleaner. We wanted issues that were personal to MacHeath (he's shaking his fist now): family, ecology, homelessness, union abuse, college athletics, justifiable homicide. We've tried to take the emotional issues and set them in the legal system. The early shows were more character-driven; our shows are more issue-driven."

Deborah buzzes. It's Vanessa Hayes, the show's postproduction supervisor in Los Angeles, calling about Episode 10's teaser.

Blatt takes the call. As he talks to Hayes, I look around. Two half-unpacked suitcases are on the floor; a stuffed Filo-Fax is sitting on the desk, on top of a pile of head-shot photographs of actors and faxes from Fox.

Sam Pillsbury, one of the show's associate producers, walks in. Blatt gets off the phone.

"Are we going ahead with the walk'n'talk near Trinity Church?" Pillsbury asks.

Walk'n'talk?

"There's this tremendous need for verbal exposition on a show like this," Pillsbury explains. "So you try to disguise it by keeping it moving. Some director once said, 'I don't care what they're saying, as long as it's moving.'"

Blatt is back on the phone. I take the opportunity to ask Pillsbury a few questions, like why is the show always running late, why are they always playing catch-up?

"It starts with the scripts," he says. "And part of it comes from the fact that Fox didn't commit to the series until the last minute. And no one wanted to pay for scripts that we weren't going to use. As a result, when you do get the go-ahead, you find yourself in the position of generating a lot of scripts quickly."

How much does a script cost?

"About twenty thousand dollars for the first draft, which can add up when you commission seven episodes. And then what happens is that Fox will wait until the last of the seven episodes before committing to do the next seven. And then you're behind again, and a bunch of us will end up in an office writing a story outline to give to a scriptwriter. And even if he's fast, we'll be working on it until the last minute."

So, do the producers generate the story ideas?

"Yes, generally we'll think up an idea for an episode and run it by Fox before we give it to a scriptwriter. Fox tends to like stories that are sensational. So we say something high-concept like 'date rape.' Then when they approve it, we have to go back and make it work as a story worth telling. So you have to be an ad guy, selling the story to them, and then you have to be a writer, to execute it. It's a very malleable exercise."

I ask Pillsbury if the show really needs all the layers of grips and gaffers.

"Shooting seven or eight minutes a day is a fucking unbelievable pace," he says. "But we can't slow up: the deadlines are too pressing. You can't afford to wait for anything. So if it comes down to adding one or two more people to guarantee that you don't wait for forty-five minutes, it's worth it. And when you keep adding one or two people, over the length of a production like this, it adds up."

Blatt hangs up, he looks at me with a kind of jet-lagged stare.

"I'll tell you what I'm trying to do with a show like Episode 11," he says. "I want to grab the viewers at the beginning of the show and hold them at the half hour."

According to the latest draft of the script, the show begins with MacHeath making love to a woman on his kitchen counter as the stalker videotapes them from a rooftop across the street. It's reasonable to assume the scene will grab viewers.

But what happens at the half hour?

"Mac gets stabbed with the poison dart," Blatt says confidently, as if amidst all the confusion, these two scenes, at least, are etched in stone.

The stalker is sitting on a couch, cradling a rifle, looking sinister. Jonathan Burkhart, the first assistant camera operator, is measuring the distance from the camera to the stalker's nose. It's about twelve feet. Then Tony Campenni pushes the dolly and camera towards the stalker. When Egleson says "stop," Burkhart measures again: five feet.

Burkhart will be pulling focus on this shot. As the camera moves in on the stalker, he'll walk next to the lens, holding a control cable, and adjusting the focus so the stalker stays sharp.

"It's a burnout job," he says. "First, you have to calculate the focus without being able to look through the lens. Then, on top of that, there's the pressure: the lights can be a little off; the props can be slightly wrong; but if the focus is off, the shot is ruined."

Above us, grips are moving large sheets of white foam core around, shaping the light into a wide shaft that falls on the stalker. The rest of the set is murkily lit, shadowy. Tom Priestly studies the effect for a few moments.

"Get me a pepper," he says to no one in particular.

There's a quick stirring among the grips and gaffers, and a small light with a long snout soon appears.

"I want it on the gun," Priestly says.

Another ripple in the grip-and-gaffer pool. A stand is positioned, sandbags are placed over the legs, and the beam is focused on the rifle.

"Let's see it with the obie," Priestly says.

A camera assistant turns on a small light on top of the camera, subtly highlighting the stalker's eyes and teeth.

"That gives his face a little more pop," Priestly says.

The responsibilities of the various grips, gaffers, and assistants on "Against the Law" are difficult to sort out. Every shot on every scene is rimmed with a bewildering number of people, most of them just standing around looking well equipped and ready, with a lot of hardware-type stuff hanging from their wide belts.

When I sought out the show's personnel list, I found that the crew includes two first assistant directors; a second A.D.; and a second second A.D.; a camera operator; a first assistant camera; a second assistant camera and a camera production assistant; three electricians, a gaffer, a best boy, and five varieties of grip: key, second, dolly, third, and fourth; three set p.a.'s, two unit p.a.'s, and three general all-around production assistants.

Surprisingly, all these bodies don't appear to slow things up on the set. In fact, unlike the situation in most bureaucracies, things get done—fast. Whenever Priestly talks, eager TV worker bees swarm all over the problem and get it right in a hurry. The grips and gaffers may look like plumbers, all loaded down with tools and tape, but they act like emergency response technicians. Still, is it really necessary to have a third and fourth grip? A second second A.D.?

I posed the question to Philip Alvare, who often works as a production manager.

"It does seem like there are more people than really necessary," he said. "But at a variety of times, throughout the course of any production, each one of these people will be called upon to perform. Their performance is critical in the execution of this particular episode. And because we do not have the information we need—that is, the script—until three days before we start shooting, it's like the less time you have to execute, the more people and the more money you need to make it happen. The deadline does not change. So the way you accomplish it is by having people waiting in the wings, because you know the inevitable will arise. It's so expensive, every minute, that it's cheaper to bring someone else on than to wait. So you have to anticipate the problems, you have to cover yourself for them. Otherwise, it's penny wise, pound foolish. That's what you need to learn: you need *these* elements now, and you don't need *those* elements yet. Or vice versa. Being able to assess that is where the experience comes in."

The film and television industry's depth of assistance apparently also gives newcomers the opportunity to get a paid position on the set, with a close-up view of the process. Doesn't it?

"That's how I got started," Alvare responds. "I was working in the theater, mostly, when I started free-lancing for local production companies in the film business as a production assistant. I p.a.'d in a lot of different departments. If you're p.a.-ing in craft service, you're basically arranging doughnuts. That's really the bottom of the heap. But if you do it well, people will take notice of you. As a production assistant, the most important thing is to be able to assume responsibility and carry it. That's the most important thing. But you become more valuable, ultimately, the more information you can store and utilize and manipulate. It's making yourself invaluable.''

When Alvare got a chance to do some location scouting, in 1983, for a Budweiser advertisement, he started to store, and utilize, and manipulate the information.

"On some jobs, location scouting is just mundane," he says. "Matching the storyboard, if you will. But as you get better at it, directors and producers start to trust your eye, which makes it more interesting."

Eventually, Alvare formed a small company with another location scout. Together they amassed a collection of more than two thousand photo files on Boston-area locations. At the same time, Alvare began to diversify into production management. When his partner moved to Los Angeles, Alvare began juggling the two jobs, depending on the production.

"Boston is a small market and the work is inconsistent," he says. "So I've been taking both jobs: location scouting and production managing. You need to diversify in a small market like Boston. Eventually I'll probably concentrate exclusively on production management."

Why?

"Because I love building the machine and setting it in motion. I think it's a very creative process. It's an odd process because it's truly collaborative. Part of the art and science of production management is learning to assess what you need, and structuring the production in a way that reflects the shape of the piece you're shooting. The way you arrange production days is very significant, for example. So there's a degree of structural elegance, in theory, to production management; but then you also have to set it in motion, to execute it, which is a long haul, which makes it interesting. And then there are certain variables that cannot be controlled, like the weather and big egos. That makes it even more interesting."

Michael O'Keefe is lying on the floor. The camera is on a small wooden stand that keeps it a few inches off the ground. MacHeath is supposed to be dying in this scene, poisoned (again) by his stalker. He looks terrible, thanks to a great makeup job. The rest of the crew looks terrible for real. It's midway through the seventh day of shooting Episode 11, and the schedule, which has been consistently slipping late, is now seriously askew: crew call was at 3:00 P.M., lunch was served at 8:45 P.M. After midnight, two crew members started wearing pajamas and bathrobes over their clothes, in silent protest of

Makeup artist Lori Hicks touching up stunt guy Brian Ricci.

the absurd hours. One grip is wearing a large piece of duct tape on his back that reads, "Today I Have a Bad Attitude." The actors are trudging between the set and their dressing rooms like zombies. And Lori Hicks, the show's makeup artist, is killing time sitting on a couch about twenty feet from the set with her feet on a low table. Also on the table: a Diet Sprite, two screwdrivers, a few old scripts, lots of clothespins, a can of 6/12, and a flashlight.

Hicks is talking about makeup.

"I only believe in a light foundation," she says. "Just enough to cover blemishes. I like a glow, I don't like a mask. Basically, everybody has lighter patches and darker patches on his face; I just deal with those, even them out. You take the reds out from around the nose and add it to the cheeks, for example. I also mix a lot of different colors, like yellows and reds. If you use just one color, it winds up looking like a mask."

What do you mean by a mask?

"Look at 'Entertainment Tonight.' Mary Hart is wearing a mask, and then there's the big hair on top, teased and sprayed. It's the Barbie look. I don't know whether it's just bad taste, or if there are other reasons for it. Or I remember I rode up the elevator with Deborah Norville once, when she was doing the 'Today' show at NBC. She was just coming in for the day, and she looked beautiful, very Swedish. And then I saw her an hour later, after makeup, and it was all gone. They had painted a face on her."

I ask her what she's using to make Michael O'Keefe look poisoned.

"Glycerin and water," she says. "You spray it on. You can get a good clammy look. Also, a little green makeup helps. A few weeks ago, I had to make up an actor to look dead. I used a little green on him too, and some gray, and a lot of white. We were shooting at a prison, and one of the prison guards told me it was very realistic.''

Out in the parking lot, Brian Ricci is sitting in his pickup truck. He's half asleep, half listening to the radio, waiting for Scene 66, when a detective sitting in a car gets shot by the stalker. The detective's car is parked a few feet away. A small device about the size of a cigarette lighter is taped unobtrusively to the bottom of the driver's window.

''We've got a small explosive charge on the window,'' Ricci explains. ''And when Dartman approaches the car, we're going to detonate the window simultaneously with the gunshot. The camera is going to be outside, facing in. We're also going to have a small cannon loaded with blood inside; and when the gun goes off, I'm going to press a button and blood is going to explode onto the windshield.''

Ricci, who also runs a karate school, got his start in show business when he was hired to coordinate a fight scene for a low-budget movie.

''After the fight, the director said to me, 'We want to do a squib hit on this guy next week. Can you take care of that?' I said, 'Sure, no problem.' Then I turned to one of my students, who was just in the fight scene, and I said, 'What the hell is a squib hit?' He didn't know either. But I had a friend in California who had worked on *The Towering Inferno,* and I called him up. He told me what it was—a gunshot effect that you control by radio—and where to get the stuff. I took it from there. Now I'm blowing up buildings. I just blew up a building last week, for 'All My Children.' The director said, 'I don't want anything left.' That's the kind of job I like.''

The actor who's playing the detective, John Grant-Phillips, is standing a few feet away.

''I was in a play a few years ago, where one of the actors was wired with squibs for a shooting scene that took place late in the play,'' he says. ''But on the first few nights, right around 8:10 the squibs would go off—that was about an hour before they were supposed to. Finally one of the grips figured it out. A guy who lived across the street had an automatic garage door opener, and his remote control unit used the same radio frequency. So every night when he came home, around 8:10 . . .''

What kind of permits and licenses do you need to do explosive special effects, I asked Ricci.

''You have to have a state license, a federal license, and a city permit,'' Ricci replies. ''You also have to have a permit from the fire department; and the fire department has to be there, and the police department.''

How about insurance? Do you have to spend a lot on that?

Ricci looks at me incredulously.

"Can you imagine telling the insurance guy that you're in the explosives business?" he asks. "They won't even talk to me."

At 2:00 A.M., Jan Egleson and Tom Priestly walk out to the parking lot to plan the shot. Paul Cote also walks out and looks around.

Will he be able to pick up the gun blast on the audio track?

"I'll record it," Cote says, "but they'll just use it in postproduction as a guide track. They'll dub in something. If they used my audio, the effect would be wimpy—kind of a 'pock' instead of a 'ppoooockkkkk!' " Cote throws his arms out to emphasize the bigness of the sound.

Egleson describes the way he wants to shoot the scene. He also tells Ricci that they're running late on the set, and it will probably be at least an hour before they'll be out here. Ricci gets back in his truck, pulls a blanket up to his chin, and clicks on the radio.

Most of the equipment on the "Against the Law" set is stenciled with "High Output," the source of the show's lighting and grip supplies. The camera dollies, the lights, the grip stands, the ladders, the generators, even the traffic cones—all are rented from High Output at a cost of close to ten thousand dollars per episode. The night before shooting started on the first episode of "Against the Law," Marcus Viscidi signed a contract with High Output that promised them $113,000 over the next twelve episodes.

Deep within the production office, where the guys with the walkie-talkies and the tape measures hang out, High Output fax order worksheets can be found with checks next to items like "Dust Off Plus refill" and "Edison plug, female." When the High Output trucks show up at the studio, guys who look like grips unload 6000-watt HMI Fresnel lights and Rosco Fog Machines.

One afternoon I trace the supply line back across the Charles River to a large concrete building in Brighton, where I meet up with Dave Hammel, one of the no-nonsense guys who runs the place. Hammel escorts me back to an open area that looks like a cross between a warehouse and an airplane hangar; two tractor-trailer trucks are being tightly loaded with equipment. Many television productions will simply rent an entire truck full of stuff from High Output. You can rent a ten-ton truck, crammed with lighting and grip equipment for $7,500 a week; smaller equipment packages start at around $3,000 a week.

I ask Hammel about the camera dollies, and he leads me over to

At High Output. Cables, lights, light stands, generators, ladders, traffic cones, dollies, fog machines, hurricane fans—to go.

a Fisher 10 dolly sitting over near a forest of grip stands. He presses a button on the handle, and the camera mount smoothly, pneumatically rises to a height of five feet.

"What you want is a solid, sturdy platform," Hammel says. "This is very solid."

How much does a Fisher Ten cost? I ask.

"You can't buy it," he says. "Fisher rents them out through authorized agents like us. We have the exclusive rights to rent Fishers for the New England area. But this dolly is insured for fifty-six thousand dollars, if that gives you an idea of its worth."

How much does it cost to rent?

"About a hundred and sixty dollars a day."

Couldn't someone create a similar dolly and sell it, allowing people to avoid the accruing rental charges?

Does the same go for the Chapman PeeWee?

"Same thing," Hammel says. "You can rent it for a hundred and sixty per day, but you can't buy it."

We walk over to a Chapman PeeWee a few yards away.

"You can see this is much smaller, easier to carry up stairs, easier to get through doorways," Hammel says. "You can pull out the wheels if you want a wider platform."

"An Italian firm just tried that," Hammel says as he puts his foot up on the PeeWee. "But this dolly has so many patents that they couldn't pull it off. In fact, Chapman sued them for patent infringement. One of these dollies spent two weeks in a New Jersey court-room last year, during the trial. And Chapman won. So we probably won't see another attempt for a while."

On the other side of the warehouse, large lights are resting on industrial shelves.

"These are HMI lights," Hammel says. "They were developed in the late seventies, and they give off twice the light of the old quartz lights. These are the lights a lot of productions like 'Against the Law' use when they need something really bright. Like when they want to fill a location with sunlight and it's pitch black outside. They can park a twelve-thousand-watt HMI on a crane outside the window, and you'll think it's high noon. The 12-K HMI will also give you good moonlight if you put it a hundred feet up on a condor crane."

I mention to Hammel that I'm having difficulty sorting out the grips from the gaffers on the set.

"Their jobs are very different," he says. "The gaffers, or electrics, their job is to get power to the heads, to the lights. So they deal with cables, and tie-ins, generators, and the lights. The gaffers support the director of photography. If a gaffer is good, he can rise to become a director of photography, because he's come up working with lights and lighting.

"Then you have the grips: they are responsible for camera support, like the dollies, and the support of the lights and the lighting equipment—flags, silks, nets. Their job is more structural. A grip, if he's good, doesn't go on to be a director or a DP. A grip hopes to rise to be a key grip, and maybe to put his own grip package of equipment together, which he can rent. A key grip can do really well: I know key grips who make ninety and a hundred thousand per year."

Is it difficult to break into the grip/gaffer ranks?

"I actually think it's easy to get into this industry," Hammel says. "The guys you see loading the trucks here, in a few years they could be making sixty thousand a year if they play their cards right."

How do you play the cards right?

"I'd say you have to do two things," Hammel responds. "First you have to give it a chance, and discover if you like it. Do you like this kind of work, or are you really more interested in being a writer or a director? Because let's face it, the real creative part of filmmaking ends with the director of photography. The writer can be creative if he's not in the studio system; also the director, the art director, and, as I said, the director of photography. But the grips or the prop guys? I mean, 'This lampshade rather than that lampshade'? C'mon. I don't see film as a collaborative art. In my opinion, the stronger and more decisive the producer and director are, the better the whole process goes. At best I would say that filmmaking is a very high collaborative craft. You've got to be happy with that if you're going to work in this area.

A High Output fax order work sheet.

HIGH OUTPUT INC.
ORDER WORKSHEET

HIGH OUTPUT, INC.
Film & Video Prod. Supplies
184 Everett St.   Brighton, MA 02134
(617) 787-4747   FAX (617) 787-4666

101 John Roberts Rd
Portland Me. 04106
Tel. 207 761-2828
Fax. 207 761-2828

Company name;   Attn.   Phone#   P.O.#

Qty.	Description	Qty.	Description	Qty.	Description	Qty.	Description
	Acetone 1 gal.		EHF		PH 213		2 x 12 x 12' common
	Adapters grnd. lift		EHG		R-20 DAN		2 x 12 x 16' common
	Allen set metric		EHZ				4 x 8 x 3/4" A/C ply
	Allen set standard		EJG				4 x 8 x 1/2" A/C ply
	Alcohol 95%		EKB				4 x 8 x 1/4" Upsom
	Arri T shirt large		EKD				4 x 8 x 1/4" Masonite
	Arri T shirt x-large		EMD			*Paint:*	
	Baby powder 9 oz.		ESR		Chalk Alpha triple		Chroma Key blue/gal.
	Battery, D cell		ESS		Chalk Railroad		Chroma Key grn./gal.
	Battery, C cell		ETB		Chamois cloth		TV white/gal.
	Battery, AA cell		ETC		Cinefoil black 12"		TV black/gal.
	Battery, AAA cell		EYL		Cinefoil black 24"		Ultimatte blue/gal.
	Battery, 9 volt		EYC		Clothespin 50 pkge.		Ultimatte grn./gal.
	Bead Board		EYE		Ditty bag canvas		Paint scraper
	Blade razor pkge.20		EYF		Ditty bag leather	*Nails:*	
	Book, ASC manual		FAD		Ditty sm. belt bag		#1 drywall by lb.
	Book, Backstage		FCB		Drywall screw 1 1/4 bx.		16D common by lb.
	Book, Gripbook		FCM		Drywall screw 1 5/8 bx.		16D duplex by lb.
	Brush, Artist 1/2"		FCR		Drywall screw 1" box		8D common by lb.
	Brush, Artist 3/4"		FCX		Drywall screw 2 1/2 bx.		8D duplex by lb.
	Brush, Artist 1"		FCZ		Drywall screw 2" box		Red Sheating 3' roll
	Brush, Paint 2 1/2"		FDA		Dust mask		1/4" Hemp by ft.
	Brush, Paint 1 1/2"		FDN		Dust Off Plus refill		1/2" Hemp by ft.
Bulbs:			FDF		Dust Off Plus System		3/4" Hemp by ft.
	15 Watt		FEL		Dust Off refill		Saftey cable 30"
	25 Watt		FEV		Duventyne 5 yd. pack		Sand bags 22lb.
	40 Watt		FEY		Duventyne bulk/yds.		Sash #4.5
	40 Watt Clear		FFM		Edison plug female		Sash #7
	40 Watt A Red		FFN		Edison plug male		Sash #10
	60 Watt T8 Clear		FFN		Ed. Quick On female		Sash chain by ft.
	60 Watt		FFP		Ed. Quick On male	*Seamless:*	
	75 Watt		FFR		Filter Fluid		Super white
	100 Watt		FFS		Flashlight, Mallory		Super black
	150 Watt		FHM		Flo. tube 4' C-50		Studio blue
	150 Watt Flood		FKW		Flo. tube 4' O-32		Slate gray
	BBA		FND		Flo. tube 8' C-50		Thunder gray
	BCA		FRK		Flo. tube 8' O-32		Studio gray
	Blue 40 Watt A		FWM		Foam Core used		Bone
	CXZ		GCA 120V		Foam Core black/white		
	CYX		GCB 30V		Foam Core white/white		Sharpie blue
	DPY		GCC 12V		Fog fluid/gallon		Sharpie red
	DSE		HMI 200 Watt		Fog fluid/liter		Sharpie black fine
	DSF		HMI 250 Watt/SE		Fog fluid mineral oil		Sharpie black x-fine
	DTY		HMI 575 Watt/GS		Glove, leather work		Write On/Wipe Off marker
	DXW		HMI 575 Par		Krazy Glue gel	*Showcard:*	
	DYG		HMI 1200 Watt/GS		Keyless Chuck 3/8"		Black/White
	DYS		HMI 1200 Watt Par		Kraft paper 48"x1000'		Matte gold
	EAL		HMI 1.2 Par lens set		Lumber crayon		Matte silver
	EBW		HMI 2500 Watt/GS		Lumber pencil		Shiny gold
	ECA		HMI 2500 Watt/SE	*Lumber:*			Shiny silver
	ECT		HMI 2500 Watt Par		1 x 12 x 16' common		
	EGR		HMI 4000 Watt		1 x 12 x 16' clear		Shurtape ATG gun
	EGT		HMI 6000 Watt		1 x 3 x 12' common		Slate blank plexi
	EGT		HMI 12000 Watt		1 x 3 x 16' common		Slate dble. side plexi
	EHC		PH 211		2 x 4 x 12' common		Slate trans. plexi
	EHD		PH 212		2 x 4 x 8' common		Sound blanket

SEE REVERSE SIDE FOR ADDITIONAL ITEMS

Sprays;
- ____ Dulling
- ____ Silicone
- ____ Cloud In A Can
- ____ Strks & Tips white
- ____ Strks & Tips brown
- ____ Strks & Tips black
- ____ Strks & Tips silver
- ____ #77 adhesive
- ____ Spray Mount
- ____ K line dulling
- ____ K line white dull'g
- ____ K line black dull'g
- ____ K line semi matte
- ____ Touch up lt. blue
- ____ Touch up lt. yellow
- ____ Touch up dk.brown
- ____ Touch up dk. blue
- ____ Mole maroon
- ____ Mole white
- ____ Glossy white
- ____ Flat white
- ____ Glossy black
- ____ Flat black
- ____ Day glo orange
- ____ Spring clamp sm.
- ____ Spring clamp med.
- ____ Spring clamp lg.
- ____ Staple 1/4" T50 box
- ____ Staple 1/2" T50 box
- ____ Staple 3/8" T50 box
- ____ Staple 5/16 T50 box
- ____ Staple gun T 50
- ____ Staple gun elec.
- ____ Staple hammer
- ____ Steel wool 8 pieces

Tape:
- ____ "Do Not Enter"
- ____ 1" black camera
- ____ 1" red camera
- ____ 1" white camera
- ____ 1" yellow camera
- ____ 1" black paper
- ____ 1" tan masking
- ____ 2" black gaffer
- ____ 2" black paper
- ____ 2" brown gaffer
- ____ 2" grey gaffer
- ____ 2" white gaffer
- ____ 2" Dble. side carpet
- ____ 2" tan masking
- ____ 2" clear packing
- ____ Black electric
- ____ Blue electric
- ____ Brown electric
- ____ White electric
- ____ Orange electric
- ____ Purple electric
- ____ Red electric
- ____ Yellow electric
- ____ 924 Dble side 1/2"
- ____ Dble. side foam
- ____ Tracing paper 54"
- ____ Tracing paper 72"
- ____ Trickline, black/ft.
- ____ Utility knife #99
- ____ Utility blade 5 pac
- ____ Visqueen blk.20x25'

- ____ Visqueen clr. 20'x 100'
- ____ Visqueen blk. 20'x 100'
- ____ White rags 25 lbs.
- ____ Wipes Kim 10"
- ____ Wire 19 guage 50'
- ____ Zipcord 18/2 black/ft.
- ____ Zipcord 18/2 white/ft.

Gels; R indicates roll / S indicates sheet
- ____ .3 ND R
- ____ .3 ND S
- ____ .6 ND R
- ____ .6 ND S
- ____ .9 ND R
- ____ .9 ND S
- ____ 1/2 White Diffusion R
- ____ 1/2 White Diffusion S
- ____ 1/2 Spun R
- ____ 1/2 Spun S
- ____ 1/2 CTB R
- ____ 1/2 CTB S
- ____ 1/2 CTO .6 ND R
- ____ 1/2 CTO R
- ____ 1/2 CTO S
- ____ 1/2 Minus Green R
- ____ 1/2 Minus Green S
- ____ 1/2 Plus Green R
- ____ 1/2 Plus Green S
- ____ 1/4 Spun R
- ____ 1/4 White Diffusion R
- ____ 1/4 White Diffusion S
- ____ 1/4 CTB R
- ____ 1/4 CTB S
- ____ 1/4 CTO R
- ____ 1/4 CTO S
- ____ 1/4 Minus Green R
- ____ 1/4 Minus Green S
- ____ 1/4 Plus Green R
- ____ 1/4 Plus Green S
- ____ 1/8 CTO R
- ____ 1/8 CTO S
- ____ 1/8 CTB R
- ____ 1/8 CTB S
- ____ Full CTO .3 ND R
- ____ Full CTO .6 ND R
- ____ Full CTO .9 ND R
- ____ Full CTO R
- ____ Full CTO S
- ____ Full CTB R
- ____ Full CTB S
- ____ Full Minus Green R
- ____ Full Minus Green S
- ____ Full Plus Green R
- ____ Full Plus Green S
- ____ Full White Diffusion R
- ____ Full White Diffusion S
- ____ Full Tough Spun R
- ____ Full Tough Spun S
- ____ Grid Cloth
- ____ Light Grid Cloth
- ____ Light Tough Spun R
- ____ Light Tough Spun S
- ____ Light Tough Frost R
- ____ Opal Tough Frost R
- ____ Opal Tough Frost S
- ____ Lt. Opal Tough Frost R
- ____ Silent Frost R
- ____ Silver Scrim R
- ____ Silver Shrink Mirror R

- ____ Soft Frost R
- ____ Tough Frost R
- ____ Tough Spun R
- ____ Tough Spun S
- ____ Tough Rolux R
- ____ Tough Rolux S
- ____ Alice Blue HT S
- ____ Alice Blue S
- ____ Apricot S
- ____ Bastard Amber S
- ____ Bastard Amber R
- ____ Blue Frost R
- ____ Bright Blue HT S
- ____ Bright Red HT S
- ____ Bright Rose S
- ____ Bright Pink S
- ____ Brushed Silk R
- ____ Chocolate S
- ____ Chrome Orange S
- ____ Clear S
- ____ Clear R
- ____ Congo Blue HT S
- ____ Cosmetic Burgandy S
- ____ Cosmetic Aqua Blue S
- ____ Cosmetic Silver Moss S
- ____ Cosmetic Peach S
- ____ Cosmetic Highlight S
- ____ Cosmetic Emerald S
- ____ Cosmetic Silver Rose S
- ____ Cosmetic Rouge S
- ____ Dark Amber HT S
- ____ Dark Green HT S
- ____ Dark Magenta HT S
- ____ Dark Blue HT S
- ____ Dark Pink S
- ____ Dark Blue S
- ____ Dark Green S
- ____ Dark Lavender S
- ____ Dark Steel Blue S
- ____ Day Light Blue S
- ____ Deep Straw HT S
- ____ Deep Blue HT S
- ____ Deep Amber S
- ____ Deep Blue S
- ____ Deep Lavender S
- ____ Deep Orange S
- ____ Fern Green HT S
- ____ Fern Green S
- ____ Fire HT S
- ____ Flame Red HT S
- ____ Flesh Pink S
- ____ Gold R
- ____ Golden Amber S
- ____ Hampshire Frost R
- ____ Hampshire Frost S
- ____ Heavy Frost R
- ____ Just Blue HT S
- ____ LCT Yellow R
- ____ LCT Yellow S
- ____ Lavender HT S
- ____ Lee Green HT S
- ____ Lee Green S
- ____ Lee UV R
- ____ Light Amber S
- ____ Light Blue HT S
- ____ Light Rose S
- ____ Light Salmon S
- ____ Light Blue S
- ____ Light Blue R

- ____ Light Red S
- ____ Loving Amber S
- ____ Magenta S
- ____ Mauve S
- ____ Med. Blue/Grn. HT S
- ____ Med. Yellow HT S
- ____ Med. Amber HT S
- ____ Med. Red HT S
- ____ Med. Blue HT S
- ____ Med. Blue/Grn. S
- ____ Med. Blue S
- ____ Middle Rose S
- ____ Mirror Silver R
- ____ Moonlight Blue S
- ____ New Hampshire Blue HT S
- ____ No Color Straw R
- ____ No Color Straw S
- ____ No Color Blue S
- ____ Orange S
- ____ Pale Green S
- ____ Pale Red S
- ____ Pale Salmon R
- ____ Pale Salmon S
- ____ Pale Navy Blue S
- ____ Pale Gold S
- ____ Pale Rose S
- ____ Pale Gold R
- ____ Pale Violet S
- ____ Pale Lavender S
- ____ Peacock Blue HT S
- ____ Peacock Blue S
- ____ Pink S
- ____ Primary Green HT S
- ____ Primary Red HT S
- ____ Primary Red R
- ____ Primary Green S
- ____ Rosy Amber S
- ____ Lee Scrim S
- ____ Slate Blue S
- ____ Smokey Pink S
- ____ Special Lavender S
- ____ Steel Blue S
- ____ Lee Straw R
- ____ Lee Straw S
- ____ Sunrise Pink S
- ____ True Blue S
- ____ White Frost R
- ____ Yellow S
- ____ Zenith Blue HT S
- ____ Zenith Blue S

Additional items not listed
- ____
- ____
- ____
- ____
- ____
- ____
- ____
- ____
- ____
- ____
- ____
- ____

"The second thing is that you have to be able to work aggressively as a member of a team. You can't go out on a delivery with a truck and get lost and just start whining about bad directions. You have to be able to take the initiative and get un-lost. Or if it's quarter to six and we've still got a truck to load, you have to be willing to stick around and work until the job is done. And then if you can work hard and take responsibility, and you're on the truck making deliveries to the set and working with the older guys, somebody's going to start taking an interest and start giving you work."

The call sheet says "Shoot Day: 8 of 8," but there isn't much "day" left as "Against the Law" trucks and trailers and generators start to close in on the Beacon Hill townhouse that serves as the exterior of MacHeath's apartment. This last day of shooting on Episode 11 won't really get started until just before sundown; it will probably go all night.

The moonlight has already arrived in the form of a large condor crane topped by a 12K HMI light from High Output. The rain, which will be delivered by one of Brian Ricci's rain towers, should be ready in a few minutes—if Ricci can generate the proper downpour. Right now the rain looks kind of thin, more like a mist. The script calls for an all-out rainstorm.

In front of the brownstone, the detective is sitting in a parked sedan. He's supposed to be guarding Mac's apartment. A few yards away, a production assistant dressed in Dartman's clothes—and hold-

The moonlight for an evening exterior: a 12K light on a Condor crane.

Brian Ricci adjusting the mist on his rain machine.

ing his gun—is waiting for the right rain. (The actor who has been playing Dartman, Steven Keats, has already returned to New York.) When he gets the go-ahead, the production assistant is supposed to quickly walk up to the driver's side of the car and raise his gun as if he's going to shoot the detective. At that point, the editor will cut to the special-effects shot that Brian Ricci made in the parking lot outside the set in Somerville.

The temperature is hovering around twenty degrees Fahrenheit. Most of the crew members are standing around, hands in pockets, shifting their weight from foot to foot. On the other side of yellow barricade tape, many Beacon Hill residents have paused to figure out what's going on. It must appear inscrutable: fifty people standing around watching a man adjusting water nozzles. It's a Friday night, "Against the Law"'s regular night on the Fox network. When pedestrians ask what show is being filmed here, one of the production assistants is adding a small plug to the basic information.

" 'Against the Law,' " he's saying. "It's on tonight, nine P.M."

Egleson and Priestly are standing behind the camera fine-tuning the lighting. The main light, of course, is the 12K light up on the crane, which is shining through Brian Ricci's mist, which is starting to get heavier.

"To see rain, you want to backlight it," Priestly says. "To see snow, you frontlight it."

Paul Koronkiewicz, the audio boom operator, is edging closer to the camera, watching his shadow.

"My job is to get the cleanest sound on the set," he says. "They'll add background, traffic, high heels later." As the boom operator, Koronkiewicz doesn't control any dials. His job is to get close, and position the microphone to get the best sound possible.

I ask him how he got started in sound.

"In film school," he replies. "In film school everyone wanted to be a director. I wanted to be a director too, but I got interested in sound. Then, pretty soon, I started doing sound for everyone's films. Now, they're all still looking for work as directors, whereas I had a skill coming out. I'm working, and I'm here on the set watching real directors work. So it's really turned out pretty well."

Now the rain, from Ricci's rain tower, is heavy, stormlike, and trained on the driver's side of the detective's car. It's surprising to see how little area he has to cover with rain to achieve a storm effect. The production assistant gets the signal, walks into the rain next to the car, and raises his gun. He looks very uncomfortable, standing under a cold shower on a twenty-degree night. Unfortunately, on the first take, he does not look as though he's been out in the rain for very long.

"He's too dry," Priestly says. "Wet him down."

The production assistant glumly walks under the rain tower and stands there for about a minute until cold water is running off his hood and coat.

On the second take, he looks convincingly wet; but as he approaches the car, he hits a patch of ice and his feet go out from under him. Immediately, at least two people yell "Salt!"

"I'm a little concerned that we're seeing too much of his face," Priestly says. "Kill that light on the sidewalk."

The third takes goes well, and the production assistant quickly disappears into a trailer.

Now the production is moving inside, to shoot the building's European-style elevator going up and going down.

"It sounds boring, but I think this is where it's at in terms of suspense," Egleson says. "The elevator's going up. Who's in it? That kind of thing."

With no one to make up, Lori Hicks is heading for her trailer. "Against the Law" will be on in about five minutes—she's not sure which episode. Would I like to watch it on the makeup room's TV?

It's Episode six, where Mac tries to save a young black man from the electric chair. I've already seen it. Hicks leaves it on, with the sound off, and pulls out a binder that contains Polaroid pictures of the "Against the Law" cast in different makeup settings. She uses them as reference shots.

One sequence of photographs shows Michael O'Keefe with a series of facial bruises.

"This was from a show where he got beat up," Hicks says. "For the scenes that were supposed to be taking place the next morning I made the bruise real red, with a little dried-up jam for the fresh scab.

Then, the next day, it gets kind of purpley and black, and it finishes up kind of greenish. But that show really drove me nuts, because it was shot all out of sequence. So they would shoot a scene that was supposed to be taking place two days later, and I would make the bruise purpley; and then in the very next scene it would be a day earlier, so I'd have to add all this red; or else it would be before he got beat up, so I'd have to take it out completely. It really drove me nuts."

Hicks also has a lot of normal-looking Polaroid portraits of O'Keefe and of the female members of the cast. On the back of the women's pictures, she has written the type of foundation she was using that day, and the brand; the type and brand of eye shadow; and the lip color.

"I really need these pictures for continuity," she says. "If we have to go back and reshoot a scene a few weeks later, it can be awful if you don't know what kind of makeup the actors were wearing."

Hicks takes her makeup kit out of a large cloth bag. ("This is the Krydon 24-color kit, which is really good," she says. "It costs about eighty dollars.") Instinctively, she starts dabbing her makeup brush into different circles.

I ask her what else she takes to the set, in addition to the Krydon makeup, which starts her rooting around in her bag.

"Let's see . . . vitamins, Kleenex, dental floss, hand lotion, Visine, stuff to make a beard, little sponges, a tear blower—"

A tear blower?

She pulls out a thin vial about the size of a cigarette.

"I got this at Frends Beauty Supply in North Hollywood," she says. "It has menthol crystals in it. If I put it in front of your eye and blow through it, tears will start to form."

On the television, the black man who is sentenced to the electric chair is sitting in his cell crying.

Did you use a tear blower on this guy? I ask.

"No, he did that himself," Hicks replies. "He was an excellent actor, and he would work himself into a state and he would cry and cry and cry. He would get into it so much during the shooting that sometimes he couldn't stop. They'd be turning off the lights and he'd still be there heaving, doing that heavy kind of weeping."

The show's hairdresser knocks on the trailer door. Lunch will be served in five minutes. Hicks and I head for a building about a block from the trailer where the show's caterer has laid out a hot meal. A group of crew members stumble in, stamping the cold from their feet. Most of them gravitate towards the soup. It's nearly ten o'clock, and the crew has at least another six hours of shooting ahead of them before Episode 11 is finished. Then, exactly twelve hours after they wrap up for the night, shooting will start on Episode 12, in which MacHeath defends a college basketball player who has lost his scholarship after a serious injury.

Another wave of grips and gaffers and actors arrives, including Michael O'Keefe, who ladles himself a large bowl of soup and sits down at my table.

"This is what I call a drive-by day," he says. "I do a lot of walking in and out of buildings, getting in and out of cars. Establishment-shot stuff."

I ask O'Keefe why he took the role of MacHeath.

"I've worked a lot, but people don't really know who I am," he replies. "I don't have a big name. I thought a television series would help that situation. So when they offered this to me, I took it."

Any surprises?

"Yeah, how unbelievably difficult it is. I really wouldn't wish this on anybody. I have to do crucial scenes at three A.M., in a day that started out at three P.M. I have to look dapper at a dinner party in black tie at four A.M. The pace is brutal, relentless, which makes it very difficult to stay focused on giving a good performance. I always feel like I'm trying to hold back this towering wave of mediocrity."

But what about the opportunity to star in your own dramatic television series?

"I have conflicting thoughts on that, sort of like the angel and devil on each shoulder. And I go back and forth between them all the time. One side is saying: 'Sure it's hard, but think how many actors would love to be in your position. Think what an opportunity this is.' Meanwhile, the other side is saying, 'Opportunity? Opportunity! (He's almost shouting now, making gestures as if he's beating something with a large stick.) I'll (now he's punctuating each word with a blow) show (wham!) you (wham!) what (wham!) I (wham!) think (wham!) of (wham!) your (wham!) opportunity (wham! wham! wham!)!' "

O'Keefe leans back in his seat as if exhausted from the beating. If he's acting, he's doing a very good job of impersonating a bone-weary leading man.

6. "AGAINST THE LAW": EPISODE 11, WEST COAST

Inside the sunbleached gate to the old MGM lot in Culver City, past open stages bursting with tropical greenery ("Hook" was shooting the day I was there), past an equipment truck emblazoned with the surly grip's motto ("YOUR poor planning does not make MY emergency"), past a small group of extras waiting outside the set of the TV show "Parker Lewis Can't Lose," and up a flight of stairs to a small second-level office, a young woman is on the phone, leaving a message on someone's answering machine. This is Vanessa Hayes, the postproduction supervisor on "Against the Law."

Hayes takes over an episode after the filming has been completed; her job ends when she delivers two 1" videotapes (a master and a protection copy) to Fox Broadcasting a few days before airdate.

Actually, Hayes doesn't wait for an episode to stop filming before she gets involved. Usually she looks at the dailies as soon as they've been flown to Los Angeles and transferred to videotape. She first started seeing dailies for Episode 11 after the third day of shooting.

"I was looking to see if the coverage was there," she says. "Jan Egleson uses a lot of pans, back and forth, and a lot of long sweeping movements. He doesn't get into coverage. Some directors always give you a lot of coverage: they'll set their master shot up, then go in and get their singles and the two shots, and get out. So then, editorially, you can go back and forth between master and singles

Vanessa Hayes in her office.

and get your coverage. Jan's style is different. So I was checking to see if there was enough for the editor to work with.''

Her early assessment?

"I thought the dailies looked good, looked fine," she says. "They were moody, they were shot well, they had a real texture to them. They looked as though they were going to cut together. The coverage was fine.

"Then Rick Westover, the editor, started working on them, and he started telling me that they weren't cutting together so well. Certain things weren't happening."

Like what?

"There were some holes, some story points that were missing. Certain show'n'tell details are missing. I've got an early edit right here. I'll show you what I mean."

Hayes inserts a tape into a VCR in her office.

On the screen, MacHeath and his girlfriend Vanessa are in a passionate embrace. She's sitting on the kitchen counter, bursting out of a very tight T-shirt; he's standing on the floor, shirtless.

"Do you see where the camera pans up and you see her nipples?" Hayes asks. "That was a little too hot for Fox. They asked us to cut around that. They also wanted us to shorten the kiss a little bit. That's a typical change."

Now MacHeath's assistant, Elizabeth, gets up from her desk and walks to the elevator.

"We'll add the elevator noises later," Hayes says. "Do you notice how dead it sounds? We'll also add inner-office sounds—computer typing, phone ringing, even traffic noise outside. It will sound a lot more alive."

Elizabeth goes into MacHeath's office.

"The strangest man delivered this," Elizabeth says, handing Mac-Heath a package.

"That line was very poorly delivered," Hayes says. "We had her do it again in postproduction."

Now MacHeath is walking out of East Boston High towards his Corvette. He opens the door and looks in with a quizzical expression.

"Okay, here's a hole," Hayes says. "He opens the door and looks down, but you don't know what he's looking at. It turns out that Dartman left a cassette on the seat for him, but you don't know that. So we used a body double out here and did an insert: we had him reach down, pick up the cassette, and look at it. I ordered up Mac-Heath's jacket and the rest of his clothing, even his gloves, from back East, I put it on his body double, and we did the scene out here. We didn't even use a Corvette, just a red car from a local car-rental agency."

A few scenes later, Dartman suddenly appears in MacHeath's basement, fooling with his phone wires.

"How did he get in the building?" Hayes asks. She sounds exasperated. "Do they give us any clue? None. Zippo. So we stretched this scene out later using a body double. We were able to show Dartman watch the house, then sneak around back and jimmy the lock. All without showing his face."

Now Elizabeth, MacHeath's assistant, is talking to him again in his office. We are seeing her in close-ups.

"We picked up those shots of her later," Hayes says. "Jan Egleson is a feature director who set things up in a feature-oriented way. It's wonderful, but television producers and television studios often want reaction shots; they want to see the person someone is talking to. So we picked up those shots of her later."

Now there's a long pan of the Boston waterfront, an establishing shot for the seafood restaurant.

"This is one of the most beautiful shots in the whole series," Hayes says. "And of course when we get to the final audio mix, you'll hear the foghorn, the water, maybe a bell buoy. Just perfect."

MacHeath is on the phone now, talking to Vanessa, his romantic interest in New York. She sounds tired.

"We had her rerecord, or loop, her performance on the other end of the phone," Hayes says. "The producer wanted her to come off more seductive."

MacHeath suddenly hangs up the phone.

"He hears something," Hayes says. "And we'll 'effect' what that something is later. Now he's grabbing a baseball bat, but it was felt that we don't really see where he grabbed the bat from, so we went back and reshot him picking the bat up."

After some fast-forwarding, we come to a scene where MacHeath gets stabbed with a poison dart; he slumps to the floor, wincing in pain.

"Michael does a lot of things really well," Hayes says, "but dying is not one of them."

"I started out with a producer when I moved here from the Bay area in 1981," Vanessa Hayes says. "The producer's name was Robert Lovenheim. We were primarily developing television movies and features. It was mostly script reading and other entry-level-type jobs. Then we went into production on a Valerie Bertinelli film, *Shattered Vows,* and I started picking up more production after that. I had a choice of either staying in development and approaching the business from that end, or getting into production. And I didn't want to do p.a. work, and I didn't have a craft, and there was no need for me to be on set. So I sort of worked my way to the back of the bus, so to speak, and ended up in postproduction. And I actually like it a lot, because it's a more comfortable place to work with producers, directors, actors, and editors.

Hayes particularly likes working with editors.

"Editors I consider to be writers, really," she says. "Because what they do is take everything that's been shot, and they have to rewrite it and put it into a form that makes sense.

"There's a common saying that you hear in production: 'We'll fix it in post.' " Hayes continues. "That's the attitude that the set takes a lot of the time. We have to go in and literally fix a lot of things that were genuine mistakes on the set. Things they didn't have the time to do or didn't think of doing. We have to fix it, whether it's a sound problem or a continuity problem—or as in this case, rewriting half the script. We end up doing it because post is the last place that you're actually able to fix the whole deal, where you're able to fill in the holes. That's more or less why I got into postproduction. It was an opportunity for me to follow a project all the way from the beginning to the very end. It's like putting a puzzle together and seeing how it fits.

"I also have aspirations to produce films, and television serials like 'Against the Law.' I'm not so interested in working on sitcoms. There's nothing there. It's step one, step two—follow the bouncing ball. But I see postproduction as my way of getting into producing. A lot of people go the whole production route, on the set. But I think it's more important for any producer to understand how the whole postproduction system works. When a film gets into postproduction, it becomes more of the film it's going to be than it was at the development and script stage."

After watching the editor's cut with Dan Blatt and taking notes on a yellow legal pad, Vanessa Hayes went back to her office and started "filling in the blanks" in Episode 11. First she arranged for the East Coast production crew to shoot some additional scenes: they needed Michael O'Keefe drinking the poisoned scotch; also a Dartman double stalking the Beacon Hill brownstone. Then she called Shahan Minassian at his studio in Burbank and reserved a day for shooting inserts. She sent a list of wardrobe needs to the East Coast wardrobe department, including Dartman's cocoa brown outback duster coat and MacHeath's rust mock turtleneck sweater. Finally she called Ron Licari, at Ellis Mercantile, with a list of the props she'd need for the insert shoot: plastic ice cubes for MacHeath's glass of scotch; an eyedropper for dispensing the poison; a police car radio; and a Mossberg pump shotgun with a case and five shells.

Licari, a laconic young man who has been at Ellis for seven years, was able to fill the order in less than an hour.

"Those are all standard items," he tells me later when I stop by on a slow midweek morning.

Licari is one of nine salesmen who work the floor at Ellis, which is located in a sprawling concrete building on North La Brea Avenue in Los Angeles. The salesmen at Ellis work standing up, at stations that resemble the small, cluttered posts manned by the traders on the floor of the New York Stock Exchange. Licari takes orders over the phone, mostly from prop masters and set decorators; then he ventures into Ellis's three-story maze of corridors and storerooms, culling props from shelves, cabinets, bins, and just plain stacks of stuff. When he heads into the storerooms, Licari always brings a cellular phone with him.

"That way I can call a client from the first floor and say, 'I'm standing here looking at about twenty police nightsticks. Is that going to be enough?' "

When Licari says this, he actually is standing on the first floor in Ellis's "cop shop," looking at twenty police nightsticks.

Police props are Ellis's biggest renters; the next biggest category is television news and still photographer props.

"Basically, most of the shows that come through here have some

The entrance to Ellis Mercantile.

sort of police scene in them," Licari says. "Or else they have a news-crew scene. It seems like no matter what the movie or television show is, there's at least one scene that involves police officers, a news team, or some still photographers. Look at 'L.A. Law': every time they come out of the courthouse, you see video cameras and press cameras. That's a big rental right there."

Ellis can, and often does, outfit an entire onscreen police department. When Licari gets a police order, he chooses the props by era and location.

"Let's say you need a police belt," he says. "You have to consider what period you're in: modern day or the nineteen-seventies. Because that makes a difference in terms of the weapon they're carrying. Most of the police officers today are carrying Berettas, which is a semiauto, that requires a different holster and a different ammo pouch.

"Nightstick styles have also changed. That's why when you call, you should know whether you want a straight-handled baton or the new modern T-handle baton. If you're doing a period film, you obviously don't want to give the policemen T-handle nightsticks."

Police badges also come in a variety of shapes and sizes. You have to be specific.

"We use an oval badge for L.A.—that's the basic shape," Licari says as he opens a drawer filled with shiny badges. "But other parts of the country use different shapes. We can usually come pretty close."

Is it difficult getting police badges?

"Yes, because the law-enforcement agencies are worried about people stealing the badges and costuming around as police officers. So in the film and television industry all the badges have to be either oversized or undersized, and they can't say specific things. For example, we cannot rent a badge that says 'Los Angles Police.' It has to say 'Metro' or 'Security.' Most of the time the police badges are thirty percent larger."

What about a gun?

"You get that in our armory. We have ten to fifteen thousand guns in there."

But first, on the way to the armory, we pass through the Western room stocked with saddlebags, powder horns, whips, Indian bows, tomahawks, war clubs, several shelves of Western holsters, Western ropes, *bandelleros,* bedrolls, lanterns, lamps, little wood-burning stoves, and an entire aisle of canteens.

" 'Young Riders' rents a lot of this stuff," Licari says. "When they were shooting that miniseries *Lonesome Dove,* they kept two salesmen tied up for several weeks."

Down the hall, Licari opens a deep drawer labeled simply "Money." It's filled with stacks of paper money, the kind you see greedy drug dealers salivating over in hotel rooms on action shows.

"You have a choice," Licari says, picking up a stack of bills and riffling it. "You can rent top-and-bottom stacks, with a printed bill on top and a printed bill on bottom, and all the rest is blank. Or you can get solid stacks, with printed bills all the way through. We also rent fake gold bars."

As we walk up a wide flight of stairs and through a hallway lined with mounted game heads, I ask Licari how long Ellis has been around.

"Since 1908," Licari says. "We started out as a little pawnshop downtown. Producers and directors started coming by looking for props; but instead of buying stuff, they always wanted to rent it. So the original owner, Ellis Zemansky, finally said, 'Okay, I'll get into the rental business.' We've been doing it ever since."

Ellis doesn't have a catalog.

"People just call us up; it's pretty much word-of-mouth," Licari says. "Or you can come in with an order, walk around the storerooms with me, and we can pull things together. Then we can either bring the stuff down or reserve it by taping it off and tagging it."

In the downstairs lobby, a thick binder details the current rental price of each item: a stunt dummy, suitable for throwing off a building, rents for $37.50 a week; a forties-era radio console rents for between $27.00 and 47.50 per week, depending on condition; a ball and chain goes for $7.50 a week.

Licari started working at Ellis in 1984.

"My father-in-law works at Columbia Pictures," he says. "He deals with Ellis a lot. And when he heard they were hiring, he said,

'Go down and give it a try.' When they hired me, there were just twelve of us. Now thirty-six people work here.''

Most of the salesmen at Ellis are generalists, with minor areas of specialization.

"My specialty is the outdoors," Licari says. "Hunting and fishing, and so on. So the guys will come to me and say, 'We need to set somebody up with a rod and reel for saltwater fishing. What should we use?' "

I ask Licari if it makes a difference if the prop is for a feature film or television.

"The only difference between big screen and television is that you have to pay closer attention to detail," he says. "Take those police badges. If you have a scene with twenty officers running by on the big screen, you may see all twenty badges. But on TV you'll probably just see the front five, and the rest of the guys are just going to be a blur."

Other rooms we walked through:

The jewelry room.

"Mostly 'Dynasty'-type stuff," Licari says as he pulls out drawers or brooches, necklaces, and earrings. "They used to like the rhinestones and the glitter stuff on the 'Dynasty' set. They wanted that real fancy, expensive look."

The basket and blanket room.

"Let's say you're doing a Viet Cong village or street market," Licari says. "You'll come in here and I'll give you a bunch of these baskets and some blankets. We did a lot of basket business with 'China Beach.' Or you've got a house, and you want to fill a closet with blankets; or an ambulance, we've got those blankets; or beach blankets; or lap blankets for a football game in a stadium."

The rubber room.

"A lot of food in here," Licari says, picking up a rubber roasted ham. "Put this on a platter, squirt it with a little glycerin to give it a moisture look, and you're all set.

"We've also got rubber cameras for those paparazzi-style camera shoots where the guy drops his camera or the movie star punches the photographer. One of these rubber cameras is a $7.50 rental. Whereas a real press camera is a $125.00 rental. And if you break it, the costs keep going up."

The armory.

"Our most popular weapons are the police revolvers, standard

Ron Licari in the Ellis armory.

four-inch revolvers," Licari says. "After that I'd say semiauto hand pistols, M-16s, Uzis, and assault pistols."

In one corner, twenty World War I–style rifles have been circled with tape. A note reads: "Hold 20 for HBO—Tales From the Crypt." In the opposite corner, suits of armor are lined up in front of hundreds of period rifles.

The armory also contains Derringers, Colt 45s, bayonets, Civil War cavalry rifles, old shotguns like the ones farmers carry in cartoons, and Russian rocket launchers.

"We used a lot of these rocket launchers in the *Rambo* movies, for the Afghan army," Licari says. "The Russian weapons go out a lot because so many Third World countries use them."

Some of the weapons in the armory are made of rubber.

"For stunts," Licari says. "Or for a scene where you have thirty extras running through a dirt field. It's a lot easier to let them walk off with a rubber gun, rather than a real gun. A lot less paperwork involved, too. To rent a rubber handgun, you're looking at $7.50 a week; $17.00 for a rubber rifle. A real automatic rifle goes for about $125.00, and you've also got to get permits."

The media room.

"These are dummy video cameras made of hard molded plastic," Licari says. "The only part that works is the little red indicator light in front, to show that the camera is on."

The media room also has shelves of Speed Graphic cameras, the 1930s-style newspaper flash cameras.

"The flashbulbs that they use are no longer manufactured," Licari says. "So they're made special, at a cost of twenty-three dollars a dozen, almost two dollars a pop. It can get expensive."

Up close, the video cameras look fake, and kind of cheesy. Licari says that doesn't matter.

"They photograph a lot better than they look in person," he says. "Remember, right now you're seeing it in three dimensions. The camera has one eye, so everything is two-dimensional, much flatter. Also, the prop will probably be on for thirty seconds at the most, and at some distance from the camera. So chances are, it will look fine. On the other hand, when you rent a prop you're not just thinking of the audience, you also have to impress the prop master, the producer, the director, and the actor—who will be handling it for a lot more than thirty seconds. So you really have to keep everything nice, even if it won't make much of a difference on the screen."

A nearby cluster of television sets, by contrast, looks real, even up close.

"They are real," Licari says. "But upstairs we do have some TV set mockups that have been gutted out so they're much lighter. They're good for moving scenes or for riot scenes where people are breaking into stores and running down the street with televisions."

As we walk down the wide stairs toward the lobby, I ask Licari if he can remember the last prop he rented that he actually saw on TV.

"It would have to be some of the things I rented to 'America's Funniest People,' like stunt dummies. Last week they had a hospital scene where somebody is supposed to get a shot. They needed an oversized syringe, and we had a big plastic one, maybe fifty cc's. I also rented them a bunch of golf clubs and bags."

Back at his desk, I ask Licari if someday he might go to work for a studio in the prop department.

"Maybe," he says. "Some guys do that. You certainly get a good view of the business from here."

"You do a lot of cheating in postproduction," Vanessa Hayes is saying. "You get to the editing stage and you realize that there's a hole in the story. The actors are usually long gone at that point, so you have to find other ways to fill it.

"Sometimes there are a lot of holes. I worked on a television movie about six years ago, a crash-and-burn film with Ken Wahl called *The Gladiator*. When we started editing the whole picture together, we discovered we were twenty minutes short. We had to go back out and do a ten-day second unit, on a schedule that was extremely accelerated. Ten days, second unit, all stunts, all crash-and-burn stuff. And all with doubles for the actors, because we lost the

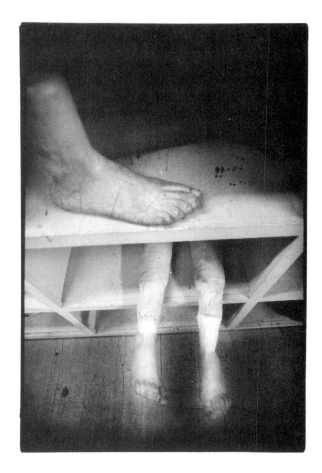

Body parts in an Ellis storeroom. Stunt dummies start at $37.50 a week. Limbs go for $15 a week, each.

A sure sign of work ahead for postproduction supervisor Vanessa Hayes and insert shooter Shahan Minassian.

actors at a certain point. And then we had to tie all this stuff into the show. It costs a lot of money to do that kind of fixing up.

"Another time, about four years ago, I worked on a Dolly Parton movie called *A Smoky Mountain Christmas*. We needed to shoot Dolly driving a pickup truck up to the Smoky Mountains. We didn't have Dolly Parton to do that. So I was Dolly Parton. I put the wig on, the makeup, the chest, the whole bit, and did the drive up to the mountains. The audience never knew the difference. I think most viewers would be surprised how much of this kind of stuff goes on."

"On Episode 11, we did most of our cheating on Shahan Minassian's insert stage in Burbank; we spent a whole day there. He does inserts for a lot of the prime-time shows. What we do is, I just bring a ¾-inch copy of the show out onto the stage and we watch it. There's usually a big "Shot Missing" billboard at each insert point. Then we just set up each insert, Shahan lights it and shoots it, and we move on to the next one."

Hayes inserts a tape marked "Inserts" into the VCR.

First we see a few short sequences of a woman's hands opening an aspirin bottle and shaking out a few aspirin tablets.

"Those are my hands," Hayes says. "We wanted to show that the girlfriend Vanessa had a bottle of aspirin in her purse. It's an important story point later on. So we shot the scenes using my hands, and inserted it."

Now Dartman is in MacHeath's basement, loading his gun.

"That's a fake brick wall that we set up on Shahan's insert stage," Hayes says. "And the Dartman is actually the prop man. I usually hire a prop man whenever there's a gun. I don't like to handle guns; and besides, there's a professional way to do it.

"There's the prop man again, or at least his hand," Hayes continues as we see a hand holding an eyedropper squeezing a few drops of something into a glass of scotch. "We fabricated that after the fact, because in the original edit, MacHeath just starts to die. Dartman tells him he poisoned his drink, but we don't see it. So we decided to make it explicit."

Next, a few shots of a car wheel spinning on some wet pavement, kicking up some water.

"We wanted to add a little action to the sequence where MacHeath's assistant Meigs steals the car," Hayes says. "So we just put some grease under one of the back wheels of the rental car, pointed a hose on it for rain, and spun it around. It will make more sense when they add the squealing sound effects."

Now the camera is shooting through a shattered car window at a bloody hand reaching for a police radio.

"They decided that they wanted the shot detective to live long

The following is a list of wardrobe needs for Insert Shoot scheduled
for Thursday, January 3, 1991 from 1:00pm on:

WARDROBE

SCN 52   Vanessa's sweater
          black pouch purse (if available)

SCN 48-53 Dartman's coco brown outback duster coat (Banana Republic)
              (belongs to actor)
          Grey hooded sweatshirt; zip front
          Grey thermal undershirt
          Fry boots (belongs to actor)

SCN 58   MacHeath's rust mock turtleneck sweater
          black belt
          blue jeans
          (NOT AN INSERT SHOT)

SCN A70   Shaner's white coat
          sweater, shirt
          Hat (actor's)

Buys: ~~Brown coat~~ ~~black belt~~

PROPS

SCN 15   Cassette with "PLAY ME" written on it) *in Mac's hand*

SCN 49   Cassette labeled with "FOUR LAST SONGS" in same color
          ink as SCN 15 cassette
          wrapping paper & bow (props)

SCN 52   Asprin
          Vanessa's purse inside pocket; purse junk

SCN 48-53 Montage:
          Mosberg pump shotgun
          5 shells
          gun case
          (from Ellis Mercantile - ask for Lance)

SCN 58   Scotch bottle
          3 glasses
          Chardonney wine

SCN A70   Car *w/ breakaway glass*
          Police car radio (Ellis Mercantile)

SCN 77   Car
          Slick grease
          water

Page Two
Insert shoot - #3516

ACTORS

SCN 49   Mac double (sitting on coach)

SCN 52   Vanessa stand-in (female)

SCN 48-53 Dartman stand-in (big male)

SCN 58   Michael O'Keefe

SCN A70   Shaner double (medium built man)

The Wardrobe/Prop list for Episode 11's insert shots.

enough to summon Meigs by radio," Hayes says. "So we took the same rental car and rolled the window down all the way. Then the prop guy took a piece of plate glass, put it on the floor, smashed it with a hammer, and hot-glued enough pieces together so that it looked as if it had a hole blown through it. Then we positioned it in the window, and put an actor in the car, and shot it so you just see his hand reaching for the microphone."

We watch a few versions of the scene. The last one looks considerably less messy.

"No blood," Hayes explains. "We shot the scene with blood and without blood, just in case the network had a problem with it."

A few days later, I stop by Shahan Minassian's insert stage in Burbank, which is large and airy and has a smooth cement floor; it looks more like a very clean garage than a stage. I find Minassian standing with a few men in front of a large television monitor watching an upcoming episode of "Jake and the Fatman." The men are Robin Madden, a producer of the show, and Todd Powers, an associate producer.

On the screen, William Conrad, the "Fatman" of the show's title, walks into an expensively decorated Los Angeles–style living room. A beautiful woman, who looks like she's trying very hard not to look guilty, escorts him to a chair. He looks down.

Suddenly the screen goes bright blue and the word INSERT appears in large letters.

After a few seconds, we see William Conrad again. "Ah, Gaulois cigarettes. Wonderful. I remember them from my early days in France."

"We want an insert of the Gaulois cigarettes on the table," Robin Madden says. "This is a key clue, and we want to see it from his point of view."

"Okay, his point of view," Shahan says.

"Do you have a table that can match her table?" Madden asks.

"Close," Shahan replies. "And I'll polish it and put a backlight on it. That hides the true color."

Minassian turns off the VCR and carries a small coffee table into the center of the stage. He polishes it, then starts arranging an ashtray and a pack of Gaulois cigarettes.

"We should smoke a few cigarettes down, for the ashtray," Madden says as he puts two in his mouth and lights them both.

I ask Madden if he shoots inserts on every episode.

"Just about," he says as he alternately drags on one Gaulois, then the other. "We shoot inserts as a way to save time and money. This

Shahan Minassian (behind camera) on his insert stage.

shot here is a good example. We need a shot of a pack of cigarettes on a table. But we don't want to take the time to light it and shoot it when all this expensive talent and crew is standing around. So we bunch all these kinds of shots together and have Shahan shoot them all at once. It's much cheaper."

"Details," Shahan says when he walks over. "That's what I shoot. You know that show 'MacGyver'? There are so many details in that show. I've shot eighty inserts for a single episode. 'Father Dowling' also has a lot of inserts. I've shot fifty for one episode."

As he's setting up the lights, carefully matching the look of the original episode, Minassian tells me that he attended UCLA; after graduation he got a job at a large Los Angeles production, the West-heimer Company.

"We worked on many of the network shows," he says. "I did a lot of work for 'Dynasty.' I did their opening title sequence."

After ten years at Westheimer, Minassian went into business for himself. The big-ticket item on his business plan was an Arriflex 35mm camera.

"It costs around sixty thousand," he says. "And by the time you put lenses on it, it's up to a hundred thousand dollars."

Now he's happy with his ashtray/Gaulois still life. He shoots about ten seconds of film, twice.

Afterwards, Minassian and Madden go back to the VCR and television monitor. They fast-forward for a while and then come to a scene in which Jake is meeting someone in a men's room. Jake makes a motion as if he's pulling something out of his trench coat.

The blue INSERT screen appears for a few seconds, and then we see the surprised reaction on the part of the other guy. Jake has just pulled out a gun, except we haven't seen it yet. That's Shahan's job.

"I've got the gun and Jake's coat," Madden says.

He places the gun on the table in front of the VCR; a minute later Todd Powers, the associate producer, arrives wearing Jake's trench coat. He's going to be Jake.

Minassian poses Powers in front of the camera and hands him the gun. Powers practices drawing the gun from inside his coat. When he gets it right, Minassian shoots about ten seconds of film, twice.

Before he goes back to the VCR for the next insert, Minassian walks into his office and emerges with a copy of a trade magazine, *International Photographer*. He folds it open to an article on "shooting stage inserts."

"In shooting inserts," the article says, "the idea is to match perfectly in all respects the originally shot scene or sequence, so that the insert will fit in unobtrusively with the leading shot and the following shot."

Later there's a paragraph on "what you need to know" to shoot an insert: "The film gauge and emulsion used; the aspect ratio used; the required length of insert; the filter pack (if any) used; the position, direction, quality (color temperature and diffusion and color gelling, if any), and relative intensity of the key, fill, top, back, kicker, foreground, and background lighting; color gels used on specific lamps; smoke, steam, or hot ice for effect; and, when applicable: the film flow rate (fps), shutter angle setting, and special matting."

"This sounds incredibly complicated," I say.

"Not if you've been doing it awhile," Minassian replies. "It's pretty simple, actually. If your inserts fall right in, you stay in business."

Larry Breslow, who edits "Against the Law"'s teasers for MGM Television, works in a small editing suite on the MGM lot. He sits in front of eight monitors and a keyboard; the small window next to

*Larry Breslow, teaser
editor.*

him has been covered with cardboard to reduce the glare on the
screens. Breslow gets a very early edit of each episode and then
spends two full days in here crafting a quick, tight, snappy thirty-
second teaser. The teaser will run at the top of the show; and if it
works, it will grab those viewers who have been slow to change the
channel after watching "America's Most Wanted," the show that
precedes "Against the Law."

The television tease is probably the most compressed video art
form. It's sort of TV haiku, a cross between a sports-highlight film
and a music video.

Like a haiku, a teaser is also slightly puzzling, because plot counts
for nothing. A good teaser is all action, all provocative dialogue, no
plot.

"I don't really care that much if it makes any sense plotwise,"
Breslow says. "I'm just looking for spicy dialogue and as much
action as I can squeeze in. The important thing is to build the jeopardy, keep the audience off balance, and hook them. Sometimes it's
even helpful to mislead the audience, in terms of the plot."

Earlier, Vanessa Hayes had told me pretty much the same thing.

"The teaser is about rhythm and the subliminal," she said. "You
don't want to just hit the nail on the head, plotwise, because you
don't really want the audience to know what the show is going to be
about. You want them to be literally teased into watching the show."

Breslow has been editing teasers for about three years. Before that
he spent ten years working at Paramount, for Gary Marshall, editing
"Laverne and Shirley," and "Happy Days" and "Mork and Mindy."
During that time, editing technology changed dramatically as
random-access, computer-based systems began to gain currency.
Breslow kept up by taking courses at night at Columbia College, a

technical college in Hollywood that specializes in motion picture and television production. One of the systems he learned was TouchVision. A few years ago, MGM Television leased some TouchVision systems to edit their dramatic series. Breslow was brought on board to craft teasers, trailers, and promos.

Breslow began working on Episode 11's teaser as soon as he received an early edit of the show. Right off, he identified a few promising scenes: the shooting of the detective, some verbal threats from Dartman, and MacHeath's getting stabbed in the leg with a poison dart. Then he started cutting them together; he didn't care about the order.

"A teaser is totally non-chronological," he says.

I have a copy of the Episode 11 teaser with me, and Breslow asks his assistant to cue it up.

Any particular instructions from the producer on this teaser? I ask.

"Dan wanted some plot, but mostly threat, quick cutting, quick action, and really succinct dialogue," Breslow answers.

The teaser begins with MacHeath sitting in his car looking worried, listening to a threatening tape that Dartman left on his car seat.

"I wanted to get to the threat right away," Breslow says. "That's to let you know that Mac's in trouble. Someone's coming after him."

Then, in very short order, MacHeath grabs Dartman by the lapels, screaming, "Who are you?" He tips over a dinner table; he gets stabbed in the leg with the dart; he says to Vanessa, "I'm having a weird day"; Dartman, up close, says, "Isn't the pain excruciating?" The detective gets shot; a car screeches around the corner; Meigs screams into a police radio, "I need some backup and an ambulance!" Then Dartman, up close, says, "I love watching you suffer." The last shot is of MacHeath slumping to the ground after being stabbed by the poison dart.

"It's great if you can leave your main character in jeopardy at the end of the teaser," Breslow says. "So you notice that we're leaving MacHeath in excruciating pain here. We don't know if he's dying or whether this guy is just playing around with him. We don't know what's going to happen to him, which is exactly the way we want the audience to feel."

The musical scoring of Episode 11 began with a spotting session in a screening room on the MGM lot. Vanessa Hayes, music editor Jeff Charbonneau, and composer Jay Gruska attended.

Composer Jay Gruska in his studio; in the background, Todd Yvega working on his Synclavier.

Gruska had watched a cassette of the show the day before. Although the episode obviously called for music that was dark and suspenseful, Gruska wanted to take a slightly different approach: instead of a traditional melodic score, he was thinking of a sound track composed of musical sound effects, "effected" pianos, and various kinds of percussion instruments.

"You know what I was thinking," Gruska recalls later. "You put a pencil inside a piano on top of the strings, or you put a dog's chain in there and play some notes, and it sounds absolutely scary and horrendous. That's the effect I was looking for."

Hayes and Charbonneau liked the idea, and for the next hour or so they watched the show, discussing the actual in-and-out points for the music. Later Jeff Charbonneau took a tape back to his Santa Monica studio and used a Macintosh-based program, Cue, to indicate where the music should start and stop.

In his Santa Monica studio, Charbonneau shows me how it works.

"First I break down the show and indicate exactly where we need music, and for how long. I print that out for Jay. Then I run a tape of the show through the Cue program, which uses vertical stripes to indicate where the music goes: when a yellow vertical stripe rolls across the screen, that means a music section is coming up. Then a green stripe rolls by, which means 'Start the music here.' When a red stripe rolls by, that's 'Stop.' "

Charbonneau leans back in his chair.

"TV music is a lot of starts and ends with no middle," he says.

Meanwhile, Gruska started pulling together some elements for the score. First he asked Todd Yvega, his semi-resident Synclavier owner-operator, to round up some gong-and-bell and ethnic drum samples. (Samples are sounds converted into digital form.)

The Synclavier, which Gruska refers to as "a quarter-million-dollar box," is a mainstay of the television music and sound effects world. Essentially, it's a large computer with the ability to sample, store, and reproduce thousands of sounds. The Synclavier that Gruska uses belongs to Yvega. Yvega rents the machine—and his extensive variety of samples—to Gruska on a long-term basis. When he's not working for Gruska, Yvega can often be found over at Frank Zappa's studio, working with Zappa's Synclavier.

One sunny afternoon, when I drive over to Studio City and park

---

Production: **AGAINST THE LAW** Production #: **3516**
Episode: **PAST PRESENT**
MUSIC SPOTTING NOTES
Friday, January 11, 1991

REEL 1 (9 Starts)

1M1	30.03	"TEASER"
d1:00:00:00		TEASER
d1:00:30:00		
Background Instrumental		

1M2	1:04.00	"MAIN TITLE"
d1:00:30:00		MAIN TITLE
d1:01:34:00		
Background Instrumental		

1M3	1:06.50	"SCORE"
d1:01:49:00		HOME MOVIE STARS-PLAYON-Mack's good buddy from the past films
d1:02:55:15		Mack and Vanessa frolicing about in Mack's flat.SEGUES to stereo
Background Instrumental		source(DVORJAK-String Serenade in E-Major ,Opus 22),on cut away
		from the weirdo's POV.Shots go to color.

1M4	46.18	"SOURCE"
d1:02:55:15		SOURCE -SEGUES from 1M3 score on CUT to interior of Mack's
d1:03:41:21		flat.DVORJAK-String Serenade in E-Major ,Opus 22.Tails on dissolve to
Background Instrumental		TIME TRANSITION to Mack and Vanessa in bed making post coital small
		talk.

1M5	12.98	"SCORE"
d1:05:51:18		DEMON DELIVERY SERVICE-Starts on CUT to interior of Mack's elevator
d1:06:04:19		as the weirdo rides up to deliver a present to Mack.Tails as the weirdo
Background Instrumental		hands Liz the package.

Music spotting notes. The left column indicates where the music should go (by time-code location), how long music should be, and the type of music required. The right column describes the scene.

in front of Gruska's suburban bungalow home, and go way around back and into a small carriage house that's been converted into a small studio, I find Gruska standing in a vortex of activity.

"We're slammin' on a Willie Nelson/Kris Kristofferson Movie of the Week," Gruska says.

One young man is moving some boxes out of the bathroom.

"We've got a guitarist coming in this afternoon to play on a part," Gruska says. "I'm going to record him in the bathroom. The acoustics are really nice in there."

Someone else is taking pages of music—flute parts that Gruska has just written out—to be photocopied. And in one corner, behind a bank of computer equipment, Todd Yvega is sorting through some samples on his Synclavier. I notice two platinum records on the wall: one by Robert Palmer, the other by Jermaine Jackson.

"I compose about nineteen minutes of music for every episode of 'Against the Law,' " Gruska says when things quiet down just slightly. "The Synclavier is the real workhorse; it's my primary instrument on the show. But I always mix it with one or two other real instruments—that tends to make a Synclavier-based score sound realer."

Aren't the Synclavier samples very authentic sounding?

"Yes, they are, but you have to play them right or they won't sound real. You might have a great harmonica sample, for example, but if you play it like a keyboard player, it's not going to sound good; it will probably sound like a cheap accordion."

Gruska usually spends from three to four days writing the sound track for an episode of "Against the Law"; he does most of his writing at the piano. It takes another one or two days to mix it to a four-track Dolby SR tape machine that he brings into his studio. He's been scoring movies and television shows since 1984 or '85.

"I was born in New York, but grew up in the Los Angeles area," he says. "I've always been in music, always been a songwriter and arranger. I did that for twenty years. Then in the mid-eighties, I decided to get into film and television work. Basically at that time I was a medium-successful songwriter with a ten-year publishing deal at Screen Gems and a relatively comfortable living. So it was a real challenge going into this field, with no guarantees. It took three or four years of me yelling out to the community, 'Hey, I can do this. I'm not just a songwriter who's going to write pop tunes as an underscorer.' It took a few years to be heard. That's the scary part. But it's like anything else: you have to walk the plank."

Gruska began by working on some TV shows with an established composer named Patrick Williams. Then he worked on a few movies as an arranger and produced a few movie scores for James Horner, like *Cocoon* and *Commando*.

"That's how I started getting into it," he says. "And pretty soon the guys I worked with and worked for started recommending me for other projects. My first opportunity to write a movie sound track came on the film *The Principal*. They called James Horner to do it but he couldn't, so he recommended me. That's sort of how it works."

Was it difficult, stylistically, making the transition from pop songwriter to film and television composer?

"It was, because it was like starting over within the same career. You come to the table with a whole new set of rules and sensibilities. First of all, when you write a pop tune it's in a vacuum. There's no picture that you're supporting. And at twenty-nine-point-eight seconds, you don't have to make this or that statement. But more than anything, the thing I needed to unlearn was pop form. Pop form has no bearing on film scoring: there's no A section or B section. That has no meaning. You're playing mood and subtext."

Has TV music changed much since you've been doing it?

"I think so. TV music got very watered down for a while. It was cheesy, synthy, synthetic-sounding. The scores didn't have musicality per se; instead, they relied on synthesizer rhythms and Xerox-sounding computer loops. The first four bars sounded just like the next four bars. Now there's a big swing back to organic, acoustic, natural settings. I think people these days appreciate flesh and bone on wood and gut."

How important is equipment?

"The quality of sound is important, but it's the quality of the writing that gets people jobs, ultimately. Because if you come out with a great-sounding thing, but the writing is skin deep, you're going to get another gig or two but it's not going to be continuous. That's especially true in television. On a feature film, it's always a new subject matter, a new setting. Everything is new, right down to the personalities of the producer/writer team. But in episodic television, you have to do something like twenty-two shows a season. So the biggest challenge is keeping it energized and fresh and interesting. You can't help but get a little derivitive. But if your original ideas were good, you can get by."

Do young musicians often ask you for advice?

"I probably talk to young musicians a few times a month, and it's always difficult to know what to say. But the general rule is: how much you love it, and how much you need it; that's what's going to keep you in there. Because you're going to hear, 'No, sorry, we're using our director's brother-in-law,' or 'Sorry, it was too fast,' or

'Sorry, we were looking for something slower.' You're going to hear that three times a day for the rest of your life. So you're going to have to cling to those few gigs that come through. After that, it's just about going to sessions, meeting composers, hanging out, doing anything. And don't just cling to doing one thing. For me the vehicle turned out to be producing for someone else for a couple of years. And I was dying. I'd be saying to myself, 'God. I could write this!' But that's what it took for me to get into it. So it comes down to how much you love it, because if you really want to do it, you're going to have to take some grief for a while."

An ADR log for Episode 11. New lines that have to be added to fill holes in the show's plot or continuity.

While Gruska was composing the score, the rest of Episode 11's sound track was starting to come together. The first order of business, for Vanessa Hayes and dialogue editor David Cantu, was co-

```
                          1990 S.S. - TrackWriter (tm)
          Company: POST SOUND CORPORATION
                          AUTOMATED DIALOGUE REPLACEMENT
          Show Title: PAST AND PRESENT                              Page:    7
          Production: LEMON SKY                    Time:14:43:58
          Project   : MACPAST   Reel No.           Date: 1/10/91
          Editor    : R. WESTOVER                                 Channels
  Loop|Start / Stop|         D e s c r i p t i o n         |1|2|3|4|5|6|7|8|
   No |
       01:37:36:07  SHANER!  COME IN, IT"S MEIGS..GET ON YOUR
    67 MEIGS      1  MOBIL CHANNEL, MAN, AND TELL ME WHAT'S
       01:37:47:01  GOING ON. SHANER, COME IN...CAN YA HEAR
                    ME!

       01:39:57:13  SUDDENLY IT BECAME APPARENT YOU WEREN'T
    68 MAC        9  THE WITNESS...YOU WERE THE MURDERER...
       01:40:00:27

       01:40:01:00  HURRY UP WITH THAT JUICE.
    69 DART MAN  11
       01:40:04:14

       01:40:13:18  HERE'S THE JUICE.
    70 CLEON      4
       01:40:15:06

       01:41:22:27  THE STORM PROBABLY KNOCKED IT OUT...
    71 GROUP      3  DOOK, THE HOUSE IS UNDER SURVEILLANCE
       01:41:24:24

       01:41:28:04  Meigs, I've got a million calls.
    72 GROUP      4
       01:41:29:11

       01:42:42:20  DAMN.
    73 MEIGS      2
       01:42:44:03

       01:42:54:12  SORRY, BUDDY, I NEED YOUR CAR
    74 MEIGS      3
       01:42:56:03

       01:42:55:17  -COP-
    75 GROUP      5  -PULLED OUT OF CAR-

       01:43:16:13  SHANER, SHANER, SHANER WAKE UP, IT'S
    76 MEIGS      4  MEIGS.  ARE YOU THERE MAN?
       01:43:21:18

       01:43:23:24  MEIGS ... IT'S SHANER ... BEEN SHOT
    77 SHANER     9  ... GET BACK-UP ...
       01:43:29:26
```

ordinating the addition of new dialogue by the principal actors. This process is called "looping," or "ADR," for "automatic dialogue replacement." There's usually some looping on every show: when a line recorded on location is obscured by a passing truck, or when an editing change makes a comment redundant or ridiculous, the actor involved simply redoes the line in a sound studio while he's watching himself on a screen. Michael O'Keefe usually budgets at least one morning per episode for ADR in a local Boston television studio.

As Episode 11 moved down the editing trail and dialogue was added and excised, it became clear that two looping sessions would be necessary: one session in New York for the guest actors who played Dartman and Vanessa; and one session in Boston for Michael O'Keefe and for the actors who played Meigs, the detective, and young Cleon.

"We had a lot of new lines that had been written; we had a lot of performance things that had to be changed," Vanessa Hayes recalls. "And it can get real dicey, in terms of filling the tracks, and blowing out lines that already exist, and putting other lines in, and putting things in people's mouths that weren't there before. It's easy if the actor has his back to you and you don't see the mouth, but anytime you're on camera, you have to be real careful of what you're going to put in people's mouths. Otherwise it's going to look like a Mexican picture dubbed in French."

By the time all the editorial changes had been made, Hayes had eight pages of additional dialogue. The insert shots of Mac drinking the poisoned scotch had to be preceded by Vanessa's calling down, "Your scotch is on the kitchen counter." The detective who's shot in front of Mac's place now lives long enough to say into his police radio, "Meigs . . . it's Shaner . . . been shot . . . get backup!"—that had to be added in the ADR session. Also, the actress who played Vanessa had to add laughing sounds to the sexual frolicking that opened the show: Fox executives wanted it to be clear that she was having fun, not being attacked. Dozens of other plot and continuity problems were also smoothed over at the ADR sessions and inserted into the final production.

The audio portion of a television show like "Against the Law" is a lush thing. Music and dialogue are only the most obvious elements: a hundred smaller noises fill the background like birds in a forest, unnoticed unless you really listen for them. The sound of footsteps on a front lawn, or a coffee cup placed on a counter, or tires on a gravel driveway—this kind of audio sweetening gives the show a luxurious, present feeling.

Sharon Michaels, who lives in a bleached-white house in North Hollywood, is responsible for much of "Against the Law" 's audio atmosphere, along with John Adams, a sound effects supervisor at Post Sound, a Los Angeles postproduction facility.

Michaels is a foley artist, which means that she makes $400 a day for adding the footsteps for all the characters, and the sound of keys jingling as they open their apartment doors, and the pushbutton sounds when they make a telephone call. None of this stuff is recorded on location—it would be too difficult; a location sound mixer like Paul Cote records almost nothing but dialogue. So most of "Against the Law" 's audio environment is added later, by a foley artist like Michaels.

The art of foley, which is named for Los Angeles sound man Jack Foley—who developed the idea in the late 1940s—is a standard item on every film and television postproduction budget.

"It's all sound effects, basically," Sharon Michaels says. "When the effecting includes footsteps, they call it foley, but it's much more than that."

Michaels does most of her work at an audio postproduction house on a foley stage, where small patches of different surfaces—cement, carpet, wood, sand, water—are built into the floor. Michaels always brings along a large collection of shoes: she wears different shoes for different characters and different situations. Michaels has two pairs of shoes for Michael O'Keefe: heavy oxford-type shoes and sneakers.

"It can get tedious," she says of her job. "Let's say O'Keefe goes from a cement sidewalk, climbs up an iron staircase, jumps onto a fire escape, and climbs into a room. I'll have to match his footsteps, at the same time I'm jumping from one surface to another on the foley stage, so that it goes along with his movements. Or he'll get up from a table and go into a bar, from carpet to wood floor. I'll walk on the carpet, matching his footsteps while watching the screen, keeping my balance and being in sync with him, and then do the same thing when he gets to the floor.

"There's tremendous pressure," she continues. "Even when they cut away from the actor and he's off camera, he's still moving. If the camera comes back to him, you still have to maintain that steady rhythm. Also, he may change his pace—and you have to stay right with him."

Michaels is a former dancer. Early in her career, she was one half of the push me-pull me animal on the movie *Dr. Doolittle*. She still has a dancer's bearing; when she picks something off the floor, she bends at the waist, keeping her legs straight.

After doing some bit parts in films and on television, she began doing foley at Columbia Pictures.

Sharon Michaels, foley artist. Her "Michael O'Keefe shoes" are the ones immediately to her right.

"They tend to use professional dancers for foley," Michaels says, "because you must be well coordinated and have a sense of time to match each step, each particular stride of the individual actors—and do it right the first or second time you see it on the screen."

Michaels has walked for George C. Scott, Barbra Streisand, and Gene Hackman. When she walks for men, she just wears heavier shoes. Years ago Michaels was hired to do the foley for the movie *Tora, Tora, Tora;* the producers delivered army boots to the foley stage for verisimilitude.

Michaels also runs the Walla Group, a small group of actors who provide background sounds and crowd noises for shows like "Against the Law." ("Walla" is an industry term that comes from the way background crowd noise often sounds on film: "walla walla walla.") On Episode 11 the Walla Group provided walla for the schoolyard, corridor, and the classroom scenes shot at East Boston High School; they also did bar walla for the scenes at the Beacon Cafe.

"We do a lot of bar and restaurant and party walla," Michaels says. "It's difficult to get party walla just right: you tend to be more boisterous than you really should be. I've often said to my people, 'This is supposed to be a party, not a rodeo.'"

When she does a foley job on a show like "Against the Law," Michaels also brings a large bag of sound props to help fill in the background.

"Every show has its own approach to background noise," she says. "'L.A. Law,' for example, is very big on chair squeaks, but they don't like a lot of movement sounds. It's a very clean-sounding show. 'Against the Law' has a more textured sound. The foley on Japanese movies is hilarious: they all scream the same way; all the punching and kicking sounds the same."

As she's talking, Michaels picks up her bag and starts taking things out.

"I remember we had a lot of key and doorknob noises on episode eleven," she says as she produces a lock, a doorknob, and a set of keys. Then a piece of leather.

"A doorknob against leather is good for a gun drawing out of a holster," she says as she rubs the doorknob against the leather with quick, sharp motions. "On 'Hill Street Blues' they liked a little metal rattle in there too."

Now she picks up the pace, and a stream of unlikely items emerges from the bag, including a pair of cocoanut halves ("still the best for horse hoofs," she says), a squeaky hinge ("everyone has to have one of these"), a Zippo lighter, an old radio ("great for buttons"), a clipboard, two feather dusters ("for the feathers of birds flying"), rubber gloves ("for passing a surgical instrument to a doctor wearing rubber gloves"), an old phone ("good for computer keys"), and a pair of handcuffs ("I wear these when I'm doing police footsteps: it adds that police jingle").

"If it's a violent show," she adds, "I'll also bring along carrots and celery for bone cracks, and grapefruits for all those squishy sounds."

John Adams, a sound effects supervisor at Post Sound in Los Angeles, also works on the sound track, providing noises that cannot be reproduced on a foley stage. Adams works in a small, cluttered office, surrounded by stacks of cassette tapes, CD's, and ½-inch reel-to-reel tapes.

"I use everything," he says. "Whatever works."

On Episode 11, Adams added a number of audio elements to the mix.

"I remember there was a shotgun blast," he recalls. "They wanted that very strong. Also, the glass breaking when the bullet went through the car window. And a storm, with rain and thunder sounds. But most of the sounds I add are much more mundane."

Like which ones?

"Like MacHeath's Corvette door closing," he says. "I put that in a lot. Also atmospheric city noises; we even put those in when Mac is in his office, as if they're coming through the window. And the phone ringing, and the lobby buzzer. Episode 11 also had a lot of elevator opens in Mac's office. I think I've done a hundred and fifty elevator opens."

Generally the very last person to work on an episode of "Against the Law" is Phil Seretti, who is responsible for mixing together all the audio elements—dialogue, music, foley, effects—into a final sound track. With the exception of titles and credits—which are tagged on at the last minute—everything has to be done by the time the show reaches Seretti.

"The way most of us in postproduction look at it," he says, "we have to pick up most of the problems that happen on the front end. And in sound, since we are the last thing that's done, we're at the very end of the schedule and the end of the budget. There's no time left, there's no money left, get it done."

At Post Sound in Hollywood, where Seretti works, they refer to the show as "Against the Wall."

"It's a horse race, every episode," Seretti says. "One of the challenges is that it's an extremely dialogue-intensive show. And since dialogue is the most important thing on any show, you want to get it as clean as you can possibly get it.

"So the first thing we work on is the dialogue," he continues. "We do a lot of cleaning and smoothing to try to make it all one performance, as much as we can. And that's always a challenge, since everything is shot on multiple days, in many different locations, and there are always audio inserts added later. But the aim is to make it all sound consistent, as consistent as possible. Then once we have the dialogue taken care of, we do the creative mixing: Is the story working? Do we want more music here or less music? Should we use the effect, or not use it? That kind of stuff.

"But first we go for consistency. That means that in those areas where we don't have real quality sound, we try to gloss in and out of the quality so that it's not noticeable, not jarring. The main idea being, don't distract the viewers from the story. If all of a sudden they hear a loop line that was done in ADR and it just stands out, if Michael O'Keefe suddenly sounds like a different man, they don't hear the words anymore. They'll say, 'Geez, who said that?' And with a show like this with rapid dialogue, they might miss three story points in thirty seconds, while their minds are settling back into the story. Or else they'll get confused, and it's like, 'I don't understand this show,' and then it's click, click, click. And they're watching something else."

When Seretti says "click, click, click," he sticks his hand out as if he's holding a remote-control unit. He also shakes his head slightly and blinks his eyes, as if a torpid viewer has just been startled.

"So the idea is to keep it very smooth," Seretti says. He slips a cassette of an early edit of Episode 11 into a videotape recorder and starts fast-forwarding through the show until he gets to a scene in which MacHeath is lying in an ambulance, talking to an Emergency Medical Technician and the detective. MacHeath has just been stabbed with the poison dart. Seretti hits play.

"You can see that when they shot the EMT and the detective, the ambulance was moving," he says. "You can see the city streets out the back window. But then when they turned around to shoot Mac-Heath, they stopped the ambulance, because there's no window behind him. They probably just had a few grips pushing the ambulance a little bit from the outside, just to give it some motion. That's why MacHeath's voice comes through much better—there's no rumbling, or engine noise. So we'll degrade the quality of the recording, so that it all sounds consistent."

You'll purposely degrade MacHeath's audio track?

"Yes, often the important thing is not to try to bring everything up to the highest level of quality, but to degrade the tracks equally so they all match. That's one of the main tricks in dialogue editing: to go against your better judgement, and make something worse, so it blends.

"You often run into this when you're working with loop lines that have been recorded in the studio circumstances. You have to degrade those loop lines to bring them down to the level of the rest of the production sound. If you look back fifteen or twenty years ago, a show like this was always shot on a soundstage, not out in the real world. One of the reasons for that was that they weren't able to carry some of the equipment out to a location; the other reason was that they needed to control the sound. That's why they were called soundstages. Their main purpose was to isolate the action from the world and make it quiet, so that anything they did on the soundstage could be duplicated soundwise.

"If you look at some of the early location-style shows from the mid seventies, you'll notice loop lines standing out just like that (he snaps his fingers). Because the technology wasn't there to make them blend in. That can be distracting. And before you know it: click, click, click."

More fast-forwarding, until we come to a scene with MacHeath talking on the phone. Seretti hits Play.

"We are now entering the realm of the futz," he says. "When we want to convey the other end of a phone conversation, we take the dialogue and squeeze it and squash it so that it sounds as if it's coming out of a phone speaker. Actually, it usually sounds worse than today's phone speakers, but it's become such a convention that people expect a futzed-up track. It's the same thing with car radios: viewers expect a tinny sound even though today's car stereos sound extremely good. The other audio convention that's a little dated is when you want to convey that an actor is thinking, you go to echo. That one really doesn't make any sense, but people are used to it by now."

Seretti fast-forwards through the rest of the show, until towards the end he comes to a scene where Dartman is sitting on MacHeath's couch holding the gun threateningly and telling his life story to his captive audience—MacHeath, Vanessa, and the school kid. It's Dartman's big scene, and the actor is getting into it, alternately yelling, whispering, then yelling again.

"This guy is really using some dynamic range," Seretti says. "He's acting. But that's a problem, because people don't listen to television very loud. When you go to a movie, the sound level is controlled; you can't change it. So you can go up and down dynamically. But at home, when you're listening to this on your television's three-inch speaker and your daughter is upstairs playing her radio and the dishwasher is going in the kitchen, the low words are going to start to disappear. And it can get annoying if you have to start straining to hear it."

Can't you just turn it up?

"Most people will not turn the volume up unless they're really, really into the story. And if they do and the commercials come blasting on, they'll turn it back down again. So what happens is that they'll just start to lose interest in the show and suddenly ask themselves, 'What am I watching this for?' And click, click, click."

So you're going to bring up the low stuff?

"Actually, we'll compress the entire performance by pulling down the top stuff to the level of the lowest stuff, and then we'll raise the entire thing to the highest acceptable limit. If you squash all the sound and bring it up to a constant equal level, it appears to be louder. It creates the illusion of loudness, and it allows us to compete with the commercials. Also, it overcomes the ambient noise in the viewers' homes. We're actually playing a trick on them to keep from losing their attention, to keep them caught up in the story. We want to hook them, and we don't want them to have to strain to enjoy the show. Because if they start to strain . . ."

I think I know what's coming. Seretti holds out his imaginary remote control.

"Click. click. click."

7. "THE ART SCHOOL GIRLS OF DOOM," NEW YORK

From the street, in this case West 24 Street in Manhattan, the entrance to Globus Studio resembles a dark cave. The brown metal doorway, scraped and dented, looks as if a lot of heavy equipment has banged through it. Inside there's a bench, a few scattered newspapers, some paper coffee cups with classical Greek designs, and a large plate glass window. On the other side of the window, a woman is sitting behind a desk cradling a phone on her shoulder. She glances up to make sure I don't look dangerous, then buzzes me in.

It's a February day in Manhattan, the kind of day that starts getting dark around 2:45 P.M. The wet snow looks dirty even before it hits the pavement. Next door, two members of striking IBEW Local #3 are burning scrap wood in a barrel to stay warm.

But inside Globus, if you walk past a table with an uninspiring tray of bagels and cream cheese, past the two couches where the makeup people hang out, step over three electric cables as thick as firehoses, and push open a thick, padded door, it gets suddenly very, very bright. As bright as high noon but without the glare. In fact, anything that *could* glare, like a shiny metal light stand, has been shrouded in black canvas and black tape or sprayed with dulling spray. The temperature is about fifty degrees warmer than outside, at least eighty degrees Fahrenheit.

At the center of this unnatural-looking glow, two glamorous-looking women, scantily clad, are lounging on pillows against a

Director Eli Noyes and the Art School Girls of Doom, on the set.

plain green seamless background. The schedule for today's shoot says simply, "Art School Girls of Doom," which will be the name of the three short segments that will be taped here over the next few days. Eventually, these segments will be included in an MTV series entitled "Liquid Television."

About ten feet away, just out of the light, director Eli Noyes and producer Prudence Fenton are sitting on canvas chairs silently, almost sullenly, pondering an industrial-looking television monitor that sits on a banged-up light blue equipment case.

On the monitor, the plain green background has been replaced with an animated, askew room. On one wall, two large cat's eyes are shifting right and left. Outside an off-center window, a cutout man holding a newspaper occasionally pops into view.

Noyes and Fenton are ramping up to what has to be a very productive two days for Colossal Pictures, which is producing the "Liquid Television" series for MTV. So far, things are not going perfectly.

In this early scene, for example, the Art School Girls are lounging at home, talking. After a few lines about the local nightclub, they decide to feed their cat. Eli Noyes is trying to carve this scene into shots. He isn't having much success.

"Let's get an establishing shot," he says at first. But when he sees what it looks like on his monitor, he changes his mind.

"Zoom in on Cody," he says. When he says it, he pushes his hands out in front of him as if he's passing a basketball.

"I'm going to try to get away from the two shot," he says to Fenton.

A few minutes pass. Noyes stares at his monitor. He asks the Art School Girls to move a little to the right, now towards the camera. He stares at the monitor some more.

"I'm trying to be cinematic and graphic at the same time," he says to Fenton.

Then standing up as if resolved, he says, "I think we should jump around a little and worry less about continuity." (He's talking to everybody in the studio now.) "If we're not wild, we shouldn't be here."

"Kill the air!" he says, and someone turns off the air conditioning.

"Roll background!" On his monitor, the cat's eyes start moving and the cutout man starts popping into the window.

"From the beginning," he says to the two women, who upon closer inspection are starting to look more like men dressed as women.

"This is fun!" he says hortatively. It's not clear whether he's talking to the actors or himself.

After the shot, Dan Leo, the rumpled author who's been hanging around the edge of the production, says, "I love this format. It's so compacted." And it does have a compacted feeling, as if traditional perspective and vanishing points have been flattened, compressed into layers of thin, two-dimensional images. The separation you expect between the actors and the background has also shrunk, leaving an image that looks vacuum-packed. When the actors are saying their lines and the background animations are moving, it looks like a cut-and-paste collage come to life.

Which is the way director Eli Noyes wants it to look. Noyes, who's tall and kind of athletic looking, has been working in New York for slightly over twenty years: as an animator, a documentary film producer, a commercial director, and a children's television producer. Noyes has made short films and clay animations for "Sesame Street"; opening graphics and network ID's for MTV and Nickelodeon; commercials for Pepsi, Reebok, Xerox, and IBM. He and Prudence Fenton just finished a very busy looking commercial for Honeycomb cereal. His work is not slick. Most of his pieces have a rough, handmade quality. "I think there's a revulsion towards slickness in the marketplace," he told an advertising industry magazine in the late eighties. "Sometimes things are more powerful because they look crude; in fact, we often spend a lot of money to make something look fresh."

On the storyboards, the style of "Art School Girls of Doom" is described as "live actors against animated backgrounds." It's a style that Noyes has been working on for a while, ever since he spent a year in the mid seventies as an artist-in-residence at WNET, the public broadcasting station in New York.

"Animators are always working in layers," he tells me later. "Even the Disney-style cel animators are basically working with layers of drawings that are stacked up on top of one another. So when I started working in video in the mid seventies and I discovered that they had this thing that allowed you to layer in video by working against a solid color—it was called chroma key. For me that was a mind-boggler, because I said, 'It's like animation, but you can do it in real time, on videotape.'

"At the time I used chroma key to do a Grimm's fairy tale, and I did something similar to what I'm doing in 'Art Girls.' I made drawings and I had a camera that just looked at the drawings. I also had an actor in a blue stage. Then I took the image of the actor and put him on my drawings. At the time I figured that it was the closest to live animation that I could ever get.

"Then the Ultimatte got invented, which was basically a refinement of chroma key, where you didn't worry so much about the fringing around people's hair. Because it's a big technical achievement to release an actor from a background color. The pixels are doing a lot of thinking there—whether they should be in or out of the picture. And the problems usually come up around the edges, especially around the hair. And if a pixel can't make up its mind, you see this blue halo that we're all familiar with from bad rock videos. When the Ultimatte solved that problem, I saw a lot of potential for this approach in television, and in film."

• • •

I asked Noyes what he meant when he said, early on, that he was trying to be cinematic and graphic at the same time.

"Most people who shoot drama are trying to make the audience think that it is actually happening in front of their eyes," he says. "So the camera becomes this witness to the action. The camera shots are chosen in such a way so as to make the audience not even know that there's a camera there—so they suspend their disbelief and enter into the emotion of the scene. And they don't realize that they've been jumping around all over the place: into close-ups and back-ups and master shots, and all that kind of stuff. And that's what a good director knows how to do. And a really good director will be able to manipulate the mise-en-scene—the choreography of the different shots—to emphasize the drama and bring to the forefront the inner thoughts of a character, because different camera positions have different emotional relationships to the characters.

"But when you get into the world of animation, a lot of those cinematic rules either break down, or aren't necessary, or you can supersede them because you're kind of in the world of comic books. You're into a graphic reality. So I had all these backgrounds, and I had to figure out how cinematic I was going to be. And how important was it to establish space or not establish space. And how important was it to cut back to them, and feel that they were in the same place, or did it matter? That was the debate."

How was it resolved?

"I sort of split the difference," he replied. "But since we were experimenting, it seemed to me that it was my responsibility to get loose with the form."

The idea for "Art School Girls of Doom" arrived at MTV as a "concept," basically a one-panel storyboard. I first saw it, along with about a dozen other "Liquid Television" concepts, in Judy McGrath's office at MTV. McGrath's official title is "senior vice president, creative director," and her job, according to a company press release, is "to chart the direction of the overall 'look' of MTV."

McGrath, who has been with MTV since its launch in 1981, used to work at *Glamour* magazine, where she was copy chief, and at *Mademoiselle,* where she was senior writer. She still dresses in the simple but elegant manner of a Conde-Nast editor. Her office is small and cluttered, and sometimes when she has visitors she shakes a small pile of M&Ms onto the desk in front of them. In one corner of her office she has an Elvis lamp that actually looks more like Joe

Piscopo. She also has a large television near her desk, always on, most of the time with the sound off.

At MTV, all the short stuff that shows up between the music videos and the commercials is referred to as interstitial programming. Interstitial programming includes station identifications, promotions, and weird little ten-second artlike pieces.

The broadcast networks run promos and station identifications, of course, but they're usually slick and formulaic. The dominant broadcast on-air style is known as "flying logos": muscle-bound computer graphics that show off how many translucent layers of 3-D imagery can tumble and swoop across the screen in :05 seconds. Some of the fledgling cable networks, like USA and HBO, aspire to this look. MTV heads in the opposite direction.

"The way HBO looks is exactly the way we should never look," McGrath says. "HBO wants to be a traditional-looking network."

MTV's on-air style, by contrast, is kind of rough, edgy, and graphic. It projects a very strong visual identity. In fact, some of the interstitial programming has probably done as much to define the MTV image as the music videos.

"The music is the most important part," McGrath says, "and our station identification is the second most important part. Basically we went on the air with videos, humans, and *these pieces*. So the interstitial programming sort of made us not a video jukebox, which is what MTV easily could have been."

From the start, MTV has taken a different approach to self-promotion. "When we first went on the air, we put out the word that we were looking for a symbol," McGrath continues. "People came in with all the obvious stuff: guitars, lots of guitars, guys with long hair, apples—because we were in New York—and musical notes, tons of notes. And that was exactly what we didn't want. I don't think we've ever had an ID on the air that has a guitar in it."

The symbol MTV settled on was the same durable typographic template they use today; the first station ID is also still current: an astronaut planting a crudely animated MTV flag on the moon.

"We tried to think about the fact that MTV was television, and what was the most important event that our generation had witnessed on television—the moon landing," McGrath recalls. "Another reason we chose the astronaut image was that it was NASA footage, so it was free, in the public domain. We got it from a friend at the National Archives in Washington, where NASA has boxes of stuff."

Since then, the interstitial stuff has stayed fresh at MTV, even as the music videos have slipped a few notches. One reason is that because MTV is rock'n'roll and youth, young animators feel that

LIQUID TELEVISION

TITLE
Dangerous Puppets

RUNNING TIME
45 seconds

SYNOPSIS
Benign, "kids' show" puppets, in normal, <u>friendly</u> environments, prove to have very short fuses and resort to excessive violence with little provocation.

EXAMPLE

EPISODE 1: Sweet, pink furred "Mr. Funny Bunny" puppet and cute "Mr. Happy Cowboy" in his plaid shirt and blue jeans are enjoying a game show, calling out the answers to the questions. Everything's fine until Mr. Funny Bunny's interupted while trying to remember the name of the "Mystery Song" by the Cowboy who blurts the wrong name out. The Bunny complains angrily. The Cowboy laughs in his face. They miss the answer when the show host announces it and the Bunny flips out. "Now we'll never know!", he screams. A moment later it's sharp blades and flying fur as the puppets wage war...

The puppets have fights with weapons that are not scaled or finished to their style. For example, Mr. Happy Cowboy has a razor blade attached to his hand or a Bic lighter set for five inch flames. They fight dirty, trying to cut each other's strings as well as attacking each other's bodies and limbs. Weapons include water, fire, blades, hammers, anything that can be attached to and manipulated by a puppet to harm or disable the other one.

TECHNIQUE
Puppets (Henson style sock and rod puppets, marionettes, paper bag puppets...any style) are shot in front of a keyable background and comp'd over background plates (or shot in front of a rear screen projection which would be cheaper and cheesier.)

KEY PERSONNEL
Tim Boxell, Director.
Puppeteers.

they can do things for MTV that they couldn't do for NBC or CBS.

MTV pays about $1000 a second for their ten-second program ID's (''what we've been paying since we went on the air,'' McGrath says). In most cases that's not quite enough to cover the production costs, but for an animation house with a hip reputation, like Colossal Pictures or Broadcast Arts, a series of MTV spots is a cost-effective loss leader. After all, if you hang out, creatively, where MTV hangs out, you're probably the perfect place to produce that next series of Swatch ads.

On the television next to McGrath's desk, four young men are waving their hair around. They look as though they've been packaged to appeal to adolescents angry at their parents. Then an odd promotional spot comes on, a low-tech-looking, animated, stop-motion collage that coalesces into the MTV logo.

Where did that come from?

''MTV Europe,'' McGrath says. ''We've gotten some great stuff from them. My only problem with the MTV Europe stuff is that it's a little long. That was twenty seconds. I like ten seconds. I like the promo to come and go and leave you wanting more, like 'What was *that?*' ''

But it was earlier, when I asked McGrath about upcoming projects, that Colossals's name first came up.

''I'm looking at some storyboards for some promo ideas that Colossal Pictures sent us,'' she replied. ''They're probably our biggest supplier. They're great. Did you ever see the promo with the MTV logo in the washing machine? That was theirs.

''They also just gave us a really terrific idea for an animation series, 'Liquid Television,' '' she continued, reaching behind her desk to produce a collection of large concept pages.

''This is kind of the way we get ideas,'' she said as she flipped through the oversized pages.

On one page, two cute puppets were pictured in front of a fifties-style dinner scene. Both were holding razors.

McGrath read the copy: '' 'Dangerous Puppets: Benign 'kid's show' puppets, in normal, *friendly* environments, prove to have very short fuses and resort to excessive violence with little provocation.' ''

''How can we say no to that?'' she asked.

Another page featured a straight photo of Mel Gibson next to a crudely altered version: minus hair, with heavier eyebrows, and a blackened tooth.

'' 'Miss Lidia's Make-Over to the Stars,' '' McGrath read. '' 'Each week, Eastern European beauty expert, Miss Lidia, alters the phys-

OPPOSITE
*"Dangerous Puppets"
concept board. This is
how Colossal Pictures
communicated the idea
to MTV.*

LIQUID TELEVISION

TITLE
Miss Lidia's Make-Over to the Stars

RUNNING TIME
45 seconds

SYNOPSIS
Each week, Eastern European beauty expert, Miss Lidia, alters the physical features of a well-known celebrity through the magic of her beauty computer.

EXAMPLE

Each segment opens with a muzak-like theme song playing behind appropriately bad titles that are superimposed over a table top shot of cosmetic products and surgeons tools in front of a PC monitor. The narrator speaks with a distinct Polish accent in a rough, condescending manner.

EPISODE 1: "Welcome to Miss Lidia's Make-Over to the Stars. Today's subject: My favorite and yours, that handsome hunk of de silver screen... Mr. Mel Gibson." Mel's image comes up on the screen to the typing on the keyboard. "We all love him...but haven't you ever wondered - 'Is that really his hair?' Let's just see what he would look like without dis toupe."

The screen splits, we hear typing again and the Mel on the right loses his hair.
"Now let's try some other hair pieces."

SUBSEQUENT EPISODES: Roseanne Barr, Tom Cruise, David Letterman, Arsenio Hall, Dan Quayle, Michael Fuchs...

TECHNIQUE

Mac II paint box alteration of still photographs transfered to video with voice over.

KEY PERSONNEL
Gordon Clark, Director / Writer.
Lidia Pryzluska, Voiceover.

ical features of a well-known celebrity through the magic of her beauty computer.'

"That's another one we like," she added.

"Now MTV is all over the world—in Japan, in Europe," McGrath continued. "There's this international, global dance we're doing, and animation travels better than almost anything, really. MTV Europe, Japan, Australia—they can all use this stuff."

She was still flipping through the pages.

"I think this could be really good," she said. She sounded as if she was thinking out loud.

"Art School Girls of Doom" started to take shape about two months before the shoot, with a flurry of preliminary meetings, phone conversations, faxes, "While You Were Out" messages, and overnight deliveries.

At Colossal East, in New York, Eli Noyes began working with three New York animators to put together the backgrounds. "I wanted streets that had some depth, rooms that seemed to be somewhere, a beach scene, stuff like that," he recalls. "We worked basically in cutouts. We also threw in some drawings that we did quickly on a Macintosh, using a very basic paint program. We'd just make simple black and white drawings, fill them in with dots or lines, print them out on the laser printer, color them in with colored pencils or markers, cut them out with a razor knife, and put them into the collage with everything else. We also used pieces of fabric."

Later, Noyes and two of the animators—Nina Crews and Ruth Rosenfeld—went down to an animation stand and composed everything into short two- and three-second animations on 35mm film. The best animations were then transferred to Beta SP videotape and edited to make endless cycles.

"We'd take a two-second animation and edit it and edit it until we made a loop out of it," Noyes recalls. "A thousand edits later you have two minutes. It seemed like a smart way to create a lot of animation for not a lot of effort or a lot of money."

In the middle of all this, Prudence Fenton (the series producer) and Eli Noyes began working on a Honeycomb cereal commercial. The commercial, which later ran incessantly on Saturday morning, turned out to be a busy, very fast paced montage of colorful, disparate images: a cartoon bee pollinates a series of purple satellite dishes; a bunch of kids and a rubbery cartoon character pop through the holes of a large piece of Honeycomb cereal; a girl in white appears with a glowing Honeycomb halo; a Honeycomb sun rises over a mountaintop; and a kid dressed as a magician—and holding a box

OPPOSITE
"Miss Lidia's Make-Over" concept board.

of Honeycomb cereal—pulls himself out of a hat. The whole pastiche is held together by a driving, jingly Honeycomb song.

"Here's the deal," Eli Noyes said when I asked him about the ad. "If you look at Saturday morning TV and there are all these people with all these cereals, trying to sell something to kids, you ask yourself, 'What am I going to tell these kids so they'll ask for this cereal over another cereal?' If you look at the Honeycomb spot, you'll see that what it's basically saying is, 'I've got an interesting shape, I've got honey *all* over me, kids like me, and I'm called Honeycomb.' That's it. So given that advertising content, which is basically making something out of nothing, the commercial has to become an exercise of style and attitude. That's what we tried to make."

While Noyes and Fenton were jamming more images into their Honeycomb spot, the day-to-day responsibility for "The Art School Girls of Doom" fell to Mark Reusch, the segment's line producer. Reusch, who sounds energetic even when he looks very tired, defines his job as essentially creative support: "My job, basically, is to make sure that Eli has everything to do his job," he says. "If Eli wants to do something some way, it's my job to figure out how it can best be done for the budget I was given. I collect the resources so that when Eli's ready to dictate, I can have everything ready for him."

The budget Reusch was given added up to $56,000 for three two-minute segments. The biggest expense, and the biggest technical headache, would be sandwiching together the actors and the animated backgrounds. Which is why one of Reusch's first calls was to Dave Satin at SMA Video in Manhattan. "Dave Satin and his partner Mike Morrissey are the only game in town," Reusch says. "A. because they're very good at it; and B. because they have really explored that technology. They are really the only true mobile Ultimatte company in New York, maybe the country. We were very lucky to get them, because they're often off in the jungles of Mexico, shooting *Predator 2,* or some other kind of feature effects work."

The cost for Satin's Ultimatte system was $5000 a day; the studio was $2500 a day. The crew—Satin, a cameraman, John Kraus, and three lighting guys and grips—ate up another $1800 a day. The crew costs were slightly higher than usual because it was a union shoot. Dave Satin is union, and he will only work with a union crew.

"In New York, you can shoot with a non-union crew," Reusch says, "but on something like this we needed specific equipment that's only operated by union people—so we had to go with a union shooting crew. The remainder of the work was non-union: all the talent was non-union, all the artists were non-union. But the shooting crew was union, and that's usually the best way to go, because the people who are the most qualified for that kind of thing are union."

Reusch also coordinated the casting sessions. "We wanted a certain Lower East Side, Village-type look," he recalls, "and it seems as if we saw dozens and dozens of those kind of people. It turned out that the women we cast were the very first people we saw. And it was only afterwards that we learned that they were transsexuals. Which means that they've actually had the operation, or they are in the process. It's an ongoing thing, apparently. So without it being our intention, that sort of added another crazy twist to the story."

"Art School Girls of Doom": segment 1, scene 3 begins with the approach of two preppily dressed young men, referred to in the script as "the Brooks brothers." Two actors, cast as the Brooks brothers, are patiently standing at one end of the Globus Studio stage against a green screen, getting a final dusting of makeup and rehearsing their lines with Eli Noyes.

In a tiny control room off to one side of the studio, Dave Satin, surrounded by tape decks and TV screens, is sitting on the edge of a high metal chair. On one side, a plate glass window looks into the studio; a thin brown curtain hangs in the doorway. His setup resembles the booth that the Wizard worked out of in Oz.

Satin is scrutinizing two monitors: one shows the Brooks brothers against the green background; the other shows the same shot, except the green screen has been replaced with an animated, cartoon-like street scene. Every few seconds a cutout taxicab slides across one of the cartoon intersections.

On the set John Kraus, the cameraman/director of photography, is sitting very comfortably on a Fisher dolly behind an Ikegami 79I television camera.

The directions on the storyboard call for the Brooks brothers to walk into the frame. I ask Kraus if the actors are going to walk towards the camera or just pretend to walk as he zooms the camera in.

"Probably both," he says. "They'll be walking forward as I'm zooming in. That's the way you like to do it, two things at a time. It's like magic: you're looking at one hand, and the other hand is doing something else."

Above us, two strong lights are bouncing light off a white panel. Two smaller lights are shining through translucent panels. The smaller lights are wrapped in black material and covered with blue and pink gels. They look like light cannons, shooting out a few soft colors from an urban sunset.

I ask Kraus why none of the lights is shining directly on the actors: all the lights are either shining through or bouncing off something.

"The softer the light, the more it wraps around your face," Kraus says. When he says this he moves his hand around his cheek in a way that brings to mind diaphanous advertisements for skin-care products.

Sometimes, a conversation with Kraus doesn't yield much hard information, the kind of data you can quantify. At one point, for example, I asked him if there is a trick to lighting for the Ultimatte.

"Sure," he replied. "The background has to happen, and the foreground has to be beautiful."

Another time I asked if he preferred shooting film to videotape.

"It depends," he said. "But video is wide open. It can be a good look."

After three takes of the Brooks brothers sort of zooming, sort of walking into the frame and saying a line ("is this a cool place?"), Dave Satin's assistant takes the tape of the best take and puts it into another deck.

"The Brooks brothers are our new background plate," Satin says.

Eli Noyes places the Art School Girls in front of the green seamless—on either side of the screen—and asks them to look over their inside shoulders at the green background. On Eli's monitor, and Dave Satin's monitor, the Art School Girls are now looking over their shoulders at the previous scene, the approaching Brooks brothers.

Noyes says, "Roll tape," and the Brooks brothers start to zoom/walk into the frame.

The Girls are standing on opposite sides of the screen. One of them says, "Uh, oh. Twerp alert."

Then Kraus zooms between them, and the Art School girls part, stage right and stage left, like a pair of sliding doors, just as the Brooks brothers, on tape, fill the frame and ask, "Is this a cool place?"

In the control room, Dave Satin is happy with the take. He's a large man who talks very fast, in a manner that projects youthful enthusiasm. Not long after we met, he told me that he's wanted to do what he does since he was six years old; he also told me that most mornings he gets up before his alarm clock goes off, that's how much he likes his job.

The Brooks brothers and the Art School Girls of Doom layered against an Ultimatted background.

The machine he's working with today, an Ultimatte 5, is "basically the same system that weather guys use," he says.

Like Eli Noyes, Satin started compositing images using a chromakey system. At the time he was a staff engineer at a large television studio in Manhattan. Then, in 1981, he worked with one of the very first Ultimattes (a prototype, actually) and he became an instant convert.

"You know Gene Shalit on Channel 4?" he asks. "Sometimes if you see old file tapes of him, there's this blue fringe in his hair. That's chroma key. Ultimatte uses a different method, so there's no key line, no edge, no fuzzy hair."

Although Satin works on all kinds of television projects, Ultimatte projects are one of his specialties. He owns two Ultimatte systems with his partner; both are busy most of the time.

"Warrant, the rock group, is using my other system right now," Satin says. "They're making a video in a studio in Brooklyn."

For "The Art School Girls of Doom," Satin has been asked to provide a look that he categorizes as "Surreal. They want to suggest, without trying to create reality, that the girls are sitting in an apartment."

The Ultimatte is often used in this self-conscious way. On MTV, for example, they use an Ultimatte to provide simple "electronic sets" behind some of the video jocks. "I call that the Colorform school of compositing," Satin says. "It looks just like they're stuck on the screen. There's nothing that ties the foreground and back-ground together."

Most of the time, Satin is asked to work in the opposite direc-tion—toward creating reality, a challenge he enjoys. "I can make a composite where all the vanishing points line up, and the guy can walk against the background plate and his feet will touch the ground," he says. "If everything's working properly and the lighting is right on, I can put two, or three, or four things together in a way that's completely believable. Some people call that virtual reality. Anyway, that's the frontier."

Later, as the Art School Girls are rehearsing their next scene—in which they visit the beach—John Kraus and Dave Satin begin a loud discussion: Dave asks John how he expects him to make a smooth matte out of the shit he's seeing on his monitor; John replies that if Dave would just hold on for one fuckin' minute, he could figure the fuckin' problem out.

When things cool down a little bit, it's decided that the problem might be dust and dirt on the green background. At that, Prudence Fenton and a few others remove their shoes, roll up some duct tape, and start dotting the background, picking up dust.

After a few more minutes of rehearsal, the sound man, who has been quietly adjusting dials in the rear of the studio, comes forward and announces that he's picking up a low hum on the audio track. Everyone pauses and listens. It sounds like a midsized car is idling next door. Mark Reusch goes to find the studio manager.

The manager arrives; everybody quiets down again.

"That's coming from Wells Fargo, next door," the manager says. "Once a week they have to recharge their generator. It only lasts about forty minutes."

"Is it major?" Noyes asks the sound man.

"It's major," he replies.

"Lunch?" Noyes asks Reusch.

"Lunch," Reusch says.

A half block away, at a nearly empty restaurant with white table-cloths, Prudence Fenton begins the story of her professional life. During her senior year at Vassar, she thought she wanted to be in newspapers, and she took a job with a small paper in Odessa, Texas. When she found that she enjoyed contributing layouts and cartoons more than articles, she came back East, to attend the Corcoran School of Art. "From there, I started thinking about animation. I got a job at Broadcast Arts, which was in Washington then. I worked there for three years, producing ads, network ID's for MTV, stuff like that.''

At the time—in the early 1980s—Broadcast Arts, along with Colossal Pictures on the West Coast, was developing a reputation as an animation/effects house with a fresh mixed-media style. By combining a variety of techniques, including claymation and stop-motion, and by using animators from the artistic fringe, Broadcast Arts was able to produce short, spunky animations that offered an up-to-date alternative to the cloyingly sweet Disney product. Advertising art directors and fledgling cable networks responded to the look; during the first four years that Fenton spent at Broadcast Arts—mostly working as a film editor and producer—the size of the staff grew from four to twenty-four.

In 1982 and 1983, Fenton won two Clio Awards, the national advertising ''Oscar,'' for her work on MTV ID's.

''I worked on about twenty-eight of them,'' she recalls. ''The pink elephant M, the M subway, the M shaving can, the M that fell to earth, the Jackson Pollock M; there was a cat that jumped over the M . . .''

Which ones won Clios?

''The M sandwich and the M subway,'' she says.

I asked her if, at $1000 a second, MTV logos were always a loss leader for Broadcast Arts.

''Oh, you don't make anything at all doing MTV ID's,'' she replied. ''If you get a group of five of them, maybe you can come out a little ahead. People just do them because they're more creative than a lot of commercials. Also, it's a good way to get started. That's why all the young animation companies do ID's. Also MTV ''Art Breaks.'' Olive Jar in Boston does them; the Quay Brothers in London have done some; we've done some.''

In 1986 Fenton started working on a new children's show, ''Pee-wee's Playhouse.'' She was the senior animation producer. The next year, after the show was a certifiable smash hit, Pee-wee (Paul Reubens) moved the production to the West Coast. Fenton moved with him, to become the show's animation/effects producer. She also worked as the executive and line producer for Peter Gabriel's ''Big Time'' music video, which was made in busy ''Playhouse'' style and which is one of the few examples of how an original video can occasionally boost a mediocre song onto the charts. I asked her how the Pee-wee experience influenced her approach to television.

''Pee-wee got pretty complex,'' she says. ''You had the animated elements—like the dinosaurs, the fridge, and the pennies—but then you also had the magic screen, and you had Pee-wee performing inside of stock footage, and how's that going to cut against the magic screen? Or against the dinosaurs? Are we going to introduce the dinosaurs, or are we just going to cut to them? The experience of putting all that stuff together was very interesting."

I asked Fenton how she answered the question she just posed.

"We just cut to things," she said. "The audience is really savvy. They've seen a lot of TV. This is especially true of an MTV audience. They're a younger audience, they don't want to be led by the hand. They're zapping around anyway. That's one of our concepts on 'Liquid TV': we want to change the channel before you do."

Did the invention of the Ultimatte make much of a difference?

"It made a big difference. The kind of matting we're doing today has gotten cleaner and cleaner. Now we're working on making our realities more interactive instead of looking more pasted on."

What's an example of a more interactive reality?

"Well, Colossal did some network ID's for the Disney Channel that featured Mickey's hands. And there's one where you see Mickey's hand steering an outboard motor in front of some waterskiing footage. And if you look at it, you see that Mickey's hand is lit to go with the stock footage: if the light in the footage is from the left, then the light on the hand is from the left. If the light is bluish in the stock footage, then there's a bluish light on Mickey's hand. Also, at one point real water splashes over Mickey's hand. That sort of bridges the two worlds."

I asked her what kind of budget she's got for "Liquid Television."
"The budget is $150,000 a show, for six shows," she said with a grimace. "That's not a lot to work with. So, for example, we said to Dave Satin, 'We'll pay you something below what you usually get on this shoot, but we'll make it up to you when we have more money for a commercial shoot.' We've had to make a lot of deals like that."

I mentioned that I saw the concept pages for the show over at MTV. Is that the way you usually pitch ideas?

"Yeah, in fact we kind of invented them. We came up with that one-page format. One of the reasons for it is that you don't want to get into storyboards until you get the okay, because storyboards take a lot of thought. With storyboards you're also giving them more than they need to know. Usually you just need to communicate a little germ of an idea. In fact, you might screw it up by storyboarding it; they may see it going in a different direction than they wanted it to go. So you have to be careful not to overdevelop."

As we got up to leave, I asked Fenton what the yelling right before lunch was all about.

"That? It was about nothing," she replied, "That's just New York; that's just the way they work here. And actually I prefer it.

Things get done. It's much better than in L.A. I remember I was doing a shoot in Los Angeles a few years ago, and it was amazing that we got anything done, everybody was so nice to one another. It really drove me nuts. I like the direct approach; I don't mind the yelling if things get done.''

Later, back in the studio, John Kraus is standing on the dolly adjusting the balance on the camera, moving it up and down, panning right and left. He looks like a distance runner limbering up before the starting gun.

Noyes, too, seems to be in a looser mood, creatively, and as he and Kraus and Satin build up momentum, the layers start piling up. A scene shot against one background turns up a few minutes later as the new background for the next scene. Then both scenes, now combined, are used as the background plate for an entirely new scene.

How long can this piling on continue?

"About seven generations, since we're working with Beta SP videotape," David Satin replies. "After that the images start to deteriorate. If we were working in high definition television, we could go on forever."

Noyes sits one of the Art School Girls close to the camera and asks Mark Reusch to paint her sunglasses the same green color as the background. Then he asks Kraus for a tight close-up. On his monitor, and Dave Satin's, the new animated background appears on the Art School Girl's sunglasses. In the next scene, when two new characters, the Surf Dudes, arrive, we see them superimposed on Cody's sunglasses, as if she were wearing mirrored sunglasses that could provide perfectly sharp, close-up reflections.

Now Noyes starts to play with the Ultimatte's odd perspective. Because the camera doesn't see the background image—only the image in front of the green screen—the background image stays the same, even if you zoom in on the actors. The result is that when you zoom in, the actors quickly grow to giantlike size, compared to their background. Similarly, when you zoom out, the actors get much smaller and the background stays the same.

So when the Art School Girls encounter their favorite rock musician, Keith, Noyes shoots Keith saying his lines close-up on one side of the screen; he looks ten feet tall. Then that shot becomes the background plate, and he zooms out and shoots the Art School Girls against it, looking up at the giant Keith like admiring ants.

Later I ask Noyes about the shot with the ten-foot-tall Keith talking to the inch-high Art School Girls. "I love that," he says.

The Art School Girls, and Keith, their idol. First Eli Noyes videotaped the girls as a distant two shot; then he zoomed in and videotaped Keith; then he used the Ultimatte to sandwich the shots together.

"And I consider that just beginning to play with the language. If I had more time and more money, I could probably push it a lot more."

How exactly would he push it?

"I think I could pick weirder camera angles, I could layer more, I could move them through the frame more," he says. "I've come to discover that there's no reason to keep them the same size. You could do cuts where they change sizes all the time."

8. COLOSSAL PICTURES, SAN FRANCISCO

A few days after the "Art School Girls" shoot, I flew to San Francisco, where Colossal Pictures is based, to see how the rest of "Liquid Television" was coming together. I didn't bother to rent a car: a previous visit to San Francisco had left me with an image of a compact, walkable city. This turned out to be a misapprehension, because Colossal Pictures is located in a gray, industrial neighborhood that's a long, unpleasant walk from almost everywhere in the city—except perhaps from Ajax Auto Dismantlers and The Frisco Cycle Center, both of which I passed the first time I walked from my hotel to Colossal. I also passed entire blocks of chain-link fence and barbed wire, and the Urn, Casket, and Funeral Art Outlet ("Open to the Public"). As I got closer to Colossal, I started to see signs of a working waterfront: spindly cranes and derricks; garbage scows and tankers. Walking the final dozen blocks along a dusty, four-lane breezeway, I saw only two other pedestrians; both were collecting redeemable bottles. By the time I arrived at the converted warehouse that serves as Colossal's headquarters, I was ready to start pricing subcompacts with low weekly rates.

Inside Colossal Pictures, the brick walls go way up to where large wooden beams intersect with air conditioning ducts and industrial lighting fixtures. The walls are decorated with castoffs from past projects: small model planes and large expanses of blue sky from *Top Gun* (Colossal did some of the effects); a rocket from an Arnold

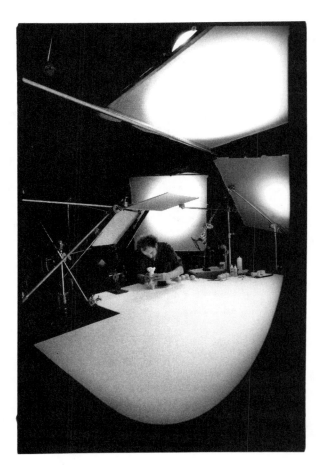

Trey Thomas animating the Pillsbury Doughboy at Colossal Pictures.

Schwarzenegger movie; a neon sign, "Dream Inn," from a Robert Palmer video; framed animation cels from an Allstate Insurance commercial; foam cutouts from a television pilot that nobody can remember; and a large, skewed, pastel television from an MTV spot. The receptionist, young, has the cheerful enthusiasm of someone who is happy just to have her foot in the door and who is probably confident that the job will lead to something else.

In industry parlance, Colossal Pictures is known as a graphics and animation house. Most of their income, about seventy percent, comes from advertising agencies who hire them to make the ads that the agencies have sold to their clients. The rest of their work consists of network ID's, music videos, and special effects for feature films. Colossal has won every major award in the moving picture field: Oscars, Clios, Emmies, and a lot of those obscure acronymic awards that only the people in the industry understand.

Colossal Pictures was formed in 1976 by two young filmmakers, Gary Gutierrez and Drew Takahashi. Gutierrez and Takahashi had met while both were working for a San Francisco filmmaker, John Korty, on an educational series for PBS, "Vegetable Soup." By the time the show was renewed, Korty had moved on to a feature film and he suggested that the two assistants join forces to produce the next season's shows. A few weeks later they set up a rough animation stand in Takahashi's basement and whimsically named their operation Colossal Pictures.

From the beginning, perhaps influenced by Korty's eclectic style, Gutierrez and Takahashi began working in a mixed-media style, melding techniques that weren't normally combined: cel animation with cutout collage; traditional puppets with stop-motion clay figures. Live actors were also part of the mix. In the Colossal lexicon, working with actors is referred to as "live action," a term that betrays the bias at Colossal, where actors are just another element to include in the mix.

Eventually, as the number of techniques they used grew, Takahashi coined a term to describe their jumbly style: blendo. Takahashi defines blendo differently depending on the day and his mood and the project he's working on; recently he described it as "a hyper jumping around from one completely different reality to another."

Today close to sixty directors, artists, producers, and technical people work at Colossal. Waves of free-lancers also wash through Colossal's facilities to work on specific projects; sometimes they stay for months at a time. Altogether, Colossal's monthly payroll frequently numbers two hundred people.

A weekly scorecard, distributed every Monday, attempts to keep track of who's doing what/where at Colossal. According to this week's rundown: the Fox network will be here on Monday to talk about some interstitial programming for their Saturday morning lineup; Mike Nichols will be in on Tuesday to plan some Disney Family Portraits for the Disney Channel; some representatives from the advertising agency Leo Burnett will be in on Tuesday to look at storyboards for a Rice Krispies advertisement; and a new Pillsbury Lovin' Lites spot, featuring the Pillsbury Doughboy, will be shooting on the stop-motion animation stage all week. "Liquid Television" has reserved an animation stand at the beginning of the week, the main edit room towards the end of the week, and the motion control camera all day Saturday.

The television production world divides itself into two large genres: "short form" comprises commercials, music videos, and miscellaneous graphic projects like show openings and network ID's; "long form" comprises just about anything $\frac{1}{2}$ hour and longer, including sitcoms, hour-long series, specials, and made-for-TV movies. In 1988, Colossal—which was short-form oriented—decided to expand into the long-form world. A new division, Big Pictures, was created to generate some projects; at the time everyone said that it was going to take at least a few years to make the transition. So far, they've been right. After two years, Big Pictures has produced a lot of proposals, a number of pilots, a cartoon series, and a network special for CBS that hasn't aired yet. They have many projects in the works.

"Liquid Television," a mixed-media animation series for MTV, is their next, best shot at breaking into the long-form world. When *Millimeter,* an industry magazine, asked Japhet Asher, the managing director of Big Pictures, to describe "Liquid Television," he said, "We're taking a lot of conventions, putting them in an animation blender, and hitting Puree."

Big Pictures consists of six people working out of a small bunkerlike office a few blocks away from the main Colossal building. When I first arrived, early one afternoon, two-thirds of Big Pictures, four people in all, were standing in front of a large television monitor watching dailies from a "Liquid Television" segment called "Dangerous Puppets."

On the screen, two cute, fuzzy puppets are making a large sandwich. There's a dispute over the mustard, which suddenly erupts into all-out fight. One of the puppets whips out a shiny electric knife and starts hacking away at his furry opponent. The violence is absurd, kind of shocking, also funny. When the screen fades to black, Prudence Fenton, who's been watching with a wry smile, says, "I think it looks good; I'm not worried about it," and then walks into her large cubicle, squints at a pink "While You Were Out" memo, and starts dialing a number on her phone.

On the other side of a thin room divider, I can hear Nicole Grindle, the coproducer of "Liquid Television," on the phone.

"Phil, would you be willing to work another project for Liquid Television?"

". . . . . . ."

"I know. We don't want people to work around the clock."

". . . . ."

"But Robin's doing too many commercials."

Now Grindle is off the phone.

"We *really* need animators," she says. "I wish I could draw."

Prudence Fenton comes out of her office to help generate some names.

"There's definitely a shortage of animators," she says. "I've lost three of my animators to the Simpsons."

Couldn't you just hire some young animators out of CalArts? I ask.

"I went to a showcase at CalArts when I was working on 'Pee-wee's Playhouse,'" Fenton says. "I was totally underwhelmed. We need animators who are fast and confident, and who know how to be funny. Recently we've had some luck recruiting from Disney. An animator at Disney can make $120,000 a year, but creatively it's not great. That gives us an opening."

Nicole Grindle is on the phone again.
    "Is she fast?"
    ". . . . ."
    "Like how much over?"
    ". . . . ."
    "Am I going to have *anything* by the twenty-second?"

Most of Colossal's projects end up on television, but the major part of the creative work originates on film. When I accompanied Prudence Fenton and Nicole Grindle to watch some dailies of "Dangerous Puppets," we found the director, Stuart Cudlitz, sitting at a large silvery Steenbeck editing console elaborately laced with 35mm film. Next to Cudlitz, long strips of film were hanging by clothespins, like celluloid laundry.

    "This is basically an editing machine for synchronizing magnetic sound track to picture," Cudlitz said of the Steenbeck. "But we're using it as an editing bench to make selects."

    Cudlitz, who has worked at Colossal since 1984, has a professorial air about him (it turns out that he lectures at San Francisco State University, and has contributed articles to *MacWORLD* magazine), so I asked him to explain the bias at Colossal towards film over videotape.

    "In this case, we shot three two-minute 'Dangerous Puppets' shows in two days, all out of sequence," he replies. "And when you have to juggle all these bits back into your story, in sequence, I find an editing bench is a lot more plastic and flexible than video editing. A lot of people in New York would probably transfer all the film to video and do a rough edit in an off-line edit suite. In California, we tend to like to handle film, and then go to electronic media with the parts we know we're going to use. That way we can spend our electronic editing time customizing the work with effects. I like to finish in the digital world, where I can use all those wonderful effects. But originating in film gives you the best quality image, and the best qualities of lighting.

    "Film is also more hands-on, and more direct, which is important because I'm on a very tight deadline.

Stuart Cudlitz at the Steenbeck editing console. Also from left to right, Karen Robert, the producer of "Dangerous Puppets," Prudence Fenton (on phone), and Nicole Grindle.

On the screen, two puppets, Mr. Funny Bunny and Mr. Happy Cowboy, are sitting on a couch watching a television game show.

"See how the lighting is flat here, like a children's show?" Cudlitz asks.

Now the puppets start to argue over answers. Soon Mr. Funny Bunny produces a straight-edge razor; Mr. Cowboy responds with a blowtorch.

"I'm going for more cinematic lighting here," Cudlitz says as the puppets back away. "More of a slasher, Sam Peckinpah look."

Later, I ask Cudlitz which tools—of all the motorized, computerized, digital tools in Colossal's kit—he considers essential.

"The Hi-8 video cameras, by Sony and others, are revolutionary in what they offer to people who are just starting to look through a camera, starting to frame images," he says. "They've got low-light sensitivity, portability, single-frame capability—generally they are versatile instruments, with better picture quality than you'd expect.

"When I teach at State and other places, I'm always amazed at the sophistication of the students in terms of animation and design because of the personal computer," he continues. "MacroMind Direc-

A frame from "Dangerous Puppets." Two benign-looking puppets with "very short fuses" starting to get violent.

tor, and other kinds of programs that allow you to string together images, have had a big influence.

"Of course, I believe that everyone should draw," he adds, almost as an afterthought. "You have to be able to get your ideas across in pictures. You don't have to draw well, but you have to be able to draw in an articulate manner. The people who are successful at this, everyone I've met, all draw.

"Even if you do it crudely and it's just thumbnail sketches, you should be able to draw sequences," he continues, gathering momentum. "You have to be able to get across to someone what kind of effect you're imagining, and be able to sort out how many different elements it takes to make that image. You have to be able to lay it out in a way that everyone can agree on.

"When they asked me to do 'Dangerous Puppets,' I spent an afternoon knocking out some crude sketches," he continues, "and those drawings turned out to be essential. Because I shot them just the way they were drawn. And because I was able to previsualize the camerawork and the edits, and draw them to the script, everyone—MTV and Big Pictures—could understand what I was planning to do. And if they wanted me to change something, they could refer specifically to a panel. We do it the same way when we're dealing with advertising agencies and feature films—it's the only way to get everyone to see it the same way. Everything comes down to story, and the best way to get story on film is to draw it first."

What about the new storyboard programs that are coming out for personal computers?

"I've reviewed some of those programs for *MacWORLD*," Cudlitz says. "And a lot of what you read about is not fully realized, or vaporware. In the meantime, the people in the industry need things that we can rely on on a daily basis. With 'Dangerous Puppets' I had to create those characters out of my head, and time was critical. The only efficient way to proceed was to draw them. I mean, we all work with computers and we believe in them, but until some of these programs take less time than drawing, we're going to draw."

At Colossal, work cubicles expand like crystals; they multiply, sub-divide, and ultimately fill up any open area with mazes of book-shelves and modular office panels. Somewhere in a maze of cubicles, behind the mailboxes and next to a bookshelf, I find Gordon Clark staring at a computer screen, juggling a few manuals on his lap, getting ready to try an Elvis hairdo on Sylvester Stallone.

Clark, an art director and writer, is nearly finished with the sixth edition of "Miss Lidia's Make-Over to the Stars," a recurring "Liquid Television" segment.

Miss Lidia's beauty computer, it turns out, is a Macintosh II, booted up with an off-the-shelf desktop program, Photoshop. Clark is using a small computerized "brush" to touch up the Elvis hairdo and a pair of trademark Elvis sunglasses, digitized from an old magazine photo of the King, getting them ready for Sly.

I ask Clark what kind of look he is going for, in the "Miss Lidia's" segments.

"Oh, cheesy," he answers right away. "I've worked with much more expensive machines, like a Quantel Paintbox, and I was surprised at how mushy and painterly things get. I much prefer the sort of cutout look, the sort of the *National Enquirer* look. Bad photo retouching is much funnier than good photo retouching."

Clark worked up a proposal for "Miss Lidia's" when the Big Pictures staff started soliciting ideas for "Liquid Television." "I heard they were looking for things that were cheap and fast to do," he recalls. "And I had always been fascinated by those old makeovers, where they bring people out of the audience and do them over. And I had heard that some hairdressers now had the capability to try different hairstyles on people. Also, I remember as a kid, messing around with pictures in magazines: erasing the eyeballs, scribbling all over some celebrity's face—I always got a big laugh out of that."

Now Clark has Sylvester Stallone on the Mac screen. He moves the Elvis sunglasses into position, sizes them, and places them on

OPPOSITE
Some drawings for "Dangerous Puppets" by Stuart Cudlitz.

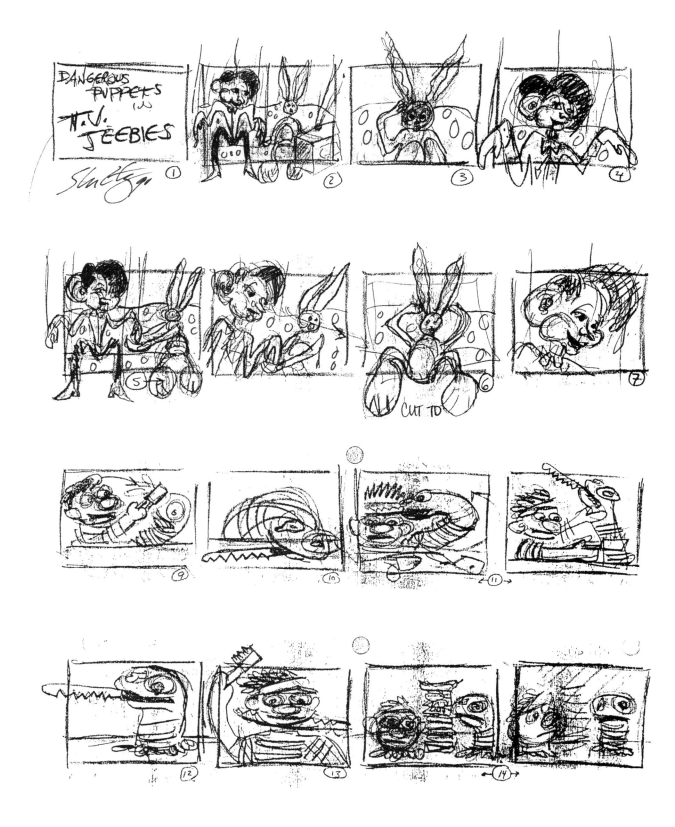

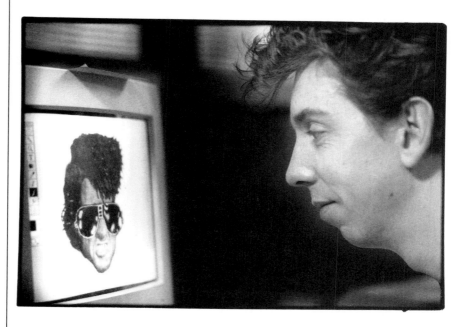

Gordon Clark views Sly Stallone with an Elvis look by "Miss Lidia."

Stallone's face. He produces the Elvis-look pompadour hairstyle from a computer file and tries that on Stallone.

Stallone looks ridiculous; Clark looks satisfied.

Clark started thinking of animation as a career when, after graduating from the University of Oregon, he got a job as a gofer on *Plague Dogs,* an animated feature movie by the same people who made *Watership Down.*

"I met a lot of people on that movie who were animators and who were making money drawing," he recalls. "That's what got me interested."

After that he began to teach himself basic animation techniques, with the aid of some friends and a few books.

"I could already draw, but there's a certain style in animation that makes it easier for everybody to draw alike. That's the point: everybody has to draw the characters the same way. And if you've got some basic drawing skills, it's not that difficult to learn."

How would you describe that style?

"It's structural. You draw through the characters. You see it in all the drawing books. You draw the head, with the crosslines in the middle of the head, and the eyes and nose and mouth in the same place. It's a technique.

"Posing was another thing. You had to be able to draw a character in different readable poses. That's pretty hard. That took the longest."

Were there any books that were valuable?

"Believe it or not, I used those Foster books you get in art stores.

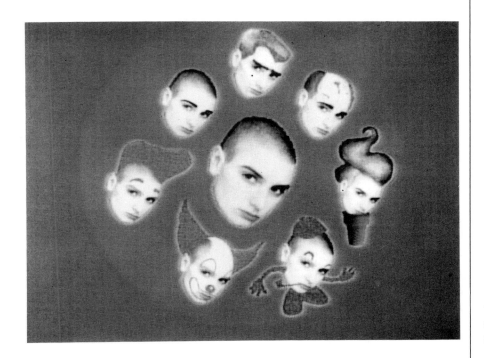

Variations on Sinead O'Connor by Gordon Clark.

I think they're written by Preston Blair: *How To Draw Animated Cartoons* and *Animated Cartoons for Beginners*. Every assistant animator had to read them. They look like some kind of joke; they look like *How to Draw Bambi* on the matchbook covers, but they actually are the main thing.

Clark landed his first real animation job at Mill Valley Animation in Mill Valley, California, doing layouts for Saturday morning cartoons. "Layouts come after storyboarding and before animation," he explains. "You're basically directing the animator: giving him a background, camera instructions, and an idea where the character is going. So you do the background, and four or five drawings, and the animator ends up doing hundreds of drawings."

One of the shows Clark worked on was "The Smurfs."

"That was easy because all the characters look alike," he says. "They just wear different hats."

Later Clark worked at Industrial Light & Magic, as a freelance special effects animator. "That was a completely different thing," he says. "You're emulating nature there, not doing cartoon stuff. Your drawing skills aren't really tested. But it's still the same principle. Mostly what you're trying to do is make your fake effect fit into a real environment. If it doesn't fit in, that really clues people in that it's fake.

"So a lot of the stuff I worked on was fix-it stuff, like shadows for the little guys in *Willow,* or shadows for the little spaceships in *batteries not included.* I also did the flash effects when the guy started shrinking in *Inner Space.* So most of the time you're trying to make it as natural as you can make something that has completely come out of somebody's head."

After three movies in a row, the pace slowed down at ILM, and Clark began working as an assistant character animator at Colossal. "That was when they were just starting to get the big cereal accounts, like Cocoa Puffs and Rice Krispies, very squash and stretch, snappy characters. And that was fine. As an assistant, that's really the most fun you can have. They're more fun to draw, and you're left with more of a challenge."

At the same time, he began working on storyboards for Drew Takahashi and other Colossal directors. "I enjoy drawing storyboards; it's like making a comic book. Also, when you work with people who are in live action, who generally can't draw, they love you. You also get away with some of your ideas. You draw something, and if the director likes it, he or she will shoot from that. That's a thrill."

Now that he's been working on the Mac, Clark is hoping to adapt it to the storyboarding process. "I'd really like to do storyboards on a Mac," he says. "On *Back to the Future,* they're already doing timing and coloring for storyboards on the Mac. That's a thrilling idea for me. I've spent a lot of time coloring with markers, and I really look forward to the day when you can have a palette of thousands of colors and you don't have to start on a new piece of paper when you discover that a color doesn't work. It will also be great to be able to time out a little storyboard film on the Mac, instead of drawing it.

"Computer magazines like *MacUser* or *AmigaWorld* are always claiming that their computers offer 'broadcast quality' or 'close-to-broadcast quality.' But wherever I've seen the artwork produced on these p.c.'s, it looks awful. The artists, by trying to emulate much more expensive machines like the Quantel Paintbox, fall so glaringly short that the results look garish, like velvet paintings."

I ask Clark his impressions of the artwork he's seen that's been produced on personal computers.

"When I look at that stuff, it always strikes me that they don't know the limitations of their medium," he says. "They aren't working within those limitations. Also for a lot of them, the machine is their baby and they're trying to push it as far as they can. Many of them don't have an art background, either. That can have an influence. I tried to incorporate the Mac's limitations into my approach to

'Miss Lidia.' I was going for a gag that the Mac could pull off."

"Okay"
"Go"
"Okay"
"Go"

Melissa Mullin holds her finger up in the air the way someone does who's just about to get off the phone. She and Denis Morella have three more frames to shoot in this sequence of "Invisible Hands."

"Okay"
"Go"
"Okay"
"Go"
"Okay"
"Go"

Melissa Mullin (above, with spot meter) and Denis Morella, working on "Invisible Hands."

"You get into a groove after a while," Mullin says when they finish, and she suddenly looks a lot more relaxed. "It's kind of funny to shoot this kind of thing: it's pretty boring, but you really have to concentrate. If you forget one thing, if you have one lapse, you can blow the entire eight hours."

This kind of thing is a cutout animation of a Richard Sala comic strip, "Invisible Hands," for "Liquid Television." Mullin, the technical director, and Morella, the director, have been working on the project for two months.

"Cutout animation is very rough," Morella says. "You can do some things every two frames, or every three frames, it really doesn't matter. You can mess up in tiny ways and nobody notices."

Morella often works in the cutout style. Oddly enough, for all its simplicity, cutout is a style that's frequently in demand by advertisers and television networks. Against a glut of computerized slickness, cutout animation has a naive clunkiness that's refreshing. Here, for example, is Morella describing how he animated his characters' mouths to match up with the sound track:

"I just drew, and cut out, three mouths for each character: open, closed, and half open," he says with a shrug. "We get by with those. We want it to be cheesy. It's okay if it comes out looking like a foreign film. Actually, when we started seeing the dailies, we were surprised it looked so good. We were afraid it would just be a 'Go Speed Racer' mouth."

A frame from "Invisible Hands." Multilayered cutout animation.

When Morella and Mullin get a good pace going, they can shoot a minute of material a day.

"We try to establish a rhythm," Mullin says. "Denis will move the artwork, and when he's ready he says, 'Go.' Then I shoot the frame, or frames, and when the camera is ready to shoot again, when I feel it's safe for him to put his hands under the camera I say, 'Okay.' And he moves the artwork a little more, says, 'Go,' and we go on like that for hours."

The camera that Mullin and Morella are working on is called a downshooter.

"It's basically a custom-made animation stand," Mullin says. "It's an old Mitchell camera that's been adapted by Fries. We just ran Unistrut up to the ceiling and mounted the camera up there pointing down. The camera is pretty simple; basically, it can zoom in, and move north, south, east, and west. Not very sophisticated, but that's all we need on a job like this."

Right now the downshooter is staring down at three very clean sheets of glass separated by a few inches of air: a multiplane setup.

"You can do things with a multiplane setup that are more interesting than flat cel work," Mullin says. "By putting the artwork on different levels, you can achieve a lot more depth. If the foreground is on the top sheet of glass and the background is on the lower two levels of glass, you really notice the increased depth of field.

"You can also throw things out of focus," Mullin continues.

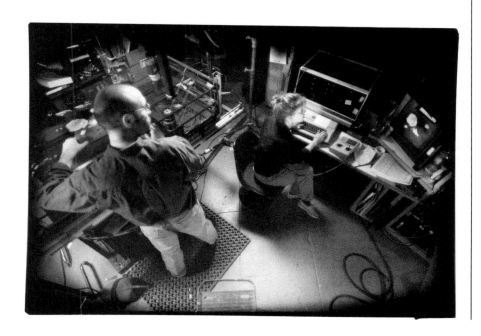

Denis Morella moving the art underneath the camera; Melissa Mullin controlling the shutter.

"You can focus on the background, and the foreground goes out of focus. We're doing a lot of selective focus on 'Invisible Hands.' It's kind of fun when things go in and out of focus, it's sort of like live action.

"Disney has a multiplane setup that's like three stories tall," Morella says. "It's thirty or forty levels high. In *Bambi* they used a multiplane to get some sense of dynamics. If you look at *Bambi* and you see the foreground moving faster than the background, that was done on the multiplane."

Melissa Mullin began working at Colossal in 1986.

"I started out in still photography," she says. "I came to Colossal as a camera assistant: I worked on live-action shoots, stop-motion, model work. I already understood how film works, how it reacts to light and how lenses work—so it was really just adapting to equipment. It took me a while to get used to the fact that everything here moves. At first I saw everything frozen into a still frame, but that changed."

For the last few years, Mullin has been working as a technical director.

"A director will have an idea how to approach a project, but he will have a lot of technical concerns, and that's where I come in," she says. "I try to come up with different methodologies for executing the idea, and then I have to make sure that everything works."

In addition to "Invisible Hands," Mullin also contributed to "Miss Lidia's Makeover." I ask whether she sees much promise in the kind of low-power computer graphics that the current line of Macintosh hardware and software delivers.

"The Macintosh definitely has its own style," she replies charitably. "But I'm not sure we've really explored that style as we could. Right now it's just trying to be animation. I think there's a much different look out there, but we're not really sure what it is. There are probably ways to use the Macintosh look and the look of the Photoshop program and make a whole new thing. It's really good for collage work, for example. Right now a lot of artists here are working on it, so it could be due for a stylistic breakthrough, an entirely new look."

Mullin has also been working with Hi-8 video cameras.

"I love that format," she says. "We're actually using it more and more, because advertising art directors associate that Hi-8 look with a kind of fun, trendy feeling. Just last week, I was using a Hi-8 camera to shoot a background out of a roller coaster. It turned out really well: unlike a lot of video, Hi-8 has a kind of grain to it. I like that look."

I ask her if she spends a lot of her time reading manuals.

"I read a lot of manuals," she responds. "I also force myself to watch a lot of television. I'm not really that wild about watching television, to tell you the truth, but I watch it to see what everybody's up to."

What specifically are you looking for?

"I'm interested in seeing what kind of techniques people are trying out. That doesn't mean that we want to emulate the techniques, but it can spark ideas, like: what if we combine what these guys are doing with the stuff we've been doing? Maybe we can make it look like something completely new."

I ask her if she watches a lot of MTV.

"A lot," she says. "MTV is fertile, the videos and the ads."

Denis Morella is just a little embarrassed to admit that his interest in animation was sparked by watching Hanna-Barbera cartoons.

"But it was before Hanna-Barbera got into "Scooby Doo" and all that horrible seventies kind of stuff," he insists. "Remember Quickdraw McGraw? The early ones were really cool. The animation was pretty limited, but they had a great design sense: the design of the characters was great, also the backgrounds. It was kind of UPA style."

UPA style?

"Sort of like the Jetsons. From the fifties and sixties, with modern but fifties-looking characters," Morella responds. "Have you ever heard of a short called 'Gerald McBoingBoing'? The animation was really simple, but it was the design that really made it. The backgrounds were real simple: they would use a few splashes of color and a few lines to create a city."

Morella talking about education (he attended the Philadelphia College of Art):

"I started out in college as an illustration major, but then I got interested in animation. Eventually I graduated with a degree in animation; the school didn't have an animation department, so they designed an animation major for me. It was fun: I had to take a certain number of classes in film, a certain number of classes in illustration, some painting classes too.

"I think I was lucky: the Philadelphia College of Art is an art school rather than an animation school, so you are exposed to a lot of painters and graphic designers. Those people tend to play with different styles of animation. Whereas if you go to CalArts, you learn about the animation business and you learn how to do it the Disney way. I think it's different on the East Coast, it's more experimental. I think that's why I felt more comfortable there. I don't do that Disney, flowing, Roger Rabbit stuff."

Morella's job at Colossal grew directly from an art project at Philadelphia College of Art.

"I did something in my junior year called 'Handicap Pig Farm,' about these two pigs who go to this handicapped pig farm to see if they want to send their son there. It's definitely black humor.

"It was all done on large index cards. I didn't use a pegging system, or even a light table. I just lined each index card up with one that I glued down on the camera bed and shot it. I did it in pencil, with watercolors over it so it has a real wobbly, loose feel to it. It still shows at festivals."

After college, Morella moved to San Francisco and started working at an ink and paint studio called Studio Actual Size. "I was coloring and inking individual frames," he says. "I worked on a lot of the early Levi's stuff. I was also doing my own paintings, and some editorial illustrations. But work was sporadic, because at the time Colossal was sort of like this Mom and Pop operation."

In 1985, Morella went to an open showcase for young animators at Colossal. He showed "Handicap Pig Farm." Afterwards a senior director at Colossal, George Evelyn, told Morella that he had already seen "Handicap Pig Farm" at an animation festival, and he thought it was one of the funniest things he had ever seen. A few weeks later, Morella started working at Colossal full-time, as an assistant animator. He has since worked as an art director, and director.

Recently Morella has noticed that the demand for animators has grown. "Many animators have migrated to L.A. because there's so much work there," he says. "It seems like every major studio is doing some kind of animated project."

The definition of animation has also broadened. "I have friends who are working at Industrial Light & Magic and they spend months doing tracer bullets," he says. "That's animation. Most people don't think of that. They think of Bugs Bunny."

Morella and Mullin are starting to set up the next scene.

For a few minutes, they stand looking at a sheet of paper on a scoffed-up table a few feet from the downshooter. The page features a drawing of a nearly bald man about to be strangled by a disembodied hand.

An element sheet for "Invisible Hands," and some cutouts.

"I call this an element sheet," Mullin says. "I made them up at the beginning of the job, one for each scene. I used a Macintosh program, Filemaker; I came up with the categories that I thought we were going to deal with. The categories differ from job to job. We recently did a job for Lexus, a car, and the element sheets had a whole different set of categories."

Next, Morella and Mullin scrutinize a page thick with crosshatchings. "Exposure sheets, which we call dope sheets." Morella says. "An editor read the sound track and broke down the dialogue into sounds on a frame-by-frame basis."

Morella moves a large cutout of the nearly bald man onto the top pane of glass. He places a cutout of the disembodied hand at about collar level.

Mullin climbs up on a platform behind Morella and starts looking though a small, gunlike apparatus. "I use a spot meter to control the exposure," she says later. "I use the zone system. Ansel Adams wrote about the zone system. It's kind of charming to read him, actually."

Now Mullin puts on heavy leather gloves; she's adjusting lights, replacing gels.

"Each of the characters has a color," she says. "Purple for the bad guy, yellow for the good guy, and so on. I also like to use a lot of blues.

"When you're working with multiplane you can really have fun

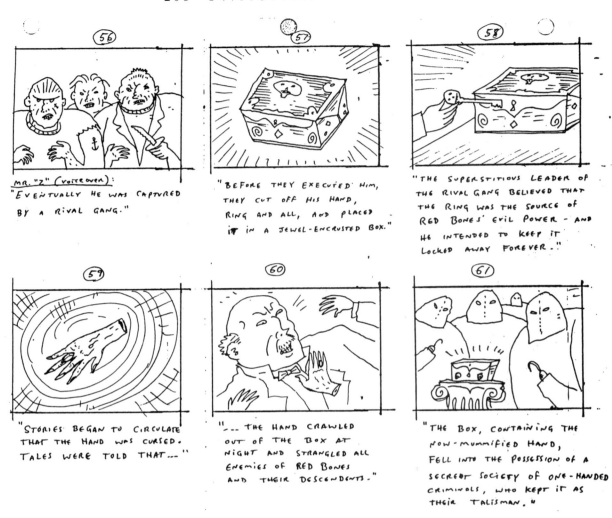

56

MR. "Z" (voiceover):
"EVENTUALLY HE WAS CAPTURED BY A RIVAL GANG."

57

"BEFORE THEY EXECUTED HIM, THEY CUT OFF HIS HAND, RING AND ALL, AND PLACED IT IN A JEWEL-ENCRUSTED BOX."

58

"THE SUPERSTITIOUS LEADER OF THE RIVAL GANG BELIEVED THAT THE RING WAS THE SOURCE OF RED BONES' EVIL POWER - AND HE INTENDED TO KEEP IT LOCKED AWAY FOREVER."

59

"STORIES BEGAN TO CIRCULATE THAT THE HAND WAS CURSED. TALES WERE TOLD THAT ---"

60

"--- THE HAND CRAWLED OUT OF THE BOX AT NIGHT AND STRANGLED ALL ENEMIES OF RED BONES AND THEIR DESCENDENTS."

61

"THE BOX, CONTAINING THE NOW-MUMMIFIED HAND, FELL INTO THE POSSESSION OF A SECRET SOCIETY OF ONE-HANDED CRIMINALS, WHO KEPT IT AS THEIR TALISMAN."

A storyboard page for "Invisible Hands."

with the lighting," she continues. "You can really create depth and space. You can put some things in shadows, and some stuff out of focus. You can light a character with a spotlight, and make a shadow on the level below him. You can also light each level separately. We're going for a film noir look on this, and we can make it so that you walk in a door and it's dark, but then the character is lit by a slash of light across his face. The background stays dark with a lot of out-of-focus, indistinguishable shapes. With multiplane, you can let certain things draw the attention, and other things be mysterious."

The producer of "Invisible Hands," Krist Ann Pehrson, arrives. She is more formally dressed; she looks tired; the phone rings.

"Margaret just called to say there's a problem with the snap-crackle-pop," she says to the person on the phone. "Frame one of the animation should work with frame ten of live action."

Denis Morella is practicing, moving the disembodied hand towards the nearly bald man's neck in increments of about a quarter inch. Morella looks absorbed. Like a baseball player in the on-deck circle, he's thinking out loud. When the disembodied hand is at the neck, Morella begins moving the nearly bald man's arms back and forth, as if in panic.

Mullin, meanwhile, is standing near a computer keyboard, looking at a video monitor. She's using a jog box to make small adjustments in the focus and the framing.

Finally, Mullin climbs back up on the platform for what she calls a "squint test."

"You have to look very carefully for reflections in the glass," she says when she's up there, squinting down at the nearly bald man.

"Ready?" Morella asks when she gets down from the platform and sits at a table loaded with electronic hardware.

"Okay," Mullin says.

"Go," Morella says.

The downshooter clicks a few times; a red light blinks on a console in front of Mullin.

"Okay," she says.

Morella moves the hand a tiny bit up towards the neck of the nearly bald man.

"Go," he says.

"Okay."

"Go."

Time passes slowly at Colossal Pictures.

"A good day's shooting is about three seconds," according to Michael Belzer, whom I find patiently animating the Pillsbury Doughboy on one of Colossal's very large shooting stages. I had wanted to talk to Belzer about some work he had done for "Liquid Television" animating a soap-on-a-rope for a segment called "Soap Opera." ("The only soap opera starring bars of soap," according to the segment's concept board.) But once I see the Doughboy standing there in front of a white seamless background, my interest shifts to the foam latex icon in front of me.

Actually, the Doughboy isn't standing; he is sort of leaning way over, holding himself up with one hand. An aluminum armature is

*Michael Belzer
animating the
Doughboy.*

holding him up from behind. And Belzer, who is twenty-six years old, is using a surface gauge to measure the distance that the Doughboy moves between shots. He's also looking at a small screen next to the camera labeled "frame grabber." By toggling a switch he can see the two previous frames, allowing him to visually compare how the current frame builds on the previous two. Occasionally he uses a wax pencil to mark a location on the monitor's screen.

A rough storyboard is taped to the seamless, just outside of camera range. It spells out the overall shape of the advertisement, which will launch a new line of cholesterol-free Pillsbury products, "Lovin' Lites." Many of Pillsbury's products debut in the fall, which Pillsbury executives refer to as "the baking season."

At this point, twenty-two seconds into the ad, the Doughboy is in the process of springing up to a standing position after doing some leg lifts. ("So do those leg lifts," the Doughboy says in the script. "Then do some fork-lifts.") Belzer, who uses a Mitchell 35mm camera that's been adapted to stop-motion work, shoots thirty frames per second. The Doughboy's spring up to a standing position will take about twenty-five frames, a morning's work. In the final advertisement, the sequence will last less than a second. (The "poke sequence," in which the Doughboy's latex tummy is given a friendly jab, lasts sixteen to eighteen frames, according to Belzer.)

Belzer moves the Doughboy up about a quarter of an inch at a time; he makes many fine adjustments—and refers to the frame grabber many times—before he shoots a frame and moves the Doughboy up another quarter inch. Watching him work is like watching someone fill out an insurance form. It's tedious.

"One of the things that makes a movement believable is giving the character a sense of weight," he says. "And the feeling of weight is something you always have to generate, because the character is usually held up by wires, or supported by an armature. First you have to figure out which direction the gravity is pulling the character, and which way his momentum is carrying him; then you have to figure out how to make it so that he looks as if he's fighting gravity. If you just pop him up like a two-by-four, that's going to look very stiff, mechanical, and not very lifelike. But if you show him sort of going down, for a crunch, and there's a little bit of anticipation, and a wink of the eye, an arch in his back, a slight compression, and then a spring up, using his arm—little things like that, the combination of a lot of little things, actually, gives the illusion that he's sort of fighting his way upwards."

One of the oldest television maxims is that people look heavier on TV. I ask Belzer if this is true for the Doughboy, because he definitely looks thinner than I remembered him. Maybe it's because he's in the middle of an athletic maneuver.

"He actually is thinner," Belzer replies. "They've slimmed him down for this campaign. His face is also a little cuter. His legs are still short, though. That's one thing that got to me right from the start: if you really look at him, he's basically a character who's been cut off at the knees. It's very difficult to make a character like that walk and look real without making him look really stubby. The other animators and I talked about it, and we decided to give him a little bounce in his step. I think that works; it gives him a little-boy quality."

Belzer began working in stop-motion when he was thirteen. His high school, Rowland High in Rowland Heights, California, had a stop-motion class that was built around Super 8 film cameras. (The program, run by Dave Master, now uses Hi-8 video cameras, which are also able to advance a frame at a time.)

Belzer discovered that although he couldn't draw ("I get lost in two dimensions," he says), he could sculpt—and mimic movement with stop-motion characters. Soon he was making his own stop-motion films in the garage with clay.

"You talk to any stop-motion animators, and that's the story they'll tell you," he says. "They saw 'Sinbad' (a sixties-era claymation children's show) or something like that, got a Super 8, went into the garage, and tried to mimic it."

Belzer's own story, however, took a dramatic turn towards the professional. Shortly after graduation from college, while casting about for stop-motion opportunities, he discovered that Art Clokey, the creator of Gumby, was gearing up for another Gumby television series. A few weeks later, after showing Clokey a tape of his student and personal projects, Belzer was animating Gumby, Pokey, and their rubbery friends five days a week.

"Gumby was down and dirty," he recalls. "Art wanted us to get eight to ten seconds done a day, which is too fast. He wanted us to shoot on twos, which means you shoot two frames for every movement instead of one. I wanted to do it on ones; it looks much better. So what often happened was that I and the other animators would try to shoot on ones, but fast enough to keep up with a schedule that was based on twos."

After a year and a half of Gumby, Belzer jumped to Colossal—which had just landed the Doughboy account and where he was assured he could take as long as it took to look right. Since then he has worked on two Doughboy campaigns; he has animated the soap-on-a-rope for "Soap Opera"; and he made two ads for Hershey Kisses with Almonds, including one where he had to make an almond fly around like a bumblebee, really mimicking the way a bumblebee moves. ("And you know that little paper flag that sticks out at the top of a Kiss?" he asks. "I had to make that stick out like a frog's tongue, grab the bumblebee, and swallow it.") He also made a group of bottle caps laugh for a Heineken commercial.

I asked Belzer about the aluminum armature holding the Doughboy up from the rear. "In the old days, we used to have to hide the support from the camera, which was a huge challenge," Belzer says. "But today, we can sort of erase the armature in the Harry system over at Western Images. That makes a tremendous difference.

"I'm grateful that I'm doing stop-motion when I am," Belzer continues. "Because of the technology. The first year that we were doing the Doughboy, Phil Kellison, who was one of the first guys to work on the Doughboy, and who lives up here in Palo Alto, came by to see what we were doing. When Kellison animated the Doughboy in the sixties, he had to hide rods and wires, whereas today we can have the Doughboy jump down a stack of books, clearly supported by a rod. Then we just take the rod out in postproduction, using the Harry. It makes it so much easier, and we can work much harder on emphasizing the character, because we don't have to worry so much about hiding the wires and the rods.

"Take a simple thing like the Doughboy's walking across the floor: he has to be screwed into the floor at each step. In the past you had to patch up the holes with putty and try to match the grain. But today you can just touch up the floor in a Harry suite and nobody knows the difference.

"Anyway, when Kellison saw how we worked he said, 'I can't even look at it. I broke my back trying to get some of the effects you

Doughboy heads, one for each of thirty sounds; the right vertical column, bottom to top, is a big smile in progress.

guys are getting with no trouble at all.' It's not like he resented it or anything, but I'd say he was pleasantly disgusted."

On a nearby table, thirty Doughboy heads sit inside a wooden box: each head represents an expression or a sound. When the script calls for the Doughboy to talk, Belzer will change the Doughboy's head every few frames, one head per sound.

"If you look in the mirror when you talk, you can see there are only just so many mouth expressions," Belzer says. "There are maybe thirty or forty sounds altogether: all the vowels, and a majority of consonants. With the Doughboy, we generally use around thirty-five heads. It's easier because he's such a happy guy. If he had a wider range of expression you'd probably have to have at least a hundred replacement heads: a sad 'O,' a happy 'O,' an angry 'O'— and that's just one vowel. It's much easier with the Doughboy because he's basically just this giddy little lobotomized piece of dough."

To get the Doughboy's heads to perfectly match the dialogue, Belzer relies on exposure sheets, which break down the prerecorded dialogue frame by frame.

"Believe it or not, there's somebody who sits in a room all day long isolating vowels and consonants and marking them down on exposure sheets," he says. "People say I have patience, but those people really have patience. There was a guy on 'Gumby'; that was his job for like a year. He broke down every sound on the Gumby sound track for thirty-three half-hour episodes."

Pillsbury's motto begins "Nothing says loving . . ." I ask Belzer how many heads it takes for the Doughboy to pronounce "loving." He thinks for a few seconds, looking up at the ceiling.

"Four heads," he says finally. "An 'L' head, an 'O' head, a 'V' head, and an 'ing' head."

A thirty-second Pillsbury Doughboy spot takes at least three weeks to animate, sometimes much longer. Belzer has spent as long as six weeks on a single spot.

"It depends on the amount of testing you do," he says. "I probably animated those Heineken bottle caps five or six different ways. The clients would look at the tests and say, 'I like a little bit of this one. Could you combine it with a little bit of the last one?' "

Belzer doesn't mind all the testing. "Good animation takes time," he says.

"My goal is to make other people believe that the Doughboy is not a stop-motion character," he continues. "I love it when people ask, 'Is the Doughboy a guy in a suit?' or 'Is the Doughboy computer-generated?' They don't know. Because it looks as though he's actually a living, breathing being. That's the reward, that's what I go for—something that doesn't look animated."

Traditional television equipment is conspicuous by its absence at Colossal. When a project reaches the stage where it needs to be polished up by high-end, high-tech machinery, Colossal producers usually bring it over to Western Images, a postproduction company located in a slightly better part of town. Western Images is a lot like the postproduction facilities in Los Angeles that spruced up "Against the Law." The difference is that Western Images concentrates on short-form material: commercials, videos, and in-house corporate projects.

Michael Cunningham, the president of Western Images, clean-cut and athletic looking, looks and acts like a senior partner at a financial services house. Even he thinks so.

"I'm like a stockbroker," he tells me over bottled water in the conference room. "I'm trying to make the right call at the right time. I'm trying to buy machines that will pay off in terms of use. We buy technology, and manipulate it to solve someone else's problem. That someone—be they an advertising agency or a production house—rents it from us to address something their customer wants. It's the classic food chain."

At the bottom of the food chain is the aspiring producer, trying to come up with a way to add some professional polish to his production. Western Images can provide it, but the rates start at hundreds of dollars an hour. I ask Cunningham if first-time producers often try to get him to advance them the production costs in return for a share of the future profits. If they do, how does he decide which producers are likely to finish the project and pay him back, and which producers are likely to get all gummed up, stop returning his calls, and eventually decide to get into a different line of work.

"I approach it this way," he says with the confident smile of someone who's found a workable solution to a difficult problem. "I tell them, 'You pay full price for the first production, then I'll cut you an amazing deal on the second.'"

Cunningham is currently betting big on a supercharged video editing and effects system, manufactured by a British company, Quantel, and named for the second in line to the British throne, Harry. A Harry suite, or system, sells for about $925,000; the addition of a few options brings the price very close to a million dollars. There are fewer than twenty Harry suites in the United States; two of them are at Western Images. Rental rates start at around $4000 a day.

How does the Harry pay for itself, in terms of use, I ask.

"A lot of our customers use the Harry to repair an image that's sometimes intentionally damaged to accomplish an effect," Cunningham replies. "The Pillsbury Doughboy doesn't stand there all by himself. He's held up by rods. Using the Harry, we can go back to those images and remove the rods, one frame at a time, so that you never see them. Or we can enhance the Doughboy, in case there's a little blemish or a seam shows. We had a case recently where the Doughboy was under the hot lights for so long that it started to peel; we used the Harry to do a little cosmetic surgery. You just use the Harry to grab an image of skin from elsewhere, soften the edges, move it over, stick it where you want it, soften the edges again, and it blends beautifully.

"The other workhorse use of the Harry is combining images," Cunningham continues. "People use it when they want to combine a number of layers on one image. Previously you had to do that with an optical printer. The Harry does most of that work now. And because it's digital, you can combine layer on top of layer in the Harry environment before there's any degradation of signal."

Most of the material that arrives at Western Images is shot on 35mm film and then transferred to videotape. "National commercials are almost always shot on thirty-five millimeter film," Michael Cunningham says, "and there's a good reason for that: nothing else looks like film. The best DP's (directors of photography) are really fine-tuned for the filmic image, in terms of lighting and so on. When you shoot film, you also have much better control of the contrast. Videotape has a pretty narrow contrast range; film's latitude is much broader. So it's there in the film record, and you can optimize those filmic qualities when you transfer to video. Whereas if you acquire it on videotape, it's there. You started with the electronic parameters, and there's no latitude to work with. When you transfer film to videotape, on a telecine, there's more control in that transfer, working with a thirty-five millimeter negative, than if you were working with an electronic original.

"For example, in the transfer process you can enlarge or push in on the image, and the resolution holds because the resolution is better in the film negative. You can push in on a film image tighter than you can on an electronic image.

"You hear a lot of talk about high definition television these days," Cunningham continues, "but in fact thirty-five millimeter is higher definition than high def. It frustrates me to see companies working on high definition acquisition formats. If you're shooting in thirty-five millimeter, you're already working in high def."

Jonathan Keeton, an editor, enters the conference room and flops down on an upholstered chair. Keeton is working in one of the Harry suites on a commercial for a line of plastic toys called Koosh Kins. It is not going well.

"We're working on a sequence where each of the little Koosh Kin creatures pops up for a half second," he says. "We worked on it yesterday and I thought we came up with something that was pretty cool looking, but it turns out to be very important to the clients that viewers know that there are six *different* Koosh Kins. They said we have to 'punch the marketing issues.' "

While Keeton is eating lunch, Cunningham takes me into the empty Harry suite. He picks up a phone and talks to somebody in a back room—where all the equipment and tape decks are kept—and asks him to load a tape into the Harry. A few seconds later, singer

Bobby McFerrin, multiplied and layered via the Harry. In some ways, the Harry stands on the shoulders of the Ultimatte. The Ultimatte was the first electronic box that was able to make multiple layers of clean video imagery possible. The Harry, by adding massive computer power and video effects to the mix, takes things—in the words of editor Bill Weber, "beyond collage to total out-there surrealism."

A Harry Suite is actually a bundle of integrated machines built around a mainframe computer: it is a film-style editor that lays the video out on a screen in "film strips" which can then be manipulated electronically to do cuts, dissolves, and wipes; it is also a compositor, which means that it can be used to combine, or composite, many layers of video. A few years ago, a multilayered look could only be achieved via the hated film optical process, which was slow and complicated; now most of these effects can be done in the Harry. The Harry also works with a Paintbox, another Quantel product, which means that at any point you can paint or manipulate individual frames. Harry also has an interface with a digital effects unit, which means that you can move any kind of footage through three-dimensional space.

A Harry suite sells in the neighborhood of $925,000; video postproduction facilities with Harry suites generally rent them out for from $4000 to $6000 a day.

———

Bobby McFerrin appears on the screen wearing a flowered shirt and holding a bottle of Ocean Spray fruit juice. Colossal used one of Western Images' Harry suites to produce a series of commercials that featured multiple Bobby McFerrins dancing around a beach musically extolling Ocean Spray products. Cunningham presses a few buttons and a filmstrip—with McFerrin's image on each frame—appears. We are now looking at the commercial a frame at a time.

Using the stylus, Cunningham begins to doodle on different frames, erasing some sections; swapping others. Bobby McFerrin "in the Harry environment" seems infinitely malleable.

Afterwards I stop into the other Harry suite, where Keeton is sitting at the console dutifully generating different backgrounds for each Koosh Kin. He looks like a schoolboy completing an onerous homework assignment.

Three representatives from Koosh Kins are sitting on a comfortable couch behind Keeton. They watch, and offer suggestions, as Keeton constructs irregular-looking geometrical shapes, fills them with color, sets them against bold backgrounds, and places a different Koosh Kin in the center of each. This goes on for more than forty-five minutes. Every five minutes or so, Keeton offers a musical selection from the Harry suite's large CD collection.

We listen to selections by Merle Saunders, Ice T, The Tom Tom Club, David Byrne, and de la Soul. At times it seems as if Keeton is paying more attention to the musical mood than he is to the Koosh Kins.

After an hour or so, just as Keeton is finishing the last Koosh Kin environment, I have to excuse myself in order to make an afternoon appointment back at Colossal. As I get up to leave, a member of the Koosh Kins creative team asks Jonathan to rewind the tape and show how the day's work will look full speed, with music and so on. Keeton obliges, and six Koosh Kin creatures zip by, one at a time, each on his own background, in just under three seconds.

Japhet Asher, managing director of Big Pictures, and Amy Capen are in Asher's office. Asher is looking at a bad photocopy of four postcards laid out on a single page. He's reading the typed caption under each card. The captions are the script for "Wish You Were Here," a low-budget segment that will run three times during every "Liquid Television" show.

Work on "Wish You Were Here" began a few months earlier when Colossal purchased the rights to a large library of postcards from a San Francisco collector. Since then Asher and two producers at MTV have been choosing groups of four postcards and constructing elliptical stories to correspond to the images.

By now, eighteen postcard stories have been written, faxed a few times between San Francisco and New York, and rewritten. Producer Amy Capen, however, hasn't been able to find the right voice-over talent.

"The stories have a kind of creepy espionage tone," she says. "So I'm looking for a British accent."

OPPOSITE
Concept board for "Wish You Were Here."

LIQUID TELEVISION

TITLE
Wish You Were Here

RUNNING TIME
1 minute

SYNOPSIS
Travelogues, intrigues, anecdotes, and adventures are developed to correspond with images from Wyatt Landesman's **Quantity Postcards** library.

EXAMPLE

1) Title Card: The back of a generic postcard with the handwritten title, "Wish You Were Here", addressed with a cancelled stamp.

2) VOICEOVER: At last, the big day was here. Grandpa and Grandma would be here soon, and so would Uncle Raymond and Aunt Edna with their adopted son William (who always smelled a little like burnt popcorn and kerosene).

3) Daddy had been shining up the Chevy all morning, and the twins had loaded the trunk with fireworks. It wouldn't be long before we were speeding out toward the cemetery, and my heart swelled with excitement.

4) And, this year was extra special, for when Mother pulled the roasting pan out of the oven, I knew it was my very own Fluffy we were basting for dinner.

TECHNIQUE
A sequence of still shots of postcards with voiceover.
Note: Acquisition of Quantity Postcards library required.

KEY PERSONNEL
Robin Steele, Director / Writer.

This morning she auditioned a Colossal animator who had recently emigrated from New Zealand, but he sounded more Australian than British. Now she has dragooned a reading out of Asher, who grew up in Britain and still maintains a slight British accent.

"Dear Mom," Asher is reading. "Went to the rendezvous with Andre. No one showed." (This caption is typed under a postcard of an empty '50s-era hotel lobby.)

"But outside his operatives attacked me with laser-guided loaves of french bread" (typed under a postcard picture of Florida jai alai players).

Amy Capen interrupts.

"Try to get into a sinister, smoky, hung-over attitude," she says.

"Wish You Were Here" is Amy Capen's first television production job. After working for a few film distribution companies, Capen was hired by Colossal two years ago to work as Asher's assistant.

"I helped Japhet put together development packages for projects he was trying to sell to networks," she recalls.

When "Liquid Television" started up, Capen was named the show's production coordinator, a job that demands a type A personality who can stay on top of a lot of details and return a lot of calls.

"I make sure that schedules get followed," she says. "Everyone involved sort of filters information through me so that I can distribute it to Prudence and Japhet and the other people who need to know these things."

"Liquid Television" will acquire approximately six minutes of independent animation for each show. Capen coordinates the acquisition process; she doesn't like it.

"First of all, I get the stuff to view," she says. "Then I have to call the people up who have stuff we want to use and send them the contract, and then deal with them being unhappy with the contract."

Why are they always unhappy with the contracts?

"The pay is very low," she replies. "At first it was two hundred and fifty dollars a minute; nobody was happy with that. Recently we doubled it to five hundred dollars a minute. Still, a lot of the artists don't like the contract. For example, we want the right to use their stuff for five years, and MTV wants the right to do just about whatever they want with any animation they purchase. Technically, MTV could run an animated segment a hundred times a day if they wanted to. Many animators just aren't interested in selling their work under those conditions. And if they are, I'm responsible for getting the contracts in, and getting the films in. It's a pretty grueling process."

Capen's work load increased dramatically a few months ago, when Japhet Asher asked her if she'd be interested in producing "Wish You Were Here."

"I had been talking to Japhet about the segment, as production coordinator," Capen recalls, "and then one day he just said, 'Why don't you do this one: it's not really that complicated, and I'll be involved as the writer.'"

Is production coordinating a standard prelude to producing?

"I believe so," Capen says. "Because it's important to know how a production works, how everything happens, from the nuts'n'bolts level. When you become a producer you're really more involved with making calls and organizing people. You're delegating, hiring people to do things. A producer is more of a facilitator. Whereas when you're production coordinating you're down there just doing it."

The budget for "Wish You Were Here" is $10,000, which sounded like plenty until Capen started negotiating for the rights to the postcard collection, which wound up costing close to $5000.

"The rights turned out to be about half of our budget," Capen says, sounding disappointed. "But the gentleman who has them knows that he has the best selection, and he knows that we want them. Also, I think he's used to dealing with people in the print field, where the price is pretty high."

Later this morning Capen will be doing a test shoot with director Phil Paternite on the Oxberry downshooter in Colossal's studio building. The Oxberry downshooter is a more sophisticated version of the overhead downshooter that Denis Morella and Melissa Mullin are using on "Invisible Hands." This downshooter not only moves east/west/north/south, up and down, but the bed on which the art rests can also move in any direction.

"We could just shoot the postcards on the floor, pointing down with a camera," Capen says, "but we want to be a little more creative than that, I guess. And the Oxberry can make some very interesting moves."

Phil Paternite, the director of "Wish You Were Here," arrives. He clears off a table and starts arranging a few elements: a vanity case covered with Astroturf that he borrowed from an artist friend, an egg carton, a dozen golf balls, a golf club, and an old reel-to-reel tape recorder.

"We want to create an environment for the postcards," he says. "We've decided to make them kind of puzzles. They do relate to the narrative, but they're kind of ambiguous."

Later this afternoon, Paternite will be moving this environment into the studio with the Oxberry for the test shoot.

"We've talked about a lot of ideas," he says. "At one point it was even suggested that we just shoot the cards with a VHS camera and make them look really low tech. But I was pushing for an overhead shot, which would give it a voyeuristic edge. I also wanted to have the postcards shot on the Oxberry, because that's a very controllable mechanism for shooting things overhead. It's repeatable, too: so we can set up a move from postcard one, to postcard two, to postcard three, to postcard four. Then we can look at it and see if we like it. If we do, the Oxberry can repeat it, exactly, for all the groups of postcards."

Paternite used an Oxberry animation stand when he was a student at Miami University of Ohio, in Oxford, Ohio, and later when he worked at a production facility, Instant Replay, in nearby Cincinnati.

"We used to use the Oxberry for real simple stuff, logos and things like that," he says. "But then we got a computer graphics system that had 3-D capability, and we sold the Oxberry."

Paternite, who has only worked on a few projects for Colossal, as a freelancer, was not surprised to find that Colossal's Oxberry is still used all the time.

"Colossal is a real interesting mix of good old-fashioned animation and new, cutting-edge ideas," he says. "I don't know of too many other places where they're working with this kind of equipment in this way. I think the difference is that Colossal seems to find the right people. So the equipment is sort of old and clunky, but the ideas are new and fresh and cool."

Back in Cincinnati, at Instant Replay, Paternite spent close to ten years working mostly on "car commercials, local ads, and industrial tapes." After hours, he often used the facility's high-end equipment to try artier projects like experimental comedy bits. Some of these projects earned him regional and national art grants. When he was offered an artist-in-residence grant from the Headlands Center for the Arts in Sausalito in 1990, he moved to California.

He began working at Colossal on a free-lance basis after a few of his art projects were featured in a San Francisco film/video series, "New American Makers."

"They have a show maybe three or four times a year," Paternite says of the "New American Makers" series. "They highlight a lot of independent film and video work. And my work was on the same bill with Tim Boxell, who works as a director at Colossal. He liked my stuff, and later he gave a copy of one of my short films to Japhet Asher."

What was the film?

"*The Creature Nights of Ohio,*" Paternite replies. "My brother used to do a lot of animal hybrid sculptures, like the jackalope, and I did these kind of ridiculous narratives about each one of them.

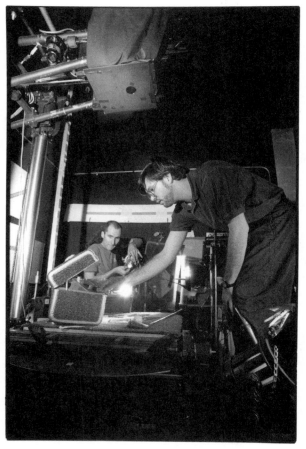

Anyway, Japhet saw it and liked it, and he called me to see if I was
interested in doing some work for Colossal and Big Pictures."

The "Wish You Were Here" test shoot went well, so Capen and
Paternite decided to reserve the Oxberry for the next morning, a
Saturday, which also happened to be my last day in San Francisco.
When I stop by on my way to the airport, the stage facility, which
has been humming all week, is quiet and nearly empty. I find Capen
and Paternite in a dark room filled with large machinery. They are
conferring with Carter Tomassi, the Oxberry operator.

The Astroturf vanity case, the golf balls, the golf club, and tape
recorder are all in place on a platform beneath a camera inside a large
mechanical-looking housing. Four postcards have been carefully arranged on this small set, in preparation for the shooting of the first
"Wish You Were Here" segment.

This is the way Amy Capen explains the upcoming shot, which
will last twenty-five seconds in the final version: "We want to start
with a wide shot, and then the camera sort of slams down—it will be
kind of a blur—to one of the cards. It will stay there for a few
seconds, and then sort of swing over to another card, stay there for

a while, and then make a sharp left over to another card, stay there, then lurch back over to the last card. We'll stay on that card for a few seconds, and then fade to black."

Although the move sounds wild and fast, it will take about ten minutes to complete as the Oxberry moves frame-by-frame through the six hundred and fifty frames that will make up the twenty-five-second sequence.

I ask Paternite why the sequence won't be shot live.

"Because we want a real erratic sweep that moves very fast, but then we want to lock very precisely on each card," he replies. "We want kind of staccato moves, a very mechanical feeling. I don't think you could do that in a live move—the camera would skid a little; you have to do it one frame at a time. Doing this on the Oxberry is a good way to sort of animate something that isn't really animated."

Before the move is executed, Paternite and Mark Kohr—a free-lance grip/gaffer/electrician/best boy who was hired for today's shoot—spend about an hour lighting the postcards, and the tape recorder, and the golf balls.

Kohr, who moves with crisp efficiency, manipulates a small array of lights and a variety of C stands, flags, nets, and scrims until the objects and postcards glow very subtly, like featured items in a department store window.

Then Carter Tomassi presses a button on his computer console, and the Oxberry starts moving down very slowly, a click of the camera's shutter indicating every frame. As the camera approaches the postcards, still clicking, the entire platform starts moving southeast. Everybody in the room is standing very still—any movement might cause a perceptible shake in the image. The camera closes in on the first postcard, moving down as the platform moves to the side. When the camera is directly over the postcard, about a hundred frames click in succession; in the final version these frames will add up to a five-second stationary shot. Then the camera starts prowling, one click at a time, towards the next postcard. The pace is glacial. When the sequence ends, ten minutes later, everybody in the room exhales audibly, shifting their weight or stretching slightly to release the tension.

A month later, back on the East Coast, I received a press release from MTV announcing the premiere of "Liquid Television" ("a combination of underground animation, over-the-edge graphics, and stories from beyond the fringe"). The next day I read an advance review of the show in *The Boston Globe* (by *Globe* TV critic Ed Siegel), that began, " 'Liquid Television' is the best thing on MTV since the early

Hardware:

Mark Kohr, grip/gaffer/electrician/best boy on the "Wish You Were Here" segment, annotates his tool apron:

"On your extreme left, that's a Maglite, a small flashlight which has a focusable beam. Very handy for seeing things under tables and places like that. And do you see that black part on the bottom? That's called a Mag Bite; it's made of hard plastic, which makes it a lot more pleasant to put the flashlight in your mouth if you have to work with both hands.

"Next to that, hanging down, is a small crescent wrench; it looks like a little toy, but I find that it comes in handy in tight situations. Above that, there's a pair of needle-nose pliers, to pull hot scrims; and a pair of big scissors to cut gels.

"See that white handle next to the scissors? That's the cap to a Mean Streak marker. It's an oil marker that writes in white; it's like lipstick, but it dries. So you can write on black tape, to label electrical connections. Next to it is a pair of black Sharpies, which will write on anything. I use them to label gels before I put on a light, because sometimes a gel will burn up, and then someone will say, "What was that gel?" And you look at it, and it's all fried, with no color, and you have no idea. So I always label them. Next you see an adjustable crescent wrench, pretty standard.

"Then you see a large pouch. Inside, I carry a circular spirit level; this one is about the size of a fifty-cent piece. I use it to level camera heads. There's also a short-handle screwdriver with a reversible blade: regular or Phillips head. I also have some hair ties in there, to keep my hair back.

"Right in the middle of the apron, that's

where I keep my tape measure and my pager.

"The pouch to the right of that is mostly filled with clothespins, which are used to keep gels on lights. I also keep some fuses in there.

"Then, hanging down, you see my gloves, to deal with hot lights, and two rolls of tape: gaffer's and paper, both black. Gaffer's tape is better for things that don't get hot; and places where you want to remove the tape afterwards. Because gaffer's tape never dries: it holds firmly, but comes off easily. You use paper tape on really hot lights, but it won't come off very easily.

"Above the gloves and tape, you see a T-handle 9/16 Allen wrench, for working with the lugs in a spider box, an electrical distribution system.

"Inside that pouch on the far right is a multimeter, to test volts, ohms, and continuity. It's like a large pencil with a digital display.

"And behind the pouch, hanging down, that's a bottle opener that I got in India. I'm not a big beer drinker, but after a job people usually like to have a few beers. That's what the opener is for."

heyday of the music video." On the day of the "Liquid Television" premiere—a Sunday—MTV ran a twelve-hour marathon of "the best animated videos of all time."

At 7:00 P.M., the first show began with one of MTV's best-known videos: Robert Palmer singing stiffly in front of a line of heavily made up models. After about ten seconds, the picture started rolling and breaking up. Then it started spinning as if in a blender, and swirled into an opening that featured a clanky musical theme (by Mark Mothersbaugh, of Devo) and a computer-generated bottle floating on a choppy computer-generated sea. On the bottle's label "Liquid Television" was written in large letters. The segments that followed were quickly paced and intensely visual. Altogether, the show looked like *Raw* magazine, televised; a gift from MTV to the art students in their television audience. It reminded me of Drew Takahashi's definition of blendo: "a hyper jumping around from one completely different reality to another." My wife thought that "Miss Lidia's Makeover" was the funniest segment.

The next time I talked to Prudence Fenton, she told me that MTV had ordered another season of "Liquid Television," for Fall 1992.

"The show started very slowly, in terms of ratings," she reported, "but now MTV is playing the hell out of it. And sometimes it triples their ratings."

I asked her if they were going to do anything differently, for the second season.

"We're casting a wider net this time," she said. "We've commissioned pieces from all over the world. We're also much more sensitive now about how long to let a piece go. That's one thing we learned in our first season: that some concepts are ten-second concepts, and some are two-minute concepts. 'Dangerous Puppets' was probably a one-minute concept; we shouldn't have tried to get three segments out of it. So we're looking harder at the concepts now; I think the show will be much tighter this time around."

Does that mean faster?

Fenton laughs.

"I have a friend who looked at "Liquid Television" and he said it made him *sick* it went so fast. And it wasn't even as fast as MTV wanted it.

"But, yes, it probably will be faster, depending on how it all cuts together when we assemble all the pieces. That's always the toughest part: trying to anticipate your remote control. We want to be able to say, 'Watch this and you won't have to change the channel.' We want to change the channel quicker than you can. That's still the challenge."

GLOSSARY

ADR——Automatic dialogue replacement, also known as "looping." When a line of dialogue is obscured by background noise, or a meddlesome executive wants to add a line to fill a perceived hole in the plot, the actor can loop the lines at an audio postproduction house. By watching himself on the screen, an actor can carefully match the new words to the movement of his lips.

Animation stand——The workhorse of the animation industry. Many animation stands are homemade, heavily customized, or just plain jury-rigged, but the basic idea is the same: an animation stand should be able to aim a camera down at a flat surface and keep the camera absolutely rock-solid-steady throughout the filming of a sequence. Camera movements of great sophistication and delicate precision are available on the high-end animation stands, the ones in the $100,000 range.

B-roll——In the news business, B-roll is archival or file footage, basically good pictures that can be added to a story. A story on seat-belt use, for example, may use B-roll footage of crash test dummies flying through windshields.

Betacam——The dominant news-gathering video format.

Biting the computer——When the anchorman doesn't quite finish his sentence before the station cuts to a commercial break, he's just bitten the computer.

Blendo——A mixed-media animation style developed by the two cofounders of Colossal Pictures: Drew Takahashi and Gary Gutierrez. Blendo often combines animation techniques that don't usually cohabitate, like stop-motion and cut-out collage.

Broadcast quality——This used to mean something, back when there were only three television networks and they pretty much agreed on technical standards. In the post–"America's Funniest Home Videos" era, everything's potentially broadcast quality.

Call sheets——The morning paper on the set of a television series, photocopied and distributed by the production department to let everybody know what everybody else is doing.

Channel Hair Loss——The kind of television you see late, late night, largely supported by Hair Club for Men, weird real estate seminars, and ads for correspondence schools.

Coffins——Shoebox-sized metal housings found outside the Capitol and the White House; they contain electronic connections that allow news crews to transmit live from these locations.

Compositing——Combining two or more video sources together to achieve layers of imagery. Ultimattes and Quantel Harrys are common compositing tools in the television world.

Coverage——Shooting the same scene from more than one angle to give the editor a variety of shots to work with.

Cutout animation——A crude animation style that consists of moving around figures that have been drawn on paper and cut out.

Dailies——The raw footage directly from the camera, developed overnight and transferred to videotape. An early indicator of how things are going.

Development hell——The weeks, months, and sometimes years that a project drags on before the money arrives and the shooting starts. What many television people are in a great deal of the time. As in: Q. "How are you doing?" A. "Terrible. I've been in development hell for two months."

Dolly——A stable camera platform able to move the camera smoothly in a number of directions.

DVE——Digital video effect. Once a video sequence is recorded digitally, it can be manipulated in all sorts of ways. Digital effects generators come in all sorts of shapes and sizes, but generally the greater the computer power, the weirder the possible digital effects.

Exposure sheets——Detailed charts that break down prerecorded dialogue into discrete sounds, primarily vowels and consonants, so that an animator knows how to shape the mouth and face on each frame of an animation.

File video——Also known as archival footage, or file footage. This is film or video that's already been shot and saved for later use. When a prominent figure dies, file video requests quickly follow.

Film-to-tape transfer——Just about all television advertisements, and most dramatic television series, are shot on 35mm film and go through a film-to-tape transfer before they are broadcast. Although the image-quality gap between film and video is shrinking, 35mm film is still the superior format.

Flying logos——Derisive term for the clichéd computer graphics used by the major networks for their on-air promotions, station identifications, and sport-show openings. Television graphics departments pay a lot of money for digital effects units that can make logos fly around the screen; that's why they do it over, and over, and over.

Foley——The art of creating all the small sounds that accompany body movement—footsteps, rustling fabric, etc.—in a postproduction audio studio.

Futz——Degrading an audio signal to create an effect. When an audio engineer wants to create the illusion of a voice on the other end of the phone line, he futzes the actor's voice.

Gaffers——Basically, the electricians on the set, who are in charge of transporting and setting up lights and the electrical cables that power them. The Best Boy is second in command.

Grips——Responsible for erecting and maintaining most of the equipment that supports the lights and cameras. Grips are also responsible for camera-moving equipment like dollies, cranes, and booms. The Key Grip is in charge; the Best Boy Grip is number two.

Harry——A supercharged video editing and digital effects system manufactured by Quantel, a British firm. A Harry system sells for about $925,000.

Hi-8——A consumer video format with professional aspirations. Like S-VHS, another ambitious consumer format, Hi-8 delivers pictures that are clearly superior to standard VHS. Both formats have started to cross over into the professional field, but Betacam and Betacam SP remain the rugged mainstay formats of the ENG industry.

HMI lights——Very powerful, very expensive lights (a 200-watt bulbs costs about $250) that throw off twice the light of traditional quartz lights.

Inserts——Material shot during postproduction and edited into the final version of a program. Inserts are shot to smooth over a break in continuity, to fill a hole in the plot, or to add details that are too time-consuming to shoot when all the actors are standing around. To work, an insert must blend in seamlessly with the rest of the production. Also called pickups.

Interstitial programming——All the semi-promotional stuff that MTV puts on between the videos and the advertisements. Interstitial programming includes station ID's, art breaks, and promotions for upcoming shows and specials.

Jerk magnet——A remote satellite television transmission truck, or sometimes even a television camera in a public place. The term recognizes the tendency of television equipment to attract meddlesome observers and would-be performers who try to squeeze into the picture. These people are also referred to as "camera lice."

Limbo set——An arrangement of seamless backdrops and lights to give the illusion that an object is floating in the middle of nowhere. The Pillsbury Doughboy is animated on a limbo set.

Location manager——The person responsible for finding locations for a film, a television program, or an advertisement.

Nat sound——For "natural sound." A documentary style that eschews voice-over narration and traditional reporter stand-ups in favor of the voices of the subjects and the sounds picked up by the on-location microphones.

Obie——A small light mounted on the camera that throws a little additional light on the subject's face.

Off-line editing——Rough editing on a simple system to work out an early version of a project.

On-line editing——The final edit, using the best, most sophisticated, available equipment.

Pepper——A very small light used either for accents or for lighting those hard-to-get places.

Photo op——An opportunity to photograph an important political figure doing something symbolic.

Pool coverage——A camera-crew reduction strategy in which one crew is chosen to provide the pictures for all the participating news agencies. Many White House events get pool coverage.

Poor man's style——A cheap way of creating the illusion that someone is riding in a car. Basically you get some grips to rock the car slightly from the outside as you move a few lights around to look like streetlights going by.

Producer——An elastic term, but generally the person who gets the project done. In television, unlike the movies, the producer is the most important single factor in the project's success or failure.

Reel——The film and video version of the resume, a collection of personal greatest hits, usually distributed on videocassette.

Second unit——A television production crew without a star. A second unit films exteriors, stunts, details, and inserts—anything that can be shot without using one of the principal actors.

Segment producer——On a talk show or magazine-style show, the person who takes responsibility for a single story or section.

Short form——Commercials, music videos, network ID's—television shorter than a sitcom.

SMPTE——The Society of Motion Picture and Television Engineers. A technical society that establishes standards for motion picture and television equipment.

Sound bite——A short comment that can easily be edited into a news item.

Spotting session——The beginning of the music scoring process. The music editor and composer watch an early edit of the show, and decide where to put the music.

Squib——A small, radio-controlled explosive pellet that simulates a gunshot wound. A squib is usually taped inside the shirt.

Stop motion——A style of animation in which a character is moved a tiny bit, a frame of film is shot, the character is moved a tiny bit more, another frame is shot, and the result, after days and days of this, is something like "Gumby."

Storyboard——A collection of single pictures, most often drawn, that outlines a planned visual sequence. All advertisements are extensively storyboarded before they are shot.

Talent——The people in front of the camera: Dan Rather and Suzanne Somers are talent.

Tear blower——A small, almost hollow vial containing menthol crystals. When air is blown through a tear blower into the eye, it causes tears to form.

Teaser——A snappy, tightly edited, thirty-second piece that runs at the top of the show. A teaser is designed to grab those viewers who have been slow to change the channel after the preceding show.

Track shot——The kind of sequence you get when you mount the camera on wheels and run it down easily-assembled tubular aluminum track.

Tungsten light——Your average, everyday light bulb.

Ultimatte——An electronic unit that allows two video sources to be seamlessly combined.

Uplink——A transmitter that can send video signals and other information up to a satellite for distribution. Also used as a verb, as in: "Can you uplink that tape to me at four P.M.?"

Video news release——A television-age update of the standard press release. Often distributed via satellite.

V.O./S.O.T.——Voice-Over/Sound on Tape. Voice-over is video that anchor people can put their voices over; in other words, pictures with a little background sound rumbling way down low. "Sound on tape" is video of people talking to the camera. A typical news segment will start with some v.o., so the anchor can introduce it; then it will cut to people talking to the camera.

Voice of God——The deep, sonorous voice often heard on automobile advertisements.

Walk'n'Talk——A standard method of disguising verbal exposition by having the characters talk while they're walking through a colorful location.

Walla——Background sound generated by actors to liven up scenes in bars, restaurants, meeting halls, courtrooms, etc. The name comes from the sound of background conversation: "Walla, walla, walla."

Wireless microphone——A microphone that uses a small transmitter about the size of a pack of cigarettes to send its signal via radio frequency. The transmitter is usually placed in a pocket or taped to the small of the back. The wireless microphone is a major advance in cable reduction, and the reason why television hosts like David Letterman are free to walk all over the place.

INDEX

Page numbers in *italics* refer to illustrations.

About the Author
David Campbell Denison has written about television for *The New York Times, Vanity Fair, The Boston Globe,* and other publications. He contributes a weekly interview column to *The Boston Globe Magazine.*